Jan & Mel,

We can't wait to
get together ... of course
you may wish to put it
off because you will have
a book report due that
day. Let us know the kid's
addresses. We would love to
send them each a copy.

Ben

Advance Praise for
The New Life Insurance Investment Advisor

"Ben Baldwin's *New Life Insurance Investment Advisor* is the definitive guide through the maze of investment oriented life insurance products proliferating in the market today. This book is absolutely indispensable for individual investors and their professional advisors. Baldwin provides a comprehensive, insightful and entertaining treatment of one of the most important tax-deferred investment options available in the 1990s."

Dr. William G. Droms, CFA
John J. Powers Jr. Professor of Finance
Georgetown University
School of Business

"*The New Life Insurance Investment Advisor* is a guide through the often complex maze of life insurance products. Ben Baldwin has written a book that should be read by anyone interested in buying or selling life insurance."

Michael Ryan, CFP, CIMA
President
Paragon Asset Management, Ltd.

"A must read for all professionals who advise clients about life insurance."

Graydon K. Calder, CLU, CFP
Chairman of the Board
Financial Planning Consultants

"Once again Ben Baldwin has provided practitioners and investors with an invaluable guide to insurance products. *The New Life Insurance Investment Advisor* is a must for the library of all financial planners."

Harold Evensky, CFP
Evensky, Brown & Katz

More Advance Praise for
The New Life Insurance Investment Advisor

"Baldwin presents essential material for all financial advisors."

Edwin P. Morrow, CLU, ChFC, CFP
President
Financial Planning Consultants, Inc.

"Mr. Baldwin's updated *New Life Insurance Investment Advisor* is not only full of understandable, factual information, it's written in such a way that it makes for interesting reading! The book is an excellent tool for all of us entrusted with the responsibility of helping people manage money and risks."

Diane P. Blakeslee, CFP, CLU
President
Blakeslee & Blakeslee, Inc.
National Certified Financial Planner of the Year (1986)

"An essential tool for any insurance agent or financial planner who wants to really understand what it is they are selling. The discussion on variable life products is the most comprehensive and understandable explanation I have read."

Gary D. Aronowitz, J.D., LL.M., CLU
Region Director, Risk Management
IDS Life Insurance Company

"*Must* reading for the insurance-needy consumer and the financial services professional alike!"

Robert A. Hewitt, Jr., CFP ChFC, CLU
Hewitt & Associates

"Ben Baldwin's book is a MUST for every attorney's library. At last, a research source to aid attorneys who advise clients on life insurance."

Robert E. Hales, Attorney at Law
Hales, Hales & George

Revised Edition

THE NEW LIFE INSURANCE INVESTMENT ADVISOR

Achieving Financial Security For You & Your Family Through Today's Insurance Products

---

BEN G. BALDWIN

PROBUS PUBLISHING COMPANY
Chicago, Illinois
Cambridge, England

ISBN 1-55738-512-2

Printed in the United States of America

BB

1 2 3 4 5 6 7 8 9 0

Dedication

To the family. My wife Maureen Margaret McGuigan, the glue that holds us all together. Her folks Leonard Michael (Pete) McGuigan, M.D. and Isabelle McGuigan. My dad and mom, Benjamin George Baldwin, Sr. and Dorothy Bell Orr Baldwin. My oldest son Benjamin George Baldwin III and his wife Rosemary Martin Baldwin. My second son Peter Michael Baldwin, his wife Susan Gough Baldwin, and their daughters Margaret McGuigan Baldwin and Eleanor Stahley Baldwin. My daughter Kathleen Marie Baldwin Leipprandt, her husband Douglas John Leipprandt, and their children Douglas Scott Leipprandt and Lauren Baldwin Leipprandt. My third son Michael Patrick Baldwin and his wife Mary Karen Barg Baldwin. And to yet unborn grandchildren. No pressure, kids.

Table of Contents

Table of Contents

Table of Contents

Preface

This book is about insurance company products, life insurance and annuities. Not just how to understand and manage them, but more importantly, how to understand and effectively manage the investment aspects involved.

No one likes to talk or think about life insurance, but most of us have it. We say we don't understand it, but we buy it anyway. Some say they don't believe in it, and that is fine. It's not a religion—it's a financial tool. We are about to treat life insurance as an investment vehicle, contrary to the conventional wisdom that cautions against mixing it with investments.

> *That's what Ellen's father told her. "Don't*
> *mix your investments with your life insurance!"*
> *he said. He was right in his day . . . but he*
> *is not right today.*

Have you looked lately at how much money you have tied up in life insurance policies? How about your parents' old policies? Those your company owns on your life or the lives of other key people in your firm? You may be among those who believe that the return on that capital isn't worth much attention or that tax or death benefits will make up for low returns.

The truth is these investment returns matter a great deal. A very substantial amount of individual and company assets are contained in the form of cash surrender values. Moreover, a large proportion of those assets may not be performing as well as they could be.

In the past, some people made a practice of financing their life insurance payments through "minimum deposit." They borrowed asset values within their policies as they grew. Income tax deductibility of the loan interest made this worthwhile. But those were the good old days, and the world has changed. Insurance companies have moved away from fixed-cost loan interest. The Internal Revenue Code of 1986 has deemed policy-loan interest as consumer interest and non-deductible; loans on contracts under previous law aren't even "grandfathered" or exempted in most cases. Most importantly, insurance companies are now offering investment alternatives worthy of consideration because they provide profitable tax-sheltered returns within the policy.

We at Baldwin Financial Systems have heard all kinds of advisors, financial planners, accountants, attorneys, trust officers and other money managers say that they don't want to manage life-insurance-policy assets because they don't understand life insurance and don't believe in it. To them we say *Read This Book!* We will give you the tools you need to manage it both profitably and efficiently.

Acknowledgments

A debt of gratitude is owed to many who were instrumental in the creation of this book. The original *Life Insurance Investment Advisor* never would have been written without the encouragement of co-author Dr. William G. Droms, CFA, professor of the Georgetown University Business School and director of Baldwin Financial Systems, Inc. He had the courage to shepherd me through the authoring process, and I am forever in his debt.

I also want to thank all of my associates in the life insurance industry, especially Marvin R. Rotter, Agency Manager of the Equitable, who has encouraged me and used the books to help new agents and their clients become more comfortable with the new life insurance products.

And then there are the consumer advocates who take it upon themselves to help the public cope with today's financial world. Financial analyst and author Terry Savage, and Loren Dunton, founder and president of the National Center for Financial Education, have been particularly encouraging and helpful in their efforts to let the public know that judicious use of today's improved insurance products can be beneficial to their economic health.

Then too there are the clients of three generations of Baldwins. You have taught us in your offices, living rooms, and at your kitchen tables what you need to know to use life insurance profitably. We thank you and have made you an integral part of this book as the audience motivating our every endeavor. We want you to know all there is to know about the products you own so they can work profitably for you.

Finally there is my wife Maureen. She is more than an editor; in truth, she could be considered my ghost writer. At times she got angry and tired but never let one detail escape careful scrutiny. Without the many hours she willingly gave, this book would never have taken form. Thank you Moses.

Ben G. Baldwin, Jr.

CHAPTER 1

The Insurance Industry Today

"Life" As We Know It

In the original 1988 edition of *The Life Insurance Investment Advisor*, this chapter began stating, "The financial services have been revolutionized . . ." Little did I know then that it was just the tip of the iceberg, that *you ain't seen nothing yet* better described the situation.

Since then, the insurance industry has been in turmoil. Insurance commissioners of various states had to take over 48 failing companies in 1989, 33 in 1990, 40 in 1991, and 19 in 1992.

Insurance commissioners take over when they question an insurance company's ability to fulfill its obligations to its policy-owners. Their first action usually is to stop or reduce payments to policy-owners. Anyone who has suffered the consequences of this action realizes that investments within insurance contracts *are* important and deserve attention. In many cases, these people regretfully learned that chasing the highest interest rate led them to the weakest insurance company. Salespeople also finally realized that those companies offering the highest commissions and interest rates were often the most vulnerable. None of us—consumers, insurance agents, insurance companies or insurance regulators—will ever be the same . . . and yet many still fall prey to making the same mistakes today.

This does not mean that the first version of *The Life Insurance Investment Advisor* is in error or no longer of value. In fact, it is valuable for its historical perspective and as a balanced, even academic, study of the industry and its products at that time. It contained statements like ". . . we hope Executive Life can pay." It couldn't! In retrospect it turned out to be one of the most traumatic of the insurance company failures.

On the last page of the original book, six rules for purchasing life insurance were offered. It is with those rules that *The New Life Insurance Investment Advisor begins.* Keep your old book because this one won't treat so academically or kindly those products that this author considers unacceptable for the new generation of life insurance buyers.

THE INSURANCE INDUSTRY TODAY

To understand life insurance it is important to appreciate the economic and sociological forces impacting the industry, causing changes in its structure and products. The objective is to select appropriate products to provide long-term satisfaction. Risk and return are very much a part of the picture, and one must understand the risks to realize the potential returns.

In *The Financial Services Shockwave,* author John Watts discusses the forces or "tidal waves" at play. The first and most obvious is the economy itself. The life insurance industry existed for almost 150 years within a very stable economy. For example, the prime rate from 1930 to 1969 ranged between 1.5 and 8.5 percent, averaging 3.62 percent in a relatively predictable economic environment. In the period from 1970 to 1979, the average rate increased to 9.63 percent, with a range of 5 to 15.5 percent. In a 60-day period in May and June of 1980, it went from a low of 12 to a high of 19, a movement of 7 percent. And between 1980 and 1982, the rate not only averaged 17.6 percent, but also experienced unprecedented volatility, ranging from 11 percent to an all-time high of 21.5 hit in December of 1980. Then came the tumble into the 1990s with long-term interest rates approaching 5.5 percent.

GOVERNMENT INTERVENTION

The second wave, government regulations, has had and will continue to have a substantial impact.

Because the industry was built in a climate of legislation, regulation, and business plans designed for a stable economy with a 3.62 percent average prime, its performance was less than satisfactory in the volatile 1970s and 1980s. In fact, in the early 1980s, the Federal Trade Commission's report on life insurance cost disclosure stated that effective price competition did not exist in the life insurance business and that rates of return were not what they could be. The government was complaining about *low* rates of return! After the blizzard of failures in the early 1990s, the government now is trying to legislate general accounts of insurance companies into safe portfolios that *will* have low rates of return.

The government-mandated portfolios of long-term bonds and mortgages that insurance companies accumulated during the long period of relatively low interest rates did look bad in the period from 1979 through 1983, especially when compared to money-market rates available. Any long-term, interest-sensitive investment vehicle will look bad in an increasing interest rate economy. We are seeing the reverse of that today.

The Tax Reform Act of 1984 created the niche market for single premium life and then snuffed it out with 1988 legislation. The insurance industry responded. It went for higher interest rates as consumers cried *"higher than the rest . . . why take less?"* Aggressive companies like Executive Life pushed the junk-bond mania beyond the limits and failed. Consumers learned, and the pendulum swung back. Their next cry, heard in 1990, was *"Rated best . . . I won't take less."* A proliferation of insurance-company-rating services sprang into prominence. Standard & Poor's, Moody's, Duff and Phelps, Fitch Financial Wire, Weiss, and A.M. Best all blessed or damned insurance companies with their ABCs and created the public demand for "AAA." Meanwhile the supply of AAA rated companies decreased to a handful.

Of course, we all criticized the government and state insurance commissioners for not correcting the problems sooner and preventing insurance company failures. Now the insurance commissioners of the various states are responding through their central organization, the National Association of Insurance Commissioners. They have decided to tell the insurance companies how much surplus (Assets in *excess* of liabilities) they need to be considered financially sound. They will call this new measure of quality the "risk-based capital ratio."

Risk-based capital means that if the insurance company has assets the commissioners define as "risky," the company needs to have more surplus than if it has assets they deem safe, such as short-term government bonds. So what do you think the insurance companies are doing? They are managing their general account investments to get high grades from the commissioners because they know that you, the public, want that *now*. Be careful! You are liable to get what you are asking for: a squeaky clean, AAA-insurance-company general account that is paying the interest you might expect from an investment of this kind. You're right, it's pretty low. In fact you might find it close to the minimum contract guarantee. How will you feel when your company skips its dividend one year or says it can only pay the minimum interest guaranteed in your universal life contract? Can you guess what we're going to be squawking about next? The return you're receiving on that whole life or universal life contract!

The third wave impacting the industry is technology. Without modern technology, we could not manage, manufacture, monitor, and service the products offered today. The technological requirements of today's marketplace have had a unique impact of their own. While tremendous capital investment is required to implement change, the expenditures for hardware, software, and education don't guarantee success. Proper identification of the problem, together with the right technology, software, and people needed, often appears to be a matter of luck. The unlucky find that they have spent substantial sums of money developing systems to handle yesterday's problems. The large, well-capitalized company has an advantage over the smaller one in coping in a world in which a system tends to be obsolete by the time it is operational. Substantial capital is required to stay current.

These tremendous costs are being incurred in a cost-conscious world that demands instant communication and total disclosure. This results in pressure on companies to reduce expenses and to increase their competitive positions and efficiency. Companies and salespeople are now required to master the technology necessary to manage the information that supports all their products and to provide the public with "usable" information. This demand brings us to the fourth wave—consumerism.

The very existence of financial planning is an example of consumerism in action. The consumer demands an understanding of how and where his or her money is to be invested. The regulators demand that the consumer receive complete disclosure. Heretofore, placing money in a whole life insurance policy was like putting it in a black box. The money went in, mysteriously did whatever it did, and neither the policy-owner nor the salesperson had usable information regarding return and expenses. That is unsatisfactory to today's consumer.

It is important to have a picture of what has been going on behind the scenes in the last few years to understand why it appears that many insurance companies are stumbling as they try to cope with change. They are being asked to both increase returns and reduce expenses. They are being asked to become more flexible, and provide more consumer information and new products, all in an environment of economic and regulatory instability. Further, the managements of these companies perceive the need to change, the time to change and the way to change at different times and in different ways. We have seen major companies start to adapt and then suddenly pull back as political forces within the company change and as new people with new views take the decision-making positions.

YOUR ALLY IN THE INSURANCE BUYING AND SERVICING PROCESS

People selling insurance products also face their own unique set of problems. Looking to their companies for leadership can be a disappointing and frustrating experience as the companies vacillate in their commitment to adapt to a consumer-oriented economy and culture. Time and time again companies that agreed to throw money into client financial-planning services neglected to also throw in the necessary talent. Instead, the money went to attractive offices and greater overhead, failing to provide a profit center because of the lack of ability and support of those occupying the offices. The typical company then terminated another "pilot" and a vice president someplace said, "See, I told you financial-planning services would be unprofitable." A step backward was taken from the idea of providing the customer base with usable, understandable information on which to base financial decisions. And the company went back to machine-gunning the public with "new and improved" products. As a result, the professional life insurance sales force actually is decreasing. We are seeing salespeople charging fees for the services they provide and severing their relationships with marginal insurance companies whose ability to cope and survive is questionable. We also are seeing salespeople severing their relationships with marginal clients, those who demand continuing services but do not pay for those services.

Professional salespeople have also changed since the first *Life Insurance Investment Advisor* was published. They have found that insurance companies they considered bastions of stability were not immune to financial problems. They have had to deal with client panic as the public press conducted a media blitz on any company subject to downgrade by one of the rating services. Those were difficult times for you and the agents. But they caused the profound rethinking evident throughout this book. You will find that my opinions are far more polarized and, more than ever before, we define quality in an insurance product to be related to policy-owner *control*. The greater your control over your insurance product, the happier you will be.

It is important to identify those companies and salespeople who will survive and prosper within the environment we have just described. Will it be the bigger companies because of their capital base and diversity? If one product is legislated out of existence, larger firms normally switch emphasis to another line or to the latest product legislated into existence. The smaller companies, many of which come into being because they recognize a niche market opened by legislative change, are exposed to a higher degree of risk. The successful niche company will either leverage success into a more diverse product line allowing it to grow, prosper, and handle the change, or face acquisition at best and bankruptcy at worst. The consumer must face the fact that dealing with a niche company carries with it the potential for company failure.

Many of the new life insurance products are securities, which changes the life insurance selection process. We are now looking for the company that in its capacity as a provider of security products has the best due diligence (thorough product examination and screening) and the best investment and product-management people within its organization. Once found, the consumer then can seek out a professional, registered company representative.

Professional salespeople constantly make demands of insurance companies. They demand quality product, superior due diligence, and sponsors that will stand behind the products and services they offer. Salespeople seek companies that will come to their defense if, as a result of a product failure, they become subject to law suit. In turn, the companies require that salespeople not sell products of competing companies and not be "dually licensed," so to speak. They demand loyalty. As a result, the consumer may find fewer salespeople willing to search the market place and act as brokers of variable products. This limits their offerings to those of the chosen company.

How do you deal with this world? The pro-active consumer will first select a quality company by asking "Will the company be there keeping its promises year-in and year-out for the rest of my life?" Secondly, "Does the company have the products I need and will it service them in the way I want them serviced?" The next choice involves the intermediary, the agent, broker, or financial planner. Never will you need an up-to-date, well-educated professional intermediary more. If he or she has not read this book, you probably know more about the new variable products than they do.

CHAPTER 2

Understanding Life Insurance

Ellen's father said, "Don't invest in life insurance. I did and it did not work for me and it won't work for you." So she didn't.

Ellen's father was wrong. He made a judgement based on obsolete information.

Have you ever heard anyone say, "I just can't understand life insurance?" What is disturbing is that this attitude is prevalent not only among the public but also among many professionals in the financial services industry. They say it as a matter of fact, as if the situation couldn't be changed. Their eyes say, ". . . and you can't make me understand it."

We have to eliminate this in ourselves and our advisors if we are to be intelligent consumers.

Doing so might be easier if we understood its origins. Insurance company marketing departments are supposed to communicate the values of life insurance to the public; instead, they sell the sizzle, not the substance. They concentrate efforts on product benefits and illustrations and camouflage product substance. This has led to poorly informed agents and consumers. To avoid having whole life compete with other investment vehicles, executives stood at their podiums and loudly proclaimed that life insurance was not an investment. In some strange way, they sought to separate the savings vehicle from an *investment* in order to avoid the need to offer a competitive return.

Consumerism, technology, the economy, and regulatory authorities have destroyed the not-an-investment myth forever by mandating transparency in products. As a result of the development of universal life and SEC regulation on variable and variable universal life, products can be divided into their component parts. Too often, articles about insurance products are written by people who received their education about a product, came to their conclusions, and are giving recommendations after two or three 10-minute phone calls with alleged experts in the field.

The experience and knowledge of the expert available to take the phone call will determine the advice printed. So be careful what you read. It is not always true and is apt to dwell on the sensational. But if you can't believe the press, who can you believe?

Yes, your chosen intermediary has a conflict of interest too. A fee-based intermediary needs to keep you paying, and a commission-based intermediary wants you to *keep* buying product. So choose an advisor who expects a *long-term* relationship with you. Well-informed advisors with integrity will then be motivated to give you advice that stands the test of time and product that is profitable, to keep your business no matter how they are compensated. The reporter, on the other hand, is catering to the needs of editors who are publishing to generate sales of their publications. The cynical public press has engendered confusion and fear in many people and made them feel *dumb* if they bought other than *no-load* products. The result in too many cases has been inaction on the part of the public. People tend to do nothing because they don't know what to do, and money that should be invested for retirement languishes in money-market funds and certificates of deposit, earning returns that will not accomplish their objectives. This is the real cost of conflict of interest in the public press, this and attracting people into investments that are inordinately high and panicking them out when they are inordinately low. Buying high and selling low causes some people never to invest again. Further, the cost is far more than will ever be incurred by paying an empathetic, caring intermediary who is trying to earn your business for life.

Expenses, mortality charges and investment results are now exposed for inspection by the consumer. Expenses and mortality charges for an insurance product can be evaluated individually, and costs and benefits of all policies compared. In addition, quantitative decision-making information is now available. Too much money is tied up in life insurance products to ignore their performance or leave their evaluation to people who have not looked at the particular product with which you are dealing.

DEFINING LIFE INSURANCE

Section 7702 of the Deficit Reduction Act of 1984 (DEFRA) defines life insurance for income tax purposes in terms of requiring an *amount at risk.* In other words, if the insured dies, the law stipulates that a significant amount of *insurance company* money must be paid out to the beneficiary. As you consider the following tests the tax law requires to determine whether a contract qualifies as life insurance, keep in mind why Uncle Sam is so concerned. He has, after all, given substantial tax breaks to life insurance. Its inside build-up occurs without taxation, giving you tax-free compounding. Its proceeds are paid at death without being subject to income tax, meaning your lifetime of compounding and the amount at risk entirely escape income taxation. That's a pretty good deal, so Uncle Sam wishes to limit how much you can put into a policy.

The definition in the law is expressed in terms of *net amount at risk,* ". . . only the excess of the amount paid by reason of the insured's death over the contract's net surrender value shall be deemed to be . . . life insurance . . . ."

DEFRA demands that this "life insurance" exist and in sufficient amount for the contract containing such net amount at risk to be deemed life insurance in accordance with the Internal Revenue Code.

The basic tests of sufficiency of net amount at risk are:

1. *Cash Value Accumulation Test.* The net cash surrender value (policy-owner current equity in the contract) cannot exceed the discounted value of the net single premium that could compound to the face amount of the policy at age 95. The discount factor

is 4 percent or the minimum rate guaranteed in the contract.

2. *Guideline Premium Requirements.* These are based upon the guideline single premium or the sum of the guideline level premiums to date.

   The guideline-single-premium portion of the test limits the amount a policy-owner may invest in a policy. You cannot pay more into a life insurance policy than the net present value of the future benefits to be paid at age 95 (face amount), discounted at 6 percent assuming the contracts stated mortality and expenses.

   The guideline level premium refers to the level annual amount that will fund the future benefits (face amount at age 95) payable to age 95, assuming the contract's stated mortality and expense charges and 4 percent interest.

3. *Cash Value Corridor Requirement* refers to the percentage relationship of the policy's death benefit to the policy-owner's equity. These percentage limitations are contained in Code Section 7702(d)(2) and are shown in Exhibit 2.1.

Internal Revenue Code Section 7702 is an historic and important document because it represents the first time life insurance has been defined for income tax purposes. In dealing with today's life insurance and these regulations, it becomes pragmatic to define life insurance as *insurance company money to be received by a beneficiary upon the death of the insured.*

Exhibit 2.1 Death Benefit Corridor:
"The death benefit may not be less than the following percentage of the cash surrender value."

Age of Insured	Amount at Risk (Life Insurance) as a % of Surrender Value	Age of Insured	Amount at Risk (Life Insurance) as a % of Surrender Value
40	250	68	117
41	243	69	116
42	236	70	115
43	229	71	113
44	222	72	111
45	215	73	109
46	209	74	107
47	203	75	105
48	197	76	105
49	191	77	105
50	185	78	105
51	178	79	105
52	171	80	105
53	164	81	105
54	157	82	105
55	150	83	105
56	146	84	105
57	142	85	105
58	138	86	105
59	134	87	105
60	130	88	105
61	128	89	105
62	126	90	105
63	124	91	104
64	122	92	103
65	120	93	102
66	119	94	101
67	118	95	100

The distinction here is that only the money that is *not* the property of the policy-owner prior to the insured's death is deemed life insurance.

If we make this distinction between policy-owner money (referred to as cash value, account value, or policy-owner equity) and the amount that is paid over and above that policy-owner money in the event of the death of the insured (insurance-company money), and refer only to the latter as life insurance, it facilitates understanding and evaluation of today's life insurance products. We buy life insurance because, in the event of our death, the life insurance company will pay our beneficiary more than what we have deposited with the company. These life-insurance-company dollars are desirable, have value, and must be paid for. If a policy should ever fail to meet these 7702 requirements and not be deemed a contract of life insurance, the primary tax advantages of life insurance would be lost and a current tax liability created.

The tax benefits of a life insurance policy are:

1. *The total death benefit* of a life insurance contract received by the beneficiary is excluded from the beneficiary's taxable income under Internal Revenue Code Section 101. This benefit would be lost if 7702 were violated and if the contract was deemed not to be life insurance. The account value of the policy would be subject to ordinary income tax to the extent that it exceeded the policy-owner's cost basis.

2. *The annual inside build-up* increases in cash value (account value), is tax-deferred during a policy-owner's lifetime, and tax-free if received as a result of the insured's death. If the contract were deemed not to

be a life insurance contract, these annual increases would be subject to current ordinary income tax.

3. *The total accumulated income*, exceeding the policy-owner's basis in the contract, would be immediately subject to ordinary income tax at the time the product failed to meet the corridor and/or percentage tests of Internal Revenue Code Section 7702.

It is obvious that Uncle Sam makes a great distinction between the living account values of a life insurance contract and the net amount at risk. It will help you to understand life insurance if you do the same. As we continue to study this situation, it becomes obvious that this *net amount at risk* is not provided by life insurance companies without a charge. There is no *free* life insurance just as there is no *free lunch*. Every policy, new or old, that includes a *net amount at risk* creates expense and mortality charges for it. The charges for insurance are taken from a policy each year either by extracting direct payment from the policy-owner or by using a part of the account value or the return earned on the account cash value to pay those expenses.

You have come a long way in understanding if you have accepted our pragmatic definition of *life insurance* as being synonymous with *net amount at risk* and have determined that you are actually paying for that at risk portion each year at increasing cost as you age. You can equate this *mortality charge* with the cost of your term life insurance. Most people are familiar with term insurance. They pay a specific amount of money for a specific amount at risk (i.e., life insurance) for a period of one year. At the end of the year, no excess premium is left over. To continue the policy, they must pay an additional premium for the next year. This is commonly referred to as *yearly renewable term insur-*

ance. Knowing what this cost is for you is another step toward understanding.

Life insurance, or net amount at risk, is paid for each year by increasing mortality costs per $1,000 of life insurance. All life insurance, including term life insurance, works exactly the same way. We can conclude, then, that *all life insurance* (net amount at risk, net coverage, excess over a contract's surrender value) *is term insurance*. All life insurance includes the cost of term insurance. The question is not, "What *kind* of life insurance is available and what should I purchase?" but rather, "I need life insurance. What is the best way for me to pay for it?"

HOW TO PAY FOR LIFE INSURANCE

You may pay for life insurance in two ways. You may purchase off-the-shelf, retail, yearly renewable term life insurance and pay for it with your after-tax income, or you may place investment funds with the insurance company, funds in excess of what is required for the yearly renewable term insurance. The insurance company will invest those extra funds on your behalf and earn a return which will *not* be subject to income tax. The insurance company will then use a portion or all of this return to pay the annual mortality and expense charges required by your life insurance contract every year. You can choose to pay for life insurance with the pre-tax earnings on your investments within the insurance policy. Under the first method, retail term life insurance, you would be paying for these same benefits with dollars that had been subject to taxation. This is better described in the *President's Tax Proposals to the Congress for Fairness, Growth and Simplicity*, of May 1985, published by Prentice Hall in *Pension and Profit Sharing Bulletin 8 Extra*, dated June 3, 1985. It explains what went on in Congressional committee meetings on the proposal to impose current taxation on the *inside build-up* of insurance—a proposal which was not successful! Following are quotes taken from the committee minutes.

Thus, a policy-owner who pays a premium in excess of the cost of insurance and loading charges for the year in which the premium is paid is, in effect, making a deposit into a savings account that earns income for the benefit of the policy-owner.

Current law permits life insurance policy-owners to earn this income on amounts invested in the policy free of current tax. This untaxed investment income is commonly referred to as inside build-up.

The document goes on to explain that if a policy-owner holds a life insurance policy until death, the investment income within the policy, which was not taxed during his or her lifetime, escapes tax permanently at the insured's death as it passes to the beneficiary without income tax. If a policyholder can avoid estate taxes as well as income taxes on the proceeds of the life insurance policy, it serves as a very efficient tool for the accumulation and transmittal of family wealth.

The proposal to tap the inside build-up went on to explain that even if the policy-owner did surrender the policy during his or her lifetime and therefore incurred ordinary income tax on the amount of policy value received in excess of the policy-owner's investment, that policy-owner has still reaped a substantial income tax benefit. This is because the tax basis in the policy "includes the portion of his premium that had been used to pay the cost of life insurance for past periods." Consequently, the income taxed to the policy-owner is reduced by the cost of the life insurance, even though this cost is a personal expense and would not be deductible if paid directly. The cost of life insurance has become equivalent to a tax deductible expense in these policies.

The proposal argued in favor of taxation of the inside build-up of life insurance for a number of other reasons.

1. The deregulation of financial institutions and various economic factors has resulted in an increase in the rate of interest/investment return paid on investments within insurance policies.

2. The investment orientation of cash-value life insurance products is increasing.

3. The favorable tax treatment of the inside build-up in an insurance policy can be obtained through a contract that provides relatively small amounts of *pure insurance coverage. Note:* the proposal refers to *pure insurance* which is also often referred to as *net amount at risk*, which we are defining as *life insurance*.

4. Comparable investment products generally are not tax-free or tax-deferred.

5. Life insurance is not subject to significant limitations on the timing and amount of contributions. (Contributions were subsequently subject to greater limitations under the tax law passed in 1988. See Modified Endowment Contract.)

6. The tax-favored treatment of the build-up within an insurance policy goes in distorted fashion more to the wealthy than to the not-so-wealthy.

When this issue comes up again in Congress, you can expect these same arguments to be presented.

It is interesting to note that our politicians are able to present the benefits of life insurance so forcefully, whereas the life insurance industry itself still seems unable to convey these same benefits without confusion.

There are many arguments against losing the tax-favored treatment of the inside build-up available within life insurance policies. Many purchasers of life insurance find the increasing after-tax cost of retail yearly renewable and convertible term insurance intolerable. Statistics from the Life Insurance Marketing Research Association (LIMRA) indicate that death benefits are paid out for only 1 percent of retail term insurance policies. The other 99 percent are dropped without value. How many families have been saved from economic ruin and having to rely on the welfare system as a result of life insurance contracts that contained the tax-favored inside build-up that stayed in force until death? How many companies and jobs have been saved by death benefits provided by this same source? Life insurance exists in its present form because it works. People buy it and keep it! It assists all of us by relieving us as taxpayers from the burden of picking up the economic cost of the deaths of others. It enhances economic independence. It rewards the thrifty and encourages self-reliance. The new theme of all legislation should be reduced reliance on government (and thus reduced taxes) and more reliance on the individual, thus encouraging individual enterprise.

Life insurance is an economic tool that not only provides security to families in the event of a death but also serves as an efficient accumulation vehicle. It is available to almost all of us to enable us to save reasonable amounts of money so that we can pay for *our own* needs during life, *our own* children's college educations, *our own* family emergencies, and *our own* retirement. At this time, government and employers cannot and will not provide for these needs. Continued need for the tax-favored nature of life insurance has never been greater.

SUMMARY

The old concepts of life insurance no longer work. The idea that we cannot divide the protection and accumulation components of a permanent life insurance policy is no longer acceptable. We must replace it with a new theory that says all life insurance is term insurance. You pay for life insurance each year whether you make the payment directly or have the payment taken from the earnings on your investment account. In the following chapters, we will review the various methods of payment, using six generic names to cover all life insurance products available today.

Exhibit 3.1 The "Menu" of Life Insurance Products

Term ONLY = Mortality and Expenses ONLY					
	General Description	*Investment*	*Investment Flexibility*	*Premium Flexibility*	*Face Amount Flexibility*
Non-Guaranteed Term	Low Cost Low Control	None	N/A	None	None
Yearly Renewable and Convertible Term	Higher Cost More Control	None	N/A	None	None
Term PLUS = Mortality, Expenses, AND Investment					
Whole Life	Dividends Provide Investment Return	Insurance Company Long-Term Bonds and Mortgages	None	None	None
Variable Life	You Direct the Investment	Common Stock Money Market etc., etc.	Maximum	None	None
Universal Life	Current Interest Rates	Short-Term Interest Investments	None	Maximum	Maximum
Universal Variable Life	Control Disclosure	Common Stock Money Market etc., etc.	Maximum	Maximum	Maximum

Source: Ben G. Baldwin 1990.

CHAPTER 3

Term Life Insurance

*Joe said, "I have investment capital but I
want it invested in my business." Joe bought
after-tax term life insurance. Dan said, "I've got
a wife and a child and I need lots of life
insurance and I can't be an investor just yet."
Dan bought after-tax term life insurance.*

The menu of life insurance products is a matrix that was developed for the Executive Financial Services Coordinators (financial-planners) of Price Waterhouse in 1985 (See Exhibit 3.1).

(Thanks for the push you gave me, Stan Breitbard!) The objective was to take all the generic forms of life insurance con-

tracts and describe them based on their major characteristics and applications. It is presented here as an aid to understanding the life insurance market place. It will help you evaluate the advantages and disadvantages of the various policies and select the one(s) appropriate for you.

While it is our objective to evaluate the investment merits of the life insurance contract, in doing so it is essential to recognize that the investment results of any contract are uniquely diminished by charges for mortality and expenses. Therefore, one must understand the alternatives. You may purchase retail term insurance, using sufficient after-tax dollars to pay yearly mortality and expense charges, or you may pay for life insurance with the pre-tax earnings on investment capital you choose to deposit with an insurance company.

The *menu* refers to two types of term coverage with accompanying charges for mortality and expenses: *non-guaranteed term* and *yearly renewable and convertible term*. Exhibit 3.2 illustrates the cost of each for a $250,000 policy for a non-smoking male.

INSURANCE COMPANY CONTROL

The premiums under Column 1 of Exhibit 3.2 are for what we refer to as *non-guaranteed term*, insurance that cannot be renewed beyond the third year and cannot be converted by the policy-owner. The insurance company can charge low rates because the insurance company *retains control*. It examines you prior to issuing the insurance and, if based on this examination the underwriters determine that you have at least a three-year life expectancy, it issues the policy, collects its three years of premium, terminates the contract at

Exhibit 3.2 Face Amount $250.000 Plus Male Preferred Non-Smoker Rates Costs per $1,000 per Year

COLUMN 1: Limited Three-Year Term Insurance. Non-Convertible.
Non-Renewable. Non-Participating
Add $50 per year policy fee for Column 1. Limited Term.

COLUMN 2: Yearly Renewable and Convertible Term
Add $50 per year policy fee for Column 2.
Yearly Renewable & Convertible Term.

Age	Col. 1	Col. 2	Age	Col. 1	Col. 2
30	.52	.96	50	1.24	2.57
35	.52	1.01	51	1.35	2.77
36	.52	1.03	52	1.48	3.00
37	.52	1.08	53	1.61	3.23
38	.52	1.10	54	1.74	3.49
39	.52	1.15	55	1.87	3.77
40	.52	1.22	56	2.22	4.08
41	.52	1.30	57	2.39	4.42
42	.60	1.38	58	2.58	4.81
43	.65	1.49	59	2.75	5.24
44	.72	1.60	60	2.93	5.75
45	.78	1.73	61	3.21	6.33
46	.87	1.88	62	3.48	7.00
47	.95	2.03	63	3.76	7.79
48	1.05	2.20	64	4.03	8.72
49	1.14	2.38	65	4.70	9.81

the end of the stated period and eliminates the risk. No wonder it is cheap! Because there is very little risk, the company can charge a great deal less for it. If it serves your objectives and those objectives don't change, the policy may be a perfect solution. The risk you take is that your personal objectives might change and/or your health might deteriorate. When the policy expires, you may have no way of obtaining a replacement.

The spectrum of *control* ranging from insurance company to policy-owner varies greatly in different policies. An experience may help to explain why I have become a *control* freak.

In the early 1980s when interest rates were at their peak, I was asked by a client to find him the *best* deal on a big term-life insurance policy. He specified that he needed it for only five years. I searched the market place and prepared a special sheet comparing 17 different policies. All had different costs for the same face amount and all gave different amounts of control to the policy-owner. The insurance companies were competing fiercely for premium income at that time because they could invest those incoming dollars at the high interest rates available in 1980.

The least expensive choice was a *re-entry* term policy that required *re-entry* in five years. Given 20/20 hindsight, it isn't surprising that it was offered by Executive Life. Re-entry means the insured has to reapply for the policy and qualify for another five years by passing a new physical exam and financial inspection. If he passed, he would get the lower re-entry rates, if he did not pass, the insurance company would charge the much higher guaranteed rates listed in the contract. This was the policy that was put in force.

Five years passed quickly and the client's dynamic life had not slowed down. He wished to continue the policy, so we applied for re-entry. I breathed a sigh of relief when he passed the physical with flying colors and expected the lower rates to be continued. But Executive Life said, "No!" It did not matter that the insured had done all that was required. Executive Life would not offer the lower rates because "its reinsurers would not provide the coverage at the lower rates." Interest rates had tumbled. They weren't that interested in the business any longer. Think of the situation both the client and I would have been in if his health had deteriorated to the point that he was no longer an acceptable risk to another company. We ceased doing business with Executive Life in 1985 and moved his term insurance coverage to a company that gave the policy-owner more control. It provided a renewability feature without an age limit and a convertibility feature that would allow the policy-owner to change that policy into any of the investment policies offered by the issuing company. We learned two lessons: one, policy-owner control costs more but it is worth it, and, two, it's amazing how needs for life insurance change over time but do not necessarily go away.

Exhibit 3.2, Column 2, shows representative rates for yearly renewable and convertible term insurance. You will note that these rates are higher simply because the insurance company now must continue to renew the policy at the policy-owner's option. The convertibility feature gives the policy-owner the added option of changing the policy to one of the alternative policies offered by the carrier. Neither option may be offered to the policy-owner without charge, so a higher premium is charged for a policy that is renewable and convertible. We refer to this as *quality* term insurance because it gives the policy-owner greater control, as opposed to non-guaranteed term which gives the insurance company control.

EARNINGS REQUIRED TO PAY PREMIUM

A non-smoking policy-owner, age 50, who needs $200,000 of insurance, could buy the non-guaranteed term insurance for $500 per year. How much will he have to earn to pay for it? The policy-owner will have to allocate earnings to pay both the insurance company and Uncle Sam.

Earnings required to net $500
$500/(1 − 30%) = $714.29

Less income-tax liability
($714.29 × 30%) =   −$214.29

Earnings minus income tax paid =
        Net Premium Payment $500.00

The policy owner actually must earn $714.29 to pay a $500 term premium. If you are in the 30% tax bracket, you have to earn $1.43 to spend $1.00 on life insurance.

OTHER TERM INSURANCE DESIGNS

There are, of course, other forms of term insurance which add features to the two basic types we have described. For example, you will find policies referred to as five-, 10-, or 20-year term policies. These designs attempt to avoid the objection people have to the annual increase in the cost of term insurance. The insurance company adds up the number of term premiums that will be required on the policy in total, divides by the number of years for which a level premium is guaranteed, discounts for the time value of money using the interest rates available at the time, and charges the resulting level premiums rather than the actual yearly renewable term rate. In this, you can see the evolution toward level premium life insurance. In effect, the insurance companies charge more in the beginning so they don't have to charge so much at the end.

Yearly renewable term insurance is normally the most efficient way to provide for life insurance needs when maximum protection is desired with the minimum current outlay of cash. We can level the cost of term insurance through the use of *mortgage term insurance*. With mortgage insurance, coverage is taken away (i.e., the amount of life insurance is reduced) and the same amount is charged each year for a smaller amount of life insurance as the policy-owner gets older. Thus, the cost per $1,000 of coverage does increase with age, but the premium stays the same because there is less coverage.

Watch out for the various level term premium policies. They may be what is referred to as *brick wall* policies. At the end of the level premium period, they may limit your rights to continue the policy at reasonable rates by putting you up against a brick wall—meaning you don't have control.

TERM-PLUS

In our redefinition of life insurance, we determined that the payment made to a beneficiary as the result of the death of an insured in an investment or term *plus* life insurance policy consisted of two parts. One was the account investment or *plus* the policy-owner had built up during the time the policy was in force prior to the insured's death. This is commonly referred to as the account value (also policy-owner equity, cash value, amount the policy-owner could have withdrawn during the insured's life). This part of the death benefit is the policy-owner's money and not the life insurance element the policy-owner wished to purchase on the insured's life. The balance of the death benefit proceeds, which we defined as life insurance, is called *net amount at risk* or *pure insurance*. This element may vary in amount each year as the investment results of the policy owner's account value vary, or it may remain fixed. It *must exist* in every contract that is to be accepted as life insurance under the Deficit Reduction Act of 1984, and it *must exist* in amounts at least sufficient to meet the cash value and corridor tests of that act to qualify as life insurance, as explained in Chapter 1. In every policy, there is a charge for each $1,000 of life insurance which increases as the insured gets older. Now, why would you choose to pay mortality and expense costs for your life insurance and, in addition, pay extra dollars into a contract to build up an investment account? Before you adopt this strategy, ask your insurance professional:

- Where will these extra funds be invested?

- What return can I expect to receive from these funds, and what risks do I take?

- How much can/should I invest?

- What control do I have over the investments within the policy?

- May I change my investment selection in the future?

In the following chapters, we will answer these questions as they pertain to the various generic life insurance contracts listed in Exhibit 3.1.

Exhibit 3.3 Term—Mortality and Expenses ONLY

	General Description	Investment Vehicle	Investment Flexibility	Premium Flexibility	Face Amount Flexibility	Appropriate for
Non-Guaranteed Term	Lowest Cost *No* Control	None	N/A	None Increases	None	Very Limited Situations
Yearly Renewable and Convertible Term	Policy-Owner Control	None	N/A	None Increases	None	Limited Cash Flow Temporary Needs Protection NOW

Source: Ben G. Baldwin 1990

CHAPTER 4

Whole Life Insurance

Hank had a whole life policy that he had borrowed against. He decided to check a little further. He found out that the policy loan not only cost him the 5% interest the insurance company was charging, but that the company also reduced his dividend as a result of the loan. He found that if he paid off the loan his dividend went up enough so that his policy increased in value, 8% annually (tax-free) without paying anything into the policy. He decided to pay off the policy loan. The insurance company was holding old high-interest-rate bonds in a decreasing interest-rate environment. As a result, his policy is working well for him.

CHAPTER 4

Whole life insurance evolved out of what were considered the negative aspects of yearly renewable term life insurance. The premium (annual cost) for term life increases each year, as shown in Exhibit 4.1.

Exhibit 4.1

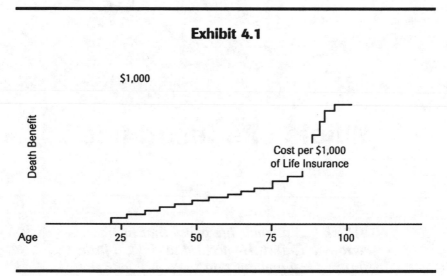

$1,000

Death Benefit

Cost per $1,000
of Life Insurance

Age   25   50   75   100

Because the premiums for the young are very low, term insurance is popular with younger-age groups. However, as age increases, the cost per $1,000 of insurance escalates to unacceptable levels. The insurance industry sought a solution to this unacceptable escalation in premium.

Whole life is a policy in which the premium remains level for the *whole* of the insured's life. It was relatively easy for the actuaries to design. The whole life premium is the result of a calculation leveling the increasing annual insurance costs and spreading them over the life of the insured. This policy is illustrated in Exhibit 4.2.

Exhibit 4.2

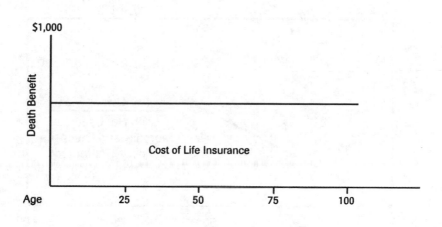

The level premiums shown in Exhibit 4.2 would be more than sufficient in the early years and less than adequate in the later years. The insufficiency in the later years would be taken from the overpayments and their earnings that compounded tax-free. Whole life policies typically are represented by Exhibit 4.3.

You will note that the portion of the contract which is life insurance (insurance-company money, net amount at risk) decreases with age. The result is that even though the cost per $1,000 increases each year as you get older, you have to buy smaller and smaller amounts eliminating both cost and life insurance by age 100, at which time you're entirely self-insured. The amount you could take out while living is equal to your death benefit. Most life insurance policies in the United States dated prior to 1977 that involve savings or investment are whole-life type policies. However, they may have different labels: family plan, 20-pay life plan, life

37

Exhibit 4.3 Conventional Whole Life Insurance Face Amount

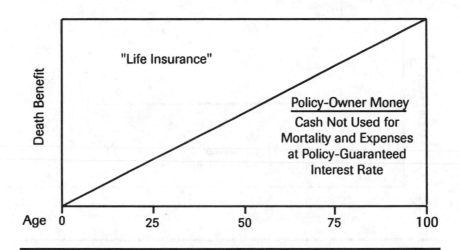

paid-up at age 65 (Exhibit 4.4), endowment plan, or some other name referring to a particular policy feature. The name may be related to the fact that the premium paying period has been adjusted to something less than the whole of the insured's life. The shortened premium-payment period is accomplished by increasing the level premium so that the required premium is collected over a shorter period of time, by age 65 rather than for the "whole of life," age 100. The dollars entering these whole life policies that are in excess of funds required for the current year's mortality and expenses are invested in the insurance company's general portfolio.

Previously, it was safe to say that this general portfolio of a life insurance company was primarily composed of long-term bonds and mortgages as dictated by the various state insurance laws. During the 1980s we learned that there can be rather different risk/reward relationships in insurance

Exhibit 4.4 Life Paid Up at Age 65

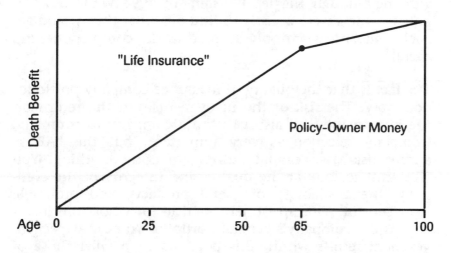

company general portfolio management. In the Baldwin United fiasco of 1983, for example, it was found that Baldwin United was investing in the stock of its own subsidiaries. In 1986-87, Executive Life had problems with the State of New York regarding the quality of its bond portfolio and the reinsurance arrangements it was using to eliminate liabilities from its books. In June of 1987, New York mandated that insurance companies licensed to do business in that state must not include more than 20 percent of "less than investment grade" bonds (junk bonds) in their general portfolios. At that time, it was reported that Executive Life of New York's portfolio contained some 57 percent of this type bond. The rest is history. Executive Life failed and was taken over by the state insurance commissioner, while the *higher than the rest, why take less?* policy-owners learned about *risk*. They found out why they should have settled for less (and gotten more!). The insurance commissioner of the State of California, John Garamendi, was named conservator of Executive Life in April of 1991. The case was still winding through the legal system in 1994 while 337,000 policy-owners were waiting to find out what they would get back. Guarantees are only as good as the company behind them!

The fact is that the quality of insurance company portfolios does vary. The risk of the investments and the return on the investments will also vary from company to company. Company selection is very important, but the "ABCs" and/or risk-based capital ratings are not everything! You will want to look at the quality and integrity of the company, the availability of useful products, and profitable management. The investment vehicle for whole life insurance is the company's general portfolio. You can expect investment results within this portfolio to parallel those of long-term bonds and mortgages (approximately 5 percent on average for the past 66 years) since that is the nature of the account. As a result of regulatory pressures, these general account portfolios have bonds of shorter maturities, fewer mortgages, and lower returns. You need to evaluate the results that can be expected from these shorter term, higher quality investments (less than 4 percent for the past 66 years) and whether you are willing to accept the risk and limitations inherent in investing in these products. Also, do you want part of these investment results expended on your behalf to pay for your life insurance? If your resolution of these considerations is a *yes*, and you do want bonds and mortgages and to have part of your return buy life insurance, then you next zero in on *company*. How does the company you're considering manage its general portfolio? What have its investment results been in the past, and what can you expect in the future? You can check the company's annual reports, Best's *Insurance Reports,* Joseph

Belth's *Insurance Forum*, and the numerous rating agencies such as S&P, Moody's, Duff and Phelps, Fitch, etc.

Best's *Insurance Reports-Life/Health* offers annual, comprehensive statistical information on the financial position, history, and operating results of life insurance companies in the United States and Canada.

The Insurance Forum is a monthly publication distributed by Joseph M. Belth, Ph.D., professor of insurance emeritus in the School of Business at Indiana University in Bloomington. He is the Ralph Nader of the life insurance industry and is admired for his tenacity in penetrating the world of insurance industry finances.

From these sources together you should be able to obtain the company's track record of portfolio rates of return, ascertain the general makeup of its portfolio, and garner an opinion from Belth on risk/reward relationships as a result of how the company is being managed.

A part of the return earned on the company portfolio is returned to the policy-owner. The policy-owner receives a return in only *one way* if the policy is a *non-participating* whole life policy. Non-participating policies do not provide dividends, rather only a guaranteed cash value. The amount is stipulated within the contract at issue and, if the policy-owner pays the stipulated premium, the guaranteed cash value is the only return earned. If the policy happens to be profitable to the insurance company, the profits will be paid to shareholders of the stock life insurance company and not to the policy-owners.

Whole life insurance policies that provide portfolio returns to policy-owners are called *participating* policies. These policies provide contractually guaranteed cash values as well as *dividends*, allowing flow-through of investment results to the policy-owner. Life insurance dividends are not like corporate dividends received for ownership of stock. They are not taxable until the amount of dividend you have received exceeds the premium paid. They are considered a return of excess premium. If the premiums paid turn out to be more than the company needs because fewer insureds died than was expected, the company's expenses were lower than expected, and/or the company's portfolio investment returns were larger than assumed, the company will return some of this excess premium to the policy-holder. It is not that difficult to predict with relative accuracy how many insureds will die each year, and expenses are not declining for most insurance companies, so you can safely figure that a substantial part of the dividends paid by participating companies come as a result of better investment results than assumed in the guarantees.

Where whole life insurance is concerned (insurance with its reserve or cash value investment within the company's general portfolio), dividends are the only way any variability of returns can be passed to the policy-owner. Because non-participating whole life policies have not been able to pass on favorable returns, the competitive position of these policies has diminished to almost nothing.

DIVIDEND CREDITING—PORTFOLIO METHOD

Insurance companies have complicated the lives of policy-owners by changing the way they credit dividends on their participating whole life insurance policies. Traditionally, they used the *portfolio* method which meant that they would determine the total investment return on the portfolio held by the company and then credit all policy-owners with their share of the divisible surplus, i.e., the rate of return that exceeded what had been guaranteed in the contracts. No attempt was made to distinguish the rate of return earned on monies invested with the company in previous years from the rate of return earned on those funds deposited recently. The portfolio method homogenized rates of return and made them more stable over time. It favored new policy-owners in periods of decreasing interest rates since they were able to invest in a portfolio that held securities with rates higher than generally would be available at the time they entered. The portfolio method was a disadvantage to new policy-owners during periods of increasing rates because they picked up investment in the older lower-interest bonds.

Long-term policy-owners were disadvantaged under this portfolio method during decreasing interest-rate periods because they had to share their higher returns with new policy-owners. But it assisted old-policy owners during periods of increasing interest rates when new policy-owners were entering with new money that could be invested at higher rates of return, thus improving overall portfolio return.

DIVIDEND CREDITING— CURRENT MONEY METHOD

Some insurance companies decided it would be more equitable to move from the portfolio method of crediting dividends to a *current money method* or *new money method*. With this method, the return earned on the money invested in the insurance policy depends on *when* the investment is made. The rate of return is determined by the rate the company is able to secure at the time the policy-owner invests. It has been referred to as the segmented or investment-block method since certain blocks of business receive different dividend amounts.

It is very difficult to determine which method of crediting dividends is the best for any one policy or policy-owner. It depends upon the market interest rates combined with policy owner's cash flow into and out of the policy, both of which are difficult to predict. This type of investment return is unique to whole life insurance policies that utilize the company's general portfolio. If you stay in a policy long enough, it is not likely to matter which method is used since time has a way of equalizing them.

LIFE INSURANCE ILLUSTRATIONS

Insurance companies typically provide *illustrations* showing how a policy might perform under various conditions. It is easy to believe there is some connection between these illustrations and reality. However, it is more likely that neither you nor your professional salesperson know the underlying assumptions. But you can be confident that those used vary from company to company, and the illustrations are *not* comparable. When you focus on policy values 10, 20 or more years into the future, you are focusing on the results of compound errors, and any resemblance between these numbers and reality is purely coincidental.

The American Society of CLU and ChFC (Chartered Life Underwriters and Chartered Financial Consultants) came out with an Illustration Questionnaire (IQ) in 1993 to help you and the professional salesperson understand the different assumptions used in illustrations. It asks the insurance company to provide answers to the following questions.

- Does what you are showing in this illustration differ from what is going on now in your company?

- Do you treat new policy-owners and existing policy-owners consistently?

- Is the number of deaths assumed in your illustration the same as your company is currently experiencing?

- Does the illustration assume that the number of people dying in the future will increase, decrease or stay the same as your current experience?

- Do the mortality costs generated by your assumptions about the number of people dying include some expenses or margin for profit?

- Do these changes vary by product?

- What is the basis for the interest rate used in the illustration?

- Is that interest rate net or gross?

- Does the interest rate illustrated exceed what you are currently earning?

- Do the expense assumptions in the illustration reflect your actual expense experience?

- If more people keep your policies than your illustrations assume, would that result in all the policy-owners getting less? (This is referred to as *lapse supported pricing*. The forfeitures paid by people terminating their policies go to support the returns earned by people who keep their policies. The catch is that if too many people keep their policies, the returns for all will be less.)

■ Do the illustrations include non-guaranteed bonuses after the policy has been held any specific number of years?

First, remember that these are not all of the questions. Second, know that there are as many answers as there are questions. Third, understand that the farther into the future you compound the difference in illustrations, the larger the deviation from the truth.

At this point you might ask, "so what can I depend on?" My advice is to depend upon your common sense and what may be referred to as *economic gravity*. Economic gravity presumes that investments will tend to do in the future what they have done over the period of recorded history. For historic returns, we commonly turn to *Ibbotson Associates' Yearbook on Stocks, Bonds, Bills and Inflation*. This book tells us that bonds have tended to provide between 5 and 5.5 percent, or 2 to 2.5 percent more than inflation. To expect bonds to do differently over the long term is to expect history to change. The economic gravity theory assumes that investment returns will vary, but tend to return to their historic norms. Based upon common sense, you could assume that the investments within your whole life policy will not defy economic gravity, and if they attempt to do so, the company could end up like Executive Life. Whole life insurance will retain its viability as a way of paying for life insurance protection because of the relative stability of returns and the fact that it is an old, familiar product. Furthermore, strategies are being used by insurance companies to enhance the rate of return. For example, dividend addition riders are being offered by some. The company constructs a paid-up additional life insurance policy maximum cash value and the lowest possible amount at risk. The objective is to provide a greater return on that supplemental additional investment. This can be accomplished because less of the rate of return on the cash value of this small additional policy must be used to cover mortality and expense charges, so the rate of return within the policy as a whole is enhanced. Companies also enter into special compensation contracts with sales representatives to defer the receipt of commissions in order to enhance front-end investment returns in policies.

DEMUTUALIZATION

Demutualization offers another opportunity to earn a return in a whole life policy. On November 6, 1986, Union Mutual, a mutual life insurance company, became UNUM Corp., a publicly traded Delaware corporation with a public offering of 22 million shares of common stock at $25.50 per share initial offering price.

On July 22, 1992, Equitable Life Assurance Society went public with shares selling at $9 per share. The stock doubled in price in six months and tripled in little more than one year. By virtue of their ownership rights in the mutual company, policy-owners were entitled to receive cash or stock from the new company. The demutualization process is a difficult one. It is almost impossible to predict what success a company will have, or what value the policy-owners will receive in exchange for their ownership rights when a company demutualizes.

THE WHOLE LIFE INVESTMENT

Once you know the nature of the investment within the whole life contract and the risk/reward relationships involved, you will want to know how much in addition to the mortality and expense charges will be required to make the investment. In other words, how much will you have to pay into that whole life policy over and above what you would pay for an equivalent amount of term life insurance.

Whole life insurance is a *fixed-premium* product. You give the insurance company your age, sex, and risk information, and the company gives you a stated level premium for the premium-paying period selected. The stated premium is billed to you each year (or for the period selected). The company cannot increase the premiums, and the only way you can reduce the cash flow into the contract is to take some of the investment results out either through the use of dividend credits, if this is a participating insurance policy, or through policy loans. Consideration of the inflexible premium requirement is an important element of financial planning. Obligatory premium payments can be a problem during periods of unemployment or high expenses. A second important element is the fact that you do not control the investment vehicle in a whole life contract. The insurance company selects the long-term bonds and mortgages and continues to invest and reinvest in the assets selected by its portfolio managers. If you decide you don't like that particular investment, you have few alternatives. You may borrow on the policy, or drop the policy and thus lose whatever life insurance has been provided. If you surrender the contract, you can expect to pay ordinary income tax on any accumulated gain, that is, any amount you receive back over what you have paid in. The net after-tax results are then available to reinvest elsewhere. Another alternative, provided you are still insurable at acceptable rates, is a *1035 tax-free exchange* of the policy. You may make an absolute assignment of the contract to the same or another company and trade the policy in on a new contract without incurring current tax liability. Once the absolute assignment is complete, the new insurance company directs the old one to drop the old policy and send a check for the proceeds directly to the new company. The new company then manages the investment as provided for under the replacement contract applied for by the policy-owner. This provides tax-free transfer of basis from the old contract and protects from current taxation that gain in the policy that otherwise would be taxable.

The unique advantage of whole life insurance is that if you pay the level premium, you have the coverage and do not have to worry about personal management of the investment vehicle. The company's long-term bond and mortgage portfolio is supposed to provide stable and historically consistent results. These results have been used to establish life insurance purchasing strategies.

Short pay, quick pay, four-pay life, and seven-pay life are premium-paying strategies frequently presented as possible with a whole life contract that normally requires premiums payable for life. These limited pay periods are made possible by using part of the investment return, dividends from the long-term bonds and mortgages, to pay the mortality and expense charges for the rest of the policyholder's life. Whether such proposals actually work or not depends upon whether the actual investment results are at least as good or better than the predicted results in the illustration presented. In the past, these strategies have worked well to minimize cash flow into a policy while maintaining life insurance protection. Actual investment results of quality companies have exceeded the illustrations in periods of increasing interest rates. There is intense competition now within the industry resulting in a tendency to stretch the high returns of the 1980s. However, since interest rates have decreased, the actual results will tend to be less than what was predicted. Policy-owners will find it necessary to pay premiums into these policies for longer periods than was shown in the illustrations. Many policy-owners also used a minimum-deposit strategy with whole life. Within a participating whole life policy, the combination of the cash value increase (guaranteed within the contract) and the dividend was more than the whole life premium. The dividend is the non-taxable return of part of the premium coming as a result of fewer death claims than anticipated and/or lower expenses or better investment results than predicted. You accessed the asset base in the policy through loans offered at somewhere between 5 and 8 percent. Therefore, if you wanted to use minimum deposit, you would instruct the company to reduce the annual premium requirement by the amount of the current dividend and pay the balance of the premium due with a loan against the policy cash value. Implicit in all these methods of limiting the amount of money going into policies was the idea that investment results from whole life policies were inferior, so it made sense to invest as little as possible.

The policy loans on those contracts increased in amount, as did interest costs. In the past, there was little reason to be concerned about a 5 percent policy loan that was deductible. Additionally, the loan didn't affect the investment results of the contract. Policy-owners received the same dividend regardless of whether they had borrowed on their policies. This strategy was particularly advantageous when interest rates were increasing in the 1970s and early 1980s. However, it was inevitable that insurance companies would have to do something about the disintermediation (people borrowing at the low 5 percent guaranteed rate to invest at higher rates of return elsewhere). The flow of funds being lent out at 5 percent when money-market mutual funds were paying rates in the high teens was devastating to insurance company portfolios. As a result, companies took the following actions.

1. They either increased the guaranteed loan interest rate on whole life policies being issued at the time to 8 percent or made the rate adjustable.

2. They made *upgrade* and *enhancement* offers to existing policy-owners, the substance being that if the policy-owner agreed to pay current market rates of interest for any loans, the company would provide higher future dividends.

3. They began issuing *conduit* type policies, such as variable and universal variable life. These are policies whereby the policy-owner accepts the return provided by market conditions and the insurance company acts as the money manager. These policies provide separate accounts, often in addition to the company's general portfolio, and after charging a management fee, pass *all* investment returns (good and bad) on to the policy-owner.

The cost of using policy loans has increased. You receive the increased dividend of the upgrade offer only if you also accept higher interest rates on any loan you may take. If you don't accept the upgrade offer, to retain low interest charges on policy loans you then accept dividends on a lower scale. Trying to quantify the actual increases in policy loan costs (increased interest costs and/or decreased dividends) as a result of these changes has added to the complexity of managing whole life policies which in effect, further increases the costs.

On top of the increased costs coming from insurance companies, the Tax Reform Act of 1986 (TRA 86) ruled out deductibility of these interest charges by both the personal and the corporate borrower in most cases. For the personal borrower, TRA-86 generally regards interest paid on policy loans as consumer interest, thereby eliminating its deductibility. But there are some exceptions. Loans to finance investments continue to be deductible to the extent of net investment income. Also, loans on policies held for trade or business purposes on the lives of officers, owners or employees generate deductible loan interest for businesses on loans aggregating no more than $50,000 per officer, employee, or owner. TRA-86 *grandfathered* policies owned for business purposes issued prior to June 21, 1986, and allows businesses to continue to deduct all policy loan interest as they did in the past. Corporations as large as Emerson Electric continue to do this despite the fact that it makes little economic sense. For business policies issued *after* June 20, 1986, only interest on loans up to $50,000 is deductible. The impact of 1) higher insurance company interest rates on policy loans, 2) lower dividends on policies with outstanding loans, and 3) reduction or elimination of policy loan interest deductibility has served to destroy the economic feasibility of the minimum deposit strategy for paying whole life insurance premiums.

But, Is It a Good Investment?

The New Life Insurance Investment Advisor is asked, "In general, do whole life policies provide an acceptable investment alternative to today's insurance buyer?"

Let's observe a good *rule of thumb*. We really know nothing about you or your specific situation. You need to know why we believe as we do and the assumptions upon which our answer is based. Our rule of thumb is *no, whole life is not an acceptable alternative* for most people today. The reasons and assumptions underlying that rule are as follows.

1. The bond mortgage general account investment in any life insurance company cannot be expected to provide in excess of 5 to 5.5 percent.

2. A bond mortgage account provides insufficient diversification for the long-term investor.

3. The creditor risk (Executive Life, Mutual Benefit Life, etc.) is unacceptable and unnecessary.

4. The policy provides the policy-owner with insufficient control over the investment.

5. The policy is a single-pocket policy. It offers only the bond mortgage account and provides no method of changing that investment if investment needs or desires change.

6. The policy is inflexible with regard to premium payment and face amount.

7. You are insurable and you will have no trouble obtaining new insurance at acceptable rates.

8. You do not intend to commit suicide or commit fraud on any of the papers you complete to obtain a policy, you can exchange your existing whole life for a more flexible contract.

When is a whole life policy a good investment?

1. When it is doing what *you* want it to do.

2. When it is providing an acceptable tax-free rate of return.

3. When you already own it and your insurability status has deteriorated for some reason.

4. When there is not an acceptable alternative.

5. When the *guaranteed* cash value is a comfort to you.

6. When the money in the policy does not represent a significant investment to you.

Caution: Do not act on any of this advice until you have thoroughly discussed it with your beneficiaries, your doctor, your tax and legal advisors, and your personal insurance and financial advisors.

Exhibit 4.5 TERM "PLUS"—Mortality and Expenses "PLUS" Additional Dollars for Investment

	General Description	Investment Vehicle	Investment Flexibility	Premium Flexibility	Face Amount Flexibility	Appropriate for
Whole Life	Fixed life Basic coverage Dividends provide investment return	Primarily insurance co. selected long-term bonds and mortgages	None. To change investment, borrowing and reinvesting is required.	None. Dividends can reduce or eliminate fixed, billed premium.	None. Want more?...Buy new, IF you can pass a physical.	The conservative older insureds Substandard insureds

CHAPTER 5

Universal Life Insurance

John bought one of the first Universal Life policies in 1981 from E.F. Hutton Life. The first-year interest rate that year was 14 percent. Policies like this are now renewing at 4 percent. When E.F. Hutton Life changed to First Capital Life, the policy no longer offered all John wanted. The economics of First Capital Life worried him. John decided to trade (1035 tax-free exchange) his First Capital policy in on a policy that gave him investment control and separate accounts. John's investment objectives have changed and he is currently considering changing the investments within his policy. John was lucky—or wise in wanting to be in control. First Capital Life did eventually fail and was taken over by the state insurance commissioner. John made it out in time.

As interest rates skyrocketed in the late '70s and early '80s, money-market mutual funds were born. The public demanded an opportunity to participate in the higher yields of the day, and the mutual fund industry responded. As interest rates went up, the return on long-term bond and mortgage portfolios of whole life insurance contracts looked worse and worse. Money moved out of insurance policies into money market accounts. In 1979, the Federal Trade Commission released its special report on the investment merits of life insurance. In 1974, Venita Van Caspel published her best-selling book *Money Dynamics*. Chapter 13 was entitled "Life Insurance, the Great National Consumer Fraud?" She too attacked the industry for inadequate returns on cash value. Nobody likes long-term bonds in a rapidly increasing interest-rate environment.

The market demanded a response and the appropriate vehicle, a money-market mutual fund, was there to provide the investment *du jour*. The market-driven insurance industry had no choice but to offer short-term money-market investments within their insurance policies instead of the long-term bonds and mortgages of whole life.

It is interesting to note that it took a life insurance company executive, John Watts, working with the brokerage firm E.F. Hutton, to get universal life into the market place. Watts was able to help brokers understand universal life as an investment alternative during a period when the stock market was not performing well. Universal life could provide tax-deferred earnings since they occurred within the insurance contract.

E.F. Hutton's success with universal life brought in small niche companies born in the days of very high interest rates. The new companies were not burdened by the baggage of large portfolios of old long-term bonds and mortgages. They were able to get a fast and effective start. The old-line life insurance companies looked fearfully at universal life as a vehicle that would create more rather than less disintermediation problems. According to a 1981 Life Insurance Management Research Association (LIMRA) study, 78 percent of the annualized premiums were for traditional cash-value life insurance, 19 percent for term insurance, and only 3 percent for the newer products. By 1986, these figures changed dramatically. Only 30 percent of the new annualized premium was going to traditional cash-value life insurance, 11 percent to term insurance, and 59 percent to investment-orientated new products.

While universal life has a number of unique characteristics, the most notable is its basic investment vehicle, current-interest-rate investments. The interest rate to be earned usually is guaranteed for one year. At the end of that year, the policy-owner is informed of the rate for the next 12-month period.

Universal life brought total disclosure to the life insurance business. The specific charges, expenses and credits are itemized and available to the policy-owner. The policies were referred to as *transparent* because of the detailed information offered for the first time. This information is essential when evaluating policies.

When you are considering putting premium into a universal life policy, ask to see the expenses and credits on a monthly basis. Those for the most current year will provide the most valid information. First-year expenses usually will be the highest as you pay to get the policy started.

You'll also want to ask:

1. What deposit do you recommend for this policy?

Questions to
ask Ameritas

Exhibit 5.1 Percentage of Annualized New Premiums

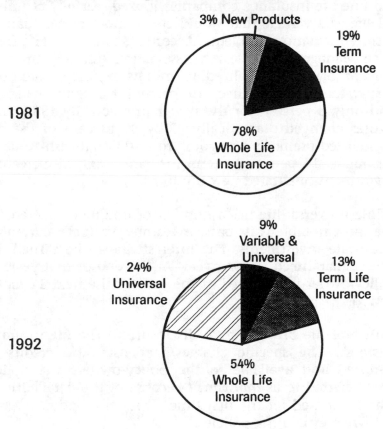

1981

3% New Products

19%
Term
Insurance

78%
Whole Life
Insurance

1992

9%
Variable &
Universal

24%
Universal
Insurance

13%
Term Life
Insurance

54%
Whole Life
Insurance

Source: Life Insurance Marketing and Research Association (LIMRA)

2. How often should I make these deposits?

3. How long should I expect to make these deposits using *conservative* interest-rate assumptions?

4. How much is taken out for state premium tax?

5. What amounts are deducted for insurance company expenses initially, and then per month?

6. What is the maximum expense charge that could be made?

7. What is the amount at risk, meaning how much life insurance is being offered by this policy under examination? Does the death benefit include my account value (Option I or A) or is it paid in addition to my account value (Option II or B)?

8. What is the current monthly cost and annual cost for this amount at risk? (You will find this referred to as the mortality charge. You will recognize it as the cost of the term insurance within the contract.)

9. What is the contractual maximum mortality charge that could be made?

10. Are there any other additional charges being made against the policy account for other policy benefits?

11. What earnings are currently being credited to the policy account on a monthly and annual basis? Historically, how much has that interest dropped in the second policy year?

12. Are any earnings guaranteed?

13. How much remains in the policy-owner's account at the end of the first month and at the end of the first year?

14. If I choose to surrender the policy at the end of the first month, how much will I receive? At the end of the first year?

15. For how long is the cash surrender value less than the account value, i.e., how long does the back-end load (expense charged if you cancel the contract before the insurance company recoups its expenses) stay in existence?

Another characteristic of universal life is that the insurance company often retains the right to change the charges it makes for mortality and expenses. It is important to know what the company is charging presently and the range within which it can charge. You will often find that charges for mortality are based on the company's current experience. Therefore, the long-term results of a universal life policy depend upon how well the company selects new insureds. Since this is an element over which you have no control, you do can only two things: 1) choose a quality company with careful underwriting standards and 2) determine whether or not the maximum potential charges for mortality guaranteed within the contract are acceptable. The maximums by statute are contained in the *1980 Commissioners Standard Ordinary Mortality Table.*

Since universal life policies are transparent, you can know charges being made for mortality at various ages. Because those charges are an important point of comparison, you also will want to check them against the various tables, benchmarks, and existing market rates for term insurance. Exhibit 5.2 provides a summary of four standard mortality tables that can be used for such comparisons. It shows how many people per 1,000 are expected to die within one year in any particular age category. The first, the American Experience table, shows how many deaths per 1,000 occurred

Exhibit 5.2 Deaths per 1,000 in
Four Statutory Mortality Tables

Age	American Experience Table	Commissioners' 1941 Table	Commissioners' 1958 Table	Commissioners' 1980 Table
20	7.80	2.43	1.79	1.90
21	7.86	2.51	1.83	1.91
22	7.91	2.59	1.86	1.89
23	7.96	2.68	1.89	1.86
24	8.01	2.77	1.91	1.82
25	8.06	2.88	1.93	1.77
26	8.13	2.99	1.96	1.73
27	8.20	3.11	1.99	1.71
28	8.26	3.25	2.03	1.70
29	8.34	3.40	2.08	1.71
30	8.43	3.56	2.13	1.73
31	8.51	3.73	2.19	1.78
32	8.61	3.92	2.25	1.83
33	8.72	4.12	2.32	1.91
34	8.83	4.35	2.40	2.00
35	8.95	4.59	2.51	2.11
36	9.09	4.86	2.64	2.24
37	9.23	5.15	2.80	2.40
38	9.41	5.46	3.01	2.58
39	9.59	5.81	3.25	2.79
40	9.79	6.18	3.53	3.02
41	10.01	6.59	3.84	3.29
42	10.25	7.03	4.17	3.56
43	10.52	7.51	4.53	3.87
44	10.83	8.04	4.92	4.19
45	11.16	8.61	5.35	4.55
46	11.56	9.23	5.83	4.92
47	12.00	9.91	6.36	5.32
48	12.51	10.64	6.95	5.74
49	13.11	11.45	7.60	6.21
50	13.78	12.32	8.32	6.71
51	14.54	13.27	9.11	7.30
52	15.39	14.30	9.96	7.96
53	16.33	15.43	10.89	8.71
54	17.40	16.65	11.90	9.56
55	18.57	17.98	13.00	10.47
56	19.89	19.43	14.21	11.46
57	21.34	21.00	15.24	12.49
58	22.94	22.71	17.00	13.59
59	24.72	24.57	18.59	14.77
60	26.69	26.59	20.34	16.08

from 1843 to 1858. (It appears that this period was a hazardous time in which to live!) Mortality rates improve as you read to the right. The 1941 table was constructed from statistics for 1930 to 1940; the 1958 table, from 1950 to 1954; and the most current 1980 table, 1970 to 1975.

FLEXIBILITY OF FACE AMOUNT AND PREMIUM

The third important characteristic of universal life is policy-owner ability to adjust the face amount and what is paid into the policy so that it fits you, rather than the other way around. You are able to change the face amount or premium level to suit your own particular needs. Once all the policy data is in the computer, it's not difficult to raise or lessen the amount at risk (life insurance). If you buy a policy and shortly thereafter elect to reduce the amount at risk, you will likely forfeit a portion of your account value in the form of a back-end load. The amount of that forfeiture will be disclosed in the contract. On the other hand, if you direct the company to increase the amount at risk, it probably will ask you to provide evidence that you are still in good health. Be sure to ask what expenses you will incur at the time of increase. With some contracts, this is the most efficient (least costly) method of increasing your coverage. The fact that universal life is flexible and can adapt to your lifestyle is important.

You'll like universal life if you prefer an investment that pays current competitive market rates of interest as opposed to the long-term bond and mortgage account returns of whole life. It also has appeal if you think you may want to use its adjustment features. The market share of this product has decreased dramatically since 1986 because of competition from variable life and decreased interest rates. In fact, it has dropped from more than 50 percent in 1986 to less than 22 percent in 1993.

Universal life transparency is exemplified in the annual report page shown in Exhibit 5.3. The policy surrender value is $343,265.56. The dollar amount of the back-end load remaining at the time is $70,928.

You can see that the amounts required to keep this policy in force are the charges for expenses ($48) and mortality for the $5,200,000 of life insurance for a male, age 70. No money went into the policy this year, and the policy costs are deducted from the investment account. Alternatively, you could use the investment feature of the policy and ask the company how much could be put in. You might wish to specify that you want to have access to this extra deposit without taxation or penalties through withdrawal or policy loan. This requires that you stay below what is called the seven-pay-maximum (see Modified Endowment Contract).

The minimum-funding level requires that there be enough money in the policy account to cover the mortality and expense charges for the year. Under a minimum-funding arrangement, the policy account could dwindle to the amount of the remaining back-end load, at which time the insurance company would call on you for more money. Unless you made a premium deposit sufficient to cover the mortality and expenses, the policy could terminate. In some cases, the company will not require payment to cover the full year, but rather a shorter period, such as one quarter. Remember that if you decide *not* to make an additional premium payment, the policy will terminate, and you will pay the back-end load within the policy. When you use a minimum-funding strategy, you really purchase yearly renewable term insurance. It generally is not economical to use a universal life policy as a term policy. The expenses of

Exhibit 5.3 Summary of Policy Values

Policy Values as of:	01/11/91	01/11/92
Face Amount	$5,200,000.00	$5,200,000.00
Death Benefit	$5,200,000.00	$5,200,000.00
Death Benefit Option	A	A
Policy Amount	$464,614.43	$414,193.56
Less: Surrender Charge	$88,578.32	$70,928.00
Outstanding Loans	$0.00	$0.00
Net Cash Surrender Value	$376,036.11	$343,265.56

Summary of Transactions Guaranteed Interest Division

		Policy Transactions	Net Amount Applied to			Cost of Insurance Monthly Processing		Interest Credited		End-of-Month
Mon Type	Effective	Gross Amount $	Expense Charges $	Policy Account $	Expense Charges	Insured Person	Additional Benefit Riders $	Unloaned Amount 8.00% $	Loaned Amount 7.00% $	Policy Account $
(A)	(B)	(C)	(D)	(E)	(F)	(G1)	(G2)	(H1)	(H2)	(J)
JAN	01/12/91	0.00	0.00	0.00	4.00	6,961.02	0.00	3,001.19	0.00	460,650.62
FEB	02/12/91	0.00	0.00	0.00	4.00	6,966.85	0.00	2,686.38	0.00	456,366.15
MAR	03/12/91	0.00	0.00	0.00	4.00	6,973.15	0.00	2,947.02	0.00	452,336.02
APR	04/12/91	0.00	0.00	0.00	4.00	6,979.07	0.00	2,826.04	0.00	448,178.99
MAY	05/12/91	0.00	0.00	0.00	4.00	6,985.18	0.00	2,893.25	0.00	444,083.06
JUN	06/12/91	0.00	0.00	0.00	4.00	6,991.20	0.00	2,773.59	0.00	439,861.45
JUL	07/12/91	0.00	0.00	0.00	4.00	6,997.41	0.00	2,838.62	0.00	435,698.66
AUG	08/12/91	0.00	0.00	0.00	4.00	7,003.53	0.00	2,811.28	0.00	431,502.41
SEP	09/12/91	0.00	0.00	0.00	4.00	7,009.70	0.00	2,693.64	0.00	427,182.35
OCT	10/12/91	0.00	0.00	0.00	4.00	7,016.05	0.00	2,755.35	0.00	422,917.65
NOV	11/12/91	0.00	0.00	0.00	4.00	7,022.32	0.00	2,639.09	0.00	418,530.42
DEC	12/12/91	0.00	0.00	0.00	4.00	7,028.77	0.00	2,695.91	0.00	414,193.56
Totals		0.00	0.00	0.00	48.00	83,934.25	0.00	33,561.36	0.00	

such a policy are typically more than a regular term policy, and you also have to contend with the back-end load.

Further there usually is a *target* premium on these flexible premium products. This is the premium the company considers adequate to maintain the policy on a long-term basis.

EFFICIENT OR *TAX-FREE TERM* FUNDING

I use the two terms to describe that point in the life of the policy when you have an amount on deposit large enough so that tax-free interest earnings are sufficient to pay for the mortality and expenses of the contract in the current year. At this point, you are buying term life insurance protection entirely with interest earnings that have not been diminished by income taxes. This type of funding allows you to pay the minimum amount possible for the protection you desire. Remember that if you're in the 30 percent tax bracket, you have to earn $1.43 in order to pay an after-tax dollar for a term premium. But if you earn interest inside a policy, you use that whole dollar, undiminished by taxes, to pay the term premium within the policy. You save 43 cents for every dollar of premium paid.

OVERFUNDING

What would happen if you decide to *overfund* your universal life policy deposit by putting in an extra $10,000 for investment purposes? Before making this decision, you need to look at whether or not the policy is a good investment alternative. What does it cost to get the money into the policy? Does the deposit increase any back-end loads? How would you get the money out if you needed it?

You know what interest your policy account is earning, you can calculate or ask what interest you may expect from the extra investment for the year. The interest earned on the money within the contract inside build-up is not subject to current income taxation. Make your decision based upon the alternative investments available at the time. Where else could you put those funds to provide higher net after-tax earnings with comparable liquidity and safety?

Some of the return you earn is used by the company to pay for your life insurance, so unless you need the insurance coverage, your returns are being reduced by unwarranted expenses.

Universal life is not without downside risk. It has now been used throughout an entire business cycle, and it came into existence at a time when interest rates were at an all-time high. At first, not even some of the agents selling it understood it, and in some cases it was improperly sold. Some policy-owners who purchased contracts in 1979 have insurance company illustrations for periods of 20 to 50 years based on 12-percent-or-more interest-rate assumptions for the entire period. Often those who bought these contracts did not even realize that part of that return would be used up in expenses and mortality charges. They bought universal life because of its associated high-gross interest-rate predictions and bad publicity surrounding whole life as interest rates rose to their 1980 levels. What was most damaging was that policy-holders determined the amount of money they would put into the universal life policy based on those high-interest-rate assumptions. As a result, they minimized their annual deposits and underfunded their contracts. As interest rates have decreased and the policy-earnings on their accounts have diminished, some of these policy-owners are finding that the earnings on their accounts are not sufficient to cover mortality and expense charges. A portion of the principal in the policy account is being utilized to cover these costs and so their policy accounts are being systematically eliminated. Also, some policy-owners regard universal life as they did whole life: they put the policies away and forget about them. They may be totally unaware of decreases in the principal amount of their account values. Unfortunately, they will be shocked when they are notified that their policy account has diminished to a level that cannot sustain the policies, and they are going to have to put in more money if they expect them to remain in force. They will receive a *call* on their policies similar to a *call* on margin accounts from stockbrokers. This is why you need to make a conscious decision about the funding level in your universal life policy and then watch it to make sure it is doing what you want it to do.

When you consider the fact that many universal life policies are underfunded because of the high long-term interest rates assumed, and add to that the following factors, you can understand the problems policy-owners may encounter if they do not actively manage their policies.

1. The insurance company can, at its discretion, increase the mortality charges up to the maximum guaranteed within the contract, e.g., from the lower current rates to 1980 Commissioners' Standard Ordinary mortality rates.

2. The insurance company can increase expense charges up to the maximum guaranteed within the contract, e.g., from $4 to $8.

3. Mortality charges will inevitably continue to rise as a result of the policy-owner's advancing age.

All factors occurring together can result in the rapid decline of an account value to zero. If, as this point approaches, your health has deteriorated to such an extent that you can no longer obtain life insurance, you would have no alternative but to meet the call for more money. In a worst-case scenario, if your resources also have decreased, you might find it difficult or impossible to meet the call and could lose your insurance coverage altogether.

Life insurance companies, insurance agents and financial planners will have a great deal of difficulty explaining this situation to these policy-owners. Policy-owners should be encouraged to maintain at least adequate funding levels, and to overfund their contracts during good times when they have excess resources and the policy is a reasonable investment alternative.

The risks in universal life are as follows.

1. The interest earnings on the policy account will move up and down as market rates fluctuate.

2. The insurance companies can and will change mortality rates.

3. The insurance companies can and will change expense charges.

4. The policy requires policy-owner management and continued vigilance.

5. Interest rates have moved from a cyclical high in December 1980 to a cyclical low in 1994. You probably won't like your policy very well when it is paying no more than the minimum guaranteed interest rate which is normally about 4 percent. If the insurance

company is maintaining a high interest rate, and paying out more than it is earning to do so, you won't like the policy for long either. Company failure is a possibility.

If you aren't aware of the risks in universal life or don't intend to deal with them, you probably would be better of with retail term life insurance.

If you look at the risks associated with universal life, you might conclude that this type of policy requires an inordinate amount of confidence in a company. The account from which you earn your interest is a part of the general account of the insurance company and could be frozen by the state insurance commissioner if the company has problems. This points out the importance of dealing with an investment-grade insurance company that is rated well by the various services. Company selection criteria are covered more extensively in Chapter 14.

MANAGEMENT

To manage your policy, you need complete, accurate, and prompt reports on what is going on within the policy. Insurance companies have the technology to track and provide this data, so ask for a current report from your agent or company. It is your money.

INTEREST RATE ADVANTAGE

Insurance companies may be able to pay slightly higher than current market interest rates on their universal life policy-owner accounts. They guarantee those rates for a 12-

month period and can be fairly sure that most of the money on which they are paying will remain with the company for more than one year. If experience bears this out, the company will be able to lend out reserves of these policies for periods somewhat longer than 12 months, and as a result, earn a higher rate of return for you.

Universal life is a *single-pocket* policy providing no investment flexibility. You may want to look at a *multiple-pocket* policy similar to your multiple-pocket 401(k) plan, so you can diversify for greater safety and higher return.

MAXIMUM-FUNDING LEVEL

If your universal life policy has proved a good place to store cash, if it has provided a competitive after-tax rate of return, you might maximum-fund it and run up against the maximum-funding level. Your policy can accept only a limited amount of money if it is to retain the tax advantages of a life insurance policy. Contact your company to find out just how much is allowed. If you want to put more money in than the code permits, you can ask to increase your death benefit. This entails expenses, additional mortality costs and proof of insurability. The increased death benefit will provide an increased maximum-funding level.

EXPENSES

Universal life is relatively new when compared to whole life. But insurance companies and their personnel are learning to manage the policy, and technology is improving. There is a possibility that the expenses associated with its management could go down. This will benefit us all—policy-owners, companies, and intermediaries. The good news is that you can watch your expenses, and you should. Complain if they are no longer competitive, and if that doesn't work, consider moving to a better contract. Do it carefully with the help of your advisors if you are attempting to do a 1035 tax-free exchange.

MORTALITY COSTS

What about mortality? Will it continue to improve as shown in Exhibit 5.2? Or will some new illness cause rates to go up to the maximum guaranteed by the contract? The AIDS threat, for example, has made insurance companies fear the latter. The risk of reduced returns as a result of increasing mortality costs is not unique to universal life. Higher death rates affect all insurance. Term rates can go up, and whole life dividends can be diminished.

MANAGING THE DEATH BENEFIT

We have been talking about the premium associated with a universal life policy. You also have the ability to manage the amount at risk—the life insurance. You will be asked whether you want Death Benefit Option I (sometimes referred to as Option A) or Option II (Option B) (Exhibit 5.4). Option I is the conventional whole life design, whereby the death benefit stays at the face amount you select when you purchase the policy (say $100,000), in spite of the fact that the account within the policy grows. Therefore, if you died and the insurance company paid off the $100,000 required, it would be partially with your own account value money and partially with insurance company money, i.e.,

Exhibit 5.4 Death Benefit Options

Issue: Who controls $ "at risk" . . .
Insurance company or policy-owner?

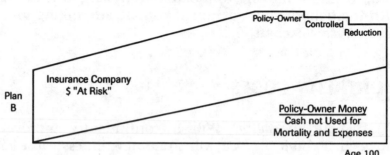

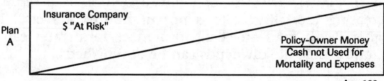

Source: Ben G. Baldwin 1991

life insurance. In effect, every time you put money into the policy, and/or the account value grows as a result of interest earnings, the amount of life insurance is decreased. Alternatively, you could request Option II (Option B) making the amount at risk a constant. That is, the insurance company promises to pay your beneficiary $100,000 of insurance company money (life insurance), *in addition to* the amount of money in your policy-owner account. In most cases, when applying for one of these policies, you will want to keep the life insurance company at risk for the maximum amount, so you will choose Option B (Option II). In the future, when you are more concerned about expenses in the policy than in the death benefit, it would be logical to switch from Option 2 to Option 1. This would result in the total death benefit being leveled to the benefit in force at the time of change. Thereafter, further increases in the account value would diminish the insurance company's amount at risk, and thereby reduce mortality charges within the policy.

You may come to a point where you want to decrease the mortality charges even more. In that case you may request that the insurance company reduce the death benefit on your policy. Do this with caution if you request such a reduction in the early years, because you may have to pay a partial surrender charge or it might cause a force-out of money from within the policy which is likely to create an income-tax liability. The insurance company will limit any death-benefit reductions that would disqualify the policy as a life insurance policy under IRC 7702. With the minimum face amount, the minimum amount of investment return from the account value will be used to service mortality charges, but the policy will still remain a life insurance policy. Earnings will remain sheltered from income taxes, and the policy will serve primarily as an investment vehicle.

Very often we find the reverse scenario when working with young policy-owners. A young couple gets married; both parties are working and are relatively independent of each other economically. They buy a universal life policy with a minimum face amount and adjust their premium payments to reach the desired funding level. At some future date, children come along, and one spouse becomes more economically dependent upon the other. In this case, the young marrieds may ask that the policy death benefit be increased. In many cases, this is far less expensive than applying for and starting a new insurance policy to increase coverage. In fact, if they had maximized premium payments while both were working, they might now decrease their cash flow into the contract while increasing the amount at risk.

CONCLUSION

The key to a proper analysis of universal life insurance is having a monthly breakdown of state premium taxes, expenses, amounts at risk, mortality charges, account values, interest earnings, and potential surrender charges. The insurance company providing the policy earns a profit (if it plans to stay in business) in a number of ways. It can profit on the expense charges by charging you more than it costs to administer the policy. There also has to be some sort of profit margin built into the mortality charges, so the charge may be for more than the mortality being experienced at the current time. In addition, the company is paying you less interest than it is earning on the policy account and/or is charging investment management fees against your account. You want your policy with a profitable company—as long as the profits and charges are reasonable.

BUT IS IT A GOOD INVESTMENT?

The New Life Insurance Investment Advisor is asked: "Generally speaking, do universal life policies provide an acceptable investment alternative to today's insurance buyer?"

Generally speaking, universal life is not an acceptable alternative for today's insurance buyer. The reasons and assumptions behind this generalization are:

1. There are better contracts available as long as you are insurable. You will have no trouble obtaining new insurance at acceptable rates.

2. You do not intend to commit suicide or commit fraud by giving false answers to any of the questions on any of the papers you complete to obtain a different policy.

3. Using historical averages, we cannot expect the one-year interest-rate guarantees provided by the insurance companies to be more than 2 percent over the inflation rate.

4. A one-year-interest account provides insufficient investment diversification for the long-term investor.

5. The creditor risk assumed when investing in the general account of an insurance company (yes, the one-year guaranteed interest account is part of the general account) is unacceptable and unnecessary.

6. You do not have control over the investments in a universal life policy.

7. The policy is a single-pocket policy. It offers only the guaranteed interest account and provides no method of changing that investment if investment needs or desires change.

When is a universal life policy a good investment?

1. When it is doing what *you* want it to do.

2. When it is providing an acceptable tax-free rate of return.

3. When you already own it and your insurability status has deteriorated for *any* reason.

4. When there is not an acceptable alternative.

5. When the *guaranteed* minimum interest rate is a comfort to you.

6. When it does not represent a significant investment to you.

Caution: Do not act on any of this advice until you have thoroughly discussed it with your beneficiaries, your doctor, your tax and legal advisors, and your personal insurance and financial advisors.

Exhibit 5.5 Term "PLUS"—Mortality and Expenses "PLUS" Additional Dollars for Investment

	General Description	Investment Vehicle	Investment Flexibility	Premium Flexibility	Face Amount Flexibility	Appropriate for
Universal Life	Current interest rate flexibility transparency	Short-term interest investments	None Borrow or Withdraw	Maximum. Enough for mortality and expenses, or as much as law allows.	Maximum Increase or decrease... Stay healthy for major increases.	Younger Insureds Variable needs Like short-term interest rate investments.

Source: Ben G. Baldwin 1990

CHAPTER 6

Variable Life Insurance

Kay purchased a variable life policy in September
of 1981 for diversification, since she already
owned a number of whole life policies.
It outperformed all, even the best of her
whole life policies.

Variable life insurance was first brought to the market place in the United States by the Equitable Life Assurance Society in 1976. It took four years of development, negotiations with the Securities and Exchange Commission (SEC) and the approval of the various state insurance commissioners to bring this revolutionary product to market. It was not until four years later that another company, John Hancock, did the same followed shortly thereafter by Monarch Life. Variable life insurance has been slow to develop for a number of reasons. First, the policy must be registered under the Securities Act of 1933 as a security. Second, the agent selling it must be registered under the Securities and Exchange Act of 1934 and must pass the National Association of Security Dealers (NASD) Series 6 Exam to obtain a license to sell it. Third, life insurance agents generally have been uncomfortable with securities. They are used to guarantees, perceive that whole life offers guarantees, and therefore have not taken to variable life.

It was in December of 1976 that the SEC came out with Rule 6E-2, providing the limited exception from sections of the Investment Company Act of 1940 that gave this product life. This rule requires that insurance companies provide an accounting to contract holders, imposes *limitations on sales charges* (there are no such SEC limitations in whole life or universal life), and requires that the insurers offer refunds or exchanges to variable-life purchasers under certain circumstances. Policy-owners also must be offered the option of returning to a whole-life type policy.

Rule 6E-2 defines variable life insurance as a policy in which *the insurance element is predominant*, the cash values are funded by separate accounts of a life insurance company, and death benefits and cash values vary to reflect investment experience. The policy also has to provide a minimum death-benefit guarantee and have mortality and expense risks borne by the insurance company. The basic policy structure is similar to whole life insurance in that a stated face amount at a stated age requires a specific, level, fixed premium payment. Once the policy is issued, the cash value of the contract increases or decreases daily depending on the investment results of the underlying investment fund. There is no guaranteed minimum below which that fund cannot fall. Fixed premium variable life contracts do guarantee that the face amount will not go below the originally issued face amount, regardless of investment experience, and that only the guaranteed level premium will be required to keep the policy in force. If investment experience is positive, on the anniversary date of the policy the face amount of the contract is adjusted upward, reflecting that investment experience. If negative, the death benefit will be adjusted downward, *but never below* the face amount originally contracted for. The original variable life policies had only a money market account and a common stock account available for investment.

You affect the investment results of a variable policy by borrowing from it. By taking a policy loan, you collateralize the equity from the underlying investment accounts. When this happens, the insurance company moves an amount equal to what you have borrowed to a loan guarantee account not subject to market risk, where it will earn one or two percent less interest than you are paying for the loan. The collateralized equity will stay in that account, securing the loan, until such time as the loan is paid off.

The principal difference between whole life and variable life is the investment factor. You will prefer the variable contract if you want the assets invested in an assortment of mutual funds, rather than in the long-term bond and mortgage portfolio typical of a whole life policy. Variable life provides downside protection basically by guaranteeing that the face amount of the policy will never be less than the originally issued face amount no matter what the investment results are, as long as the scheduled premiums are paid. *This guarantee is not available in universal life or in universal variable.* Guaranteed death benefits require guaranteed premiums. Variable life provides the potential for future growth of the death benefit if the investment experience proves to be favorable. Exhibit 6.1 shows the common

Exhibit 6.1 Annual Rates of Return within Variable Life Insurance Common Stock Account

Year Ending December 31	Common Stock
1976	9.2%*
1977	–9.2
1978	8.2
1979	29.8
1980	50.1
1981	–5.8
1982	17.6
1983	26.1
1984	–2.0
1985	33.4
1986	17.3
1987	7.5
1988	22.4
1989	25.6
1990	–8.1
1991	37.9
1992	3.2
1993	24.8

*Unannualized from the inception date.

stock investment experience of early variable life policy-owners.

A LIMRA study entitled *The Performance of Variable Life* reported that only three companies sold equity-based variable life insurance prior to 1981. Variable life sales also represented only 1 percent of the life insurance market. By 1981, there were approximately 10 companies selling the product and market share had increased to 2.5 percent of the ordinary life premium. LIMRA reported that variable life sales remained fairly flat at 3 percent in 1986. This seems a rather inauspicious beginning for a product born in 1976. Its growth was inhibited by insurance company costs of development, the licensing requirements for agents, and the agents' discomfort with mutual fund products.

The Equitable now has more than 17 years of experience with this product. According to its prospectus, it has an historical net rate of return in its common stock account for that period of 14.3 percent per year. This rate exceeds the Standard and Poor's (S&P 500) average for the same time. Those figures substantially outperformed the typical rate of return in conventional whole life insurance contracts. It is time for consumers to take notice of these alternatives—and they are. Variable products accounted for a 6 percent market share in 1991, 9 percent in 1992, and a projected 14 percent to 15 percent in 1993.

The key advantage of variable life is that you have the *ability to direct your account* value to the investment of choice from among those offered. Further, a variety of new accounts are being added. You now will find not only the money market and common stock accounts that were in the early policies, but also aggressive stock accounts; balanced, global and bond funds; high-yield bond funds; guaranteed interest accounts; zero-coupon accounts; and even some real estate accounts.

Even though higher expenses have been associated with first-generation variable life insurance policies, they have offered the highest net return available from a life insurance policy from 1976 to the present when invested in the common stock account.

These policies must be sold with a prospectus that divulges more information regarding the workings of a life insurance policy than ever before. The data has to be extracted from the prospectus to be useful but you will find that easier than you think. You and your agent may not be accustomed to doing this with life insurance, but we are all getting better, and the prospectus is a great source of quality information.

When these policies work efficiently, your investment in the contract provides you with life insurance protection, a family of mutual funds for your investments, professional management, and the ability to redirect your investments. All this can be accomplished without incurring income-tax liability as you move your assets within the contract. The shelter of the contract protects interest, dividends, and capital gains from current income taxation. The sale of one fund and purchase of another within the contract is *not a taxable event.*

A disadvantage of the fixed-premium variable life policy is that once you have purchased it, you cannot increase or decrease the amount to be paid into it. It is designed to be a level premium contract and *you* cannot dictate the terms. This also can be considered an advantage since you are required to keep up your investments in the contract and this may be just the incentive you need to continue investing. We have seen too many people interpreting the *flexibility of investment* feature in universal policies as *an excuse to not invest.* Instead, they choose to spend, which is often detrimental to their economic well-being.

The amount of life insurance is fixed at its minimum level upon the date of purchase. The face amount varies thereafter only as a result of positive and negative investment account results above the initial face amount. This policy does offer a unique advantage in that even if investments results are disastrously poor, you will never be called upon to pay a larger premium than contracted for originally, nor can the face amount of your policy decrease below that at which you originally purchased it. This is unique to fixed-premium variable life and is not available with *any* other type of policy.

While early variable life policies have had positive investment results, the product has been slow to catch on with the public, the insurance sales force, and the financial-planning and investment communities. Many times life insurance agents drag their feet because of their relatively conservative backgrounds and training as well as the additional licensing and educational requirements for selling this product. Investment advisors have been reluctant to recommend it, in spite of its long history of credible results, because many planners have their minds so set against *mixing insurance and investments* that they have not stopped to study it. The planning community will have to become more aware as more clients ask about it. You may personally have to encourage them to do so.

Variable life does require a level premium which is substantially higher than that required by a yearly renewable and convertible term insurance policy, so the decision to invest that additional capital is an important one. Just as you inquire about expenses, management fees, and other factors when you decide to make an investment within a mutual fund, you will need to make similar inquiries when you are about to invest in variable life.

Fixed-premium variable life lacks flexibility of premium and face amount. Universal variable life, introduced in 1985, brought both flexibility of premium and death benefits to the variable life policy.

As we discuss universal variable life insurance in the following chapters, keep in mind that when you move from a fixed-premium variable life contract to a universal variable life contract, you are exposing yourself to an additional downside risk. With universal variable, if expenses and mortality costs increase to the maximum contractually allowable level and investment results are negative, the contract could require a premium higher than the guaranteed level premium in a variable life policy to keep it in force.

BUT IS IT A GOOD INVESTMENT?

The New Life Insurance Investment Advisor is asked: "Generally speaking, do variable life policies provide an acceptable investment alternative for today's insurance buyer?" The rule of thumb is *yes*, variable whole life is an acceptable alternative for today's insurance buyer. Implicit in the assumption that it could be good for you are the following considerations.

1. You are insurable. You will have no trouble obtaining a new variable life insurance policy at acceptable rates.

2. You do not intend to commit suicide or perjure yourself by giving fraudulent information on any of the papers you complete to obtain a policy.

3. The creditor risk of the insurance company issuing the policy as relates to the death benefit and any general account investment alternatives are not a concern for you.

4. The policy provides you with sufficient control over the investment.

5. The policy is a multiple-pocket policy (provides a variety of investment alternatives).

6. The policy is inflexible with regard to premium payment and face amount, and this limitation is considered desirable or acceptable to you.

When is a variable life policy a good investment?

1. When it is doing what *you* want it to do.

2. When it is providing an acceptable tax-free rate of return.

3. When you already own it and your insurability status has deteriorated for any reason.

4. When there is not an acceptable alternative.

Caution: Do not act on any of this advice until you have thoroughly discussed it with your beneficiaries, your doctor, your tax and legal advisors, and your personal insurance and financial advisors.

Exhibit 6.2 Term "PLUS"—Mortality and Expenses "PLUS" Additional Dollars for Investment

	General Description	Investment Vehicle	Investment Flexibility	Premium Flexibility	Face Amount Flexibility	Appropriate for
Variable Life	You direct the investment	Common stock Bond funds Guaranteed interest rates Zero coupons Money markets etc., etc...	Maximum Your decision Split it, move It, etc.	None Fixed premium remains level. Loans available	None Want more?... Buy new, IF you can pass a physical.	The investor. An alternative to... Buy term, invest difference.

CHAPTER 7

Understanding Universal Variable Life Insurance

In 1993, Kay traded in her life insurance policy for a universal variable life insurance policy without having to pay income taxes at that time on the profit in the policy in accordance with Section 1035 of the Internal Revenue Code. She did it to reduce expenses, increase flexibility, and have more room for investment. It is working well.

PROLOGUE

We're here! This is the chapter I've been eager to get to, and you should be happy to have made it, too! This product is why *The New Life Insurance Investment Advisor* exists. Universal variable is "the financial product of the century," a veritable financial Swiss army knife, a product that is capable of helping nearly everyone. It is a very efficient life insurance and investment product for the consumer. Efficient in that, generally speaking, costs are competitive and investments are tax-sheltered, diversified and productive. That may be a pretty big statement and one you may see contradicted in the popular press—but don't believe everything you read. Unfortunately, many publishers of periodicals just want to keep you buying their publications and just give you meaningless generalizations. It would be better if they gave you the information you need to do your own analytical work. You have a very short list of questions to get answered to determine if a universal variable life insurance product is efficient for *you*.

1. Are the term life insurance costs (mortality costs) of the product competitive and acceptable to you?

2. Are the expenses associated with the contract acceptable, and do you expect them to be offset by the income-tax savings on your investment capital and the income tax and transaction cost savings as you move money among the various mutual funds (separate accounts) within the contract?

3. Is this a profitable product to the company issuing it?

4. Is the mutual fund family within your contract broad enough and performing well enough that it is likely to provide good investment opportunities for the rest of your life?

5. Do you expect to maximum-fund the policy as soon and as often as practical and possible for you? Remember, the cost benefit ratio of these products works best when you maximum-fund your policy.

Those are the questions, and the answers are not that difficult to get. Do not accept inaccurate generalizations such as those published in *The Wall Street Journal* of August 12, 1993, i.e., "It's the most expensive form of insurance you can buy," which is simply false, or "annual costs may exceed 4 percent of your investment in some policies," which has no meaning since they have no idea how much money you intend to invest in your contract.

THE BASICS

Universal variable life insurance is created from a combination of universal life, which provides flexibility of face amount and premium payments, and variable life, which provides flexibility of investment. The combined flexibility makes it unique.

Whole life insurance, on the other hand, dictates the investment vehicle, premium amount and face amount. It leaves little room for change. In 1976, variable life came along and allowed the policy-owner to dictate the investment vehicle but continued to insist upon a level face amount and a level premium payment throughout the policy lifetime. In 1979, universal life came along and gave the public the investment vehicle it seemed to want at that time—money-market types of accounts. Universal life allowed the policy-owner to decide on the amount of the premium, within certain parameters, and the size of the policy face amount and permitted change of these decisions to suit personal objectives over time. Since 1981, the consumer has seen the rate of return diminish on interest-rate-sensitive accounts and is becoming increasingly disenchanted with interest-only contracts. Universal life had 8 percent of the market in 1985, 35 percent in 1986, and was dropping below 22 percent in 1993. The market share lost is being gained by universal variable, the product with three-way flexibility that first came to the market in late 1985.

Universal variable generates new enthusiasm because it is not only a second-generation variable life policy, but also a second-generation universal life policy. You can go into a universal variable policy and have its performance emulate that of the old universal life. Just use the guaranteed-interest account available within the contract as your only investment. In fact, you may find that the expenses and back-end loads are lower in universal variable than they are in universal life. Thus, a universal variable policy may make a more cost-effective universal life policy (just using the guaranteed-interest account) than a regular universal life policy. The universal variable policy is a security and, as such, its expense-loading is limited by the Securities Act of 1940.

TRANSFERRING REINS TO THE POLICYHOLDER

The three strings of insurance company control—investment vehicle, face amount and premium payment—have all been cut. In a universal variable policy, you the policy-owner now control your face amount, premium allocation and investment. You may direct the insurance company to bill you a certain amount at specific times, to increase or decrease your face amount, to change the allocation of incoming deposits in the various investment accounts, and to move existing investment from one policy account to another. You may make withdrawals and/or borrow using your policy as collateral. In some policies, you may be able to dictate the account charged for the expenses and mortality costs.

Pruco Life, a subsidiary of Prudential Life, was the first to market a universal variable life product in 1985 closely followed by Equitable Life in 1986. By 1993, the product reached critical mass, meaning there were many more products available to the consumer and more respected companies were offering it.

There are now information services, such as *Morningstar's Life and Annuity Sourcebook* published each year in Chicago, that provide up-to-date information on both the companies providing these products and the performance of the underlying investment accounts.

FINANCIAL EVALUATION OF UNIVERSAL VARIABLE

Financial evaluation of a universal variable life policy is very similar to the process followed for universal life. It requires a monthly illustration over a number of years based on an agreed-upon premium and specified assumed rate of return, and a year-by-year illustration to age 95 based on the assumed premium input requested. The latter shows when back-end loads are no longer a factor and the possible failure of the policy if the illustrated premium results in a

Exhibit 7.1 Specimen Variable Universal Annual Report
Summary of Policy Values

Policy Values as of:	11/01/92	11/01/93
Face Amount	$550,000.00	$746,243.45
Death Benefit	$729,727.88	$746,243.45
Death Benefit Option	B	A
Policy Account	$179,727.88	$226,062.72
Less: Surrender Charge	$2,777.50	$2,777.50
Outstanding Loans	$0.00	$0.00
Net Cash Surrender Value	$176,950.38	$223,285.22

Additional Benefit Riders as of 11/01/93   Insurance Amount

Summary of Loan Activity

Beginning Balance 11/01/92	$0.00
Plus New Loans:	$0.00
Interest Charged:	$0.00
Less Loan Repayments:	$0.00
Interest Paid:	$0.00
Ending Balance 11/01/92	$0.00

5.75% will be credited to the unloaned portion of your guaranteed interest division until 11/01/94.

Exhibit 7.1 Continued

Summary of Transactions All Divisions

	Policy Transactions		Monthly Processing			Cost of Insurance		End-of-Month Policy Account		
			Net Amount Applied to							
Mon Type	Effective	Gross Amount $	Expense Charges $	Policy Account $	Expense Charges $	Insured Person $	Additional Benefit Riders $	Investment Gain or Loss $	Policy Account $	Cash Surrender Value $
(A)	(B)	(C)	(D)	(E)	(F)	(G1)	(G2)	(I)	(J)	(K)
NOV	11/02/92	0.00	0.00	0.00	5.00	114.58	0.00	10,270.82	189,879.15	187,101.65
DEC	12/02/92	0.00	0.00	0.00	5.00	114.58	0.00	2,214.47	191,974.04	189,196.54
JAN	01/02/93	0.00	0.00	0.00	5.00	114.58	0.00	2,955.87	194,810.33	192,032.83
FEB CHDB	02/02/93	0.00	0.00	0.00	0.00	0.00	0.00	0.00		
	02/02/93	0.00	0.00	0.00	5.00	114.58	0.00	−4,632.19	190,058.56	187,281.06
MAR	03/02/93	0.00	0.00	0.00	5.00	115.47	0.00	2,846.59	192,784.68	190,007.18
APR	04/02/93	0.00	0.00	0.00	5.00	116.25	0.00	−353.94	192,309.49	189,531.99
MAY	05/02/93	0.00	0.00	0.00	5.00	115.40	0.00	7,212.43	199,401.52	196,624.02
JUN	06/02/93	0.00	0.00	0.00	5.00	113.86	0.00	2,481.15	201,763.81	198,986.31
JUL	07/02/93	0.00	0.00	0.00	5.00	113.52	0.00	3,679.66	205,324.95	202,547.45
AUG	08/02/93	0.00	0.00	0.00	5.00	112.69	0.00	0.00		
PREM	08/23/93	5,000.00	100.00	4,900.00	0.00	0.00	0.00	10,264.98	220,372.24	217,594.74
SEP	09/02/93	0.00	0.00	0.00	5.00	109.54	0.00	3,507.88	223,765.58	220,988.08
OCT	10/02/93	0.00	0.00	0.00	5.00	108.67	0.00	2,410.81	226,062.72	223,285.22
TOTALS			100.00	4,900.00	60.00	1,363.72	0.00	42,858.53		

policy that is underfunded. The guaranteed illustration shows the downside risk if the insurance company increases its expense-loading and/or mortality costs to the maximum allowable under the contract. The rate of return illustrated on the account values within the contract should be the rate *you* consider conservatively sustainable in the future.

Exhibit 7.1 is an actual annual report on the inner workings of the policy. You want to be able to identify charges for state premium taxes, expenses and administrative charges, and mortality charges. When ordering illustrations from the insurance company, take advantage of break-points (face amount levels at which mortality or expense charges decline). Life insurance, like eggs, can be cheaper per $1,000 when you buy larger face amounts.

Exhibit 7.2 provides a list of the various costs of term insurance for a male, age 50.

You will note that the term rate within the universal variable policy for a 50-year-old male is $3.52 per $1,000 per year, which is 26 cents per $1,000 per year more than the cost of retail term insurance. Column 2 makes the assumption that this purchaser is in the 30-percent marginal income tax bracket. The numbers given in column 2 indicate how much money the individual *must earn* to pay the amount required in column 1. This points out that once the mortality charge within the universal variable life policy is being paid with the pre-tax earnings on the investment within the contract, the cost ($3.52 per $1,000) would be almost as low as the cheapest form of term life insurance ($3.21 per $1,000). The fact that term costs within the policy can be paid using untaxed investment earnings offers our 50-year-old male non-smoker the opportunity to save $1.14 per $1,000 of coverage per year (retail term would cost $4.66; universal variable term, $3.52).

Exhibit 7.2 Cost of Term Insurance
(Male, Age 50, Non-smoker)

Scale	Column 1 Annual Cost per $1,000	Column 2 Col. 1 ÷ 1(1–.30)= Pre-Tax Earnings Necessary to Service Premium (30% Tax Bracket)
American Experience Table	$13.78	
Commissioners 1941 Table	12.32	
Commissioners 1958 Table	8.32	
Commissioners 1980 Table	6.71	
PS 58 Table	12.67	
Uniform Premium Table 1	5.76	
Smoker YRT* (under $200.000)	6.47	$9.24
Smoker YRT (over $200.000)	5.75	8.21
Non-Smoker YRT (under $200.000)	3.99	5.70
Universal Variable ($200.000 and up)	3.52	3.52
Non-Smoker YRT ($200.000 and up)	3.26	4.66
Cheap Term, Smoker	2.88	4.11
Cheap Term, Non-smoker	2.50	3.57
Three-Year Term (Cheapest)	2.25	3.21

*Yearly Renewable and Convertible Term Insurance.

With this information, you can decide which is the most efficient and practical way to pay for your desired insurance protection. If you decide that buying term insurance using untaxed investment earnings is an efficient method, then you can evaluate the investment alternatives and flexibility available within the various policies and choose one appropriate to your needs. Check the track records of the separate accounts available within the policies you are considering.

You also will want to identify and match your investment objectives with the proper investment alternatives and investment managers in your policy.

EXPENSES IN UNIVERSAL VARIABLE

"Ben, why should I read all this? I just saw in *The Wall Street Journal* that variable life is the most expensive form of insurance you can buy!"

You should read all this because *The Wall Street Journal* is wrong. Variable universal life is most likely the most profitable life insurance one can buy. But the financial reporters do bring up an important point. You do need to examine the policy offered you, or even the policy you already own, to know whether the expenses are competitive and acceptable. Generalizations from *The Wall Street Journal* are unacceptable! So, let's do it!

The three elements (expense, mortality, and investment) of investment-type life insurance vary in degree of importance. As Exhibit 7.3 shows, the investment element is the part of the policy that impacts your economic well-being the most. It can make a relatively expensive policy, such as the first generation of variable life in 1976, outperform its less expensive competitors by a substantial margin. Just as those 1976 variable life policies did that invested in the stock mutual funds when compared to all whole life and universal life policies issued at that time!

Exhibit 7.3 The Life Policy Recipe

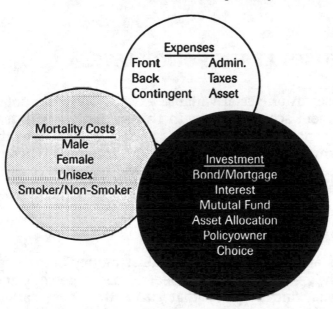

Source: Ben G. Baldwin 1993

Expenses are important, but the media puts so much emphasis on them that many people become paralyzed or wallow around in a potpourri of what they perceive as low-load or no-load products improperly applied to their situations. This is where people lose the most, while thinking they are actually saving.

It does cost money to invest. It also costs money to get assistance with your investing. Why is it that when it comes to financial products and services, the most important things you do with your money, you are least willing to pay for help? Do you expect a free lunch? Keep in mind that even the *best* often hire coaches to help them do even better and money coaches can be worth their weight in gold.

EXPENSES AT THE POLICY LEVEL

Expenses in universal variable exist at both the policy and investment account levels. In this section we will deal with the expenses you incur before your money gets to the mutual funds (sub-accounts or separate accounts). These are insurance company charges that cover its costs, commissions to intermediaries, company profit provisions, etc.

FRONT SALES LOAD

This is an expense charged against money being deposited into the policy. You can expect to pay 4 percent and with luck may find a policy that drops the charge after some stipulated sum has been paid. There are some policies that charge no front-end sales load and some with front-end loads of up to 8.5 percent.

Front Sales Load

Low	Average	High
0%	4%	8%

STATE PREMIUM TAXES

You will not be the first to be surprised (and annoyed) to find that here is another place taxes get you. There are state premium taxes deducted from every dollar you pay into a

Exhibit 7.4 State of Residence Premium Taxes

ST	CURR TX	ST	CURR TX	ST	CURR TX
AL	3.300	KY	3.000	OH	2.500
AK	2.700	LA	2.750	OK	2.250
AZ	2.000	ME	2.000	OR	2.250
AR	2.500	MD	2.000	PA	2.000
CA	2.350	MA	2.000	PR	4.000
CO	2.250	MI	1.330	RI	2.000
CT	2.000	MN	2.000	SC	0.750
DE	2.000	MS	3.000	SD	2.500
DC	2.250	MO	2.000	TN	2.000
FL	1.750	MT	2.750	TX	2.400
GA	2.250	NE	1.000	UT	2.250
GU	1.000	NV	3.500	VT	2.000
HI	2.750	NH	2.000	VI	5.000
ID	3.000	NJ	2.100	VA	2.250
IL	2.000	NM	3.000	WA	2.000
IN	2.000	NY	0.920	WV	3.000
IA	2.000	NC	2.023	WI	2.000
KS	2.000	ND	2.000	WY	1.200

policy that go to your state of residence. (Exhibit 7.4 shows the premium tax in your state.)

With your universal variable life policy, you're likely to see this tax come out in the front-end sales charge, e.g., 4 percent for the company and 2 percent for the state, for a total of 6 percent of your investment. The insurance companies do not have a choice with state premium tax. Some policies may not show it coming out, but you can bet it is being paid.

BACK-LOADS/CONTINGENT DEFERRED SALES CHARGES/SURRENDER CHARGE

The back-end load is the amount of the policy account value you forfeit if you surrender (terminate) your policy. It reimburses the insurance company for expenses that have not yet been recovered.

It is important to note how this surrender charge or contingent deferred sales charge is limited and when it is no longer a threat. If you plan to invest substantially above the basic premium, be careful to determine how such contributions will effect surrender charges. Also, if you decide that you want to reduce your face amount while the surrender charge still is applicable, you will need to determine how much of the surrender charge will be applied as a result. Normally no more than a pro-rata share would be deducted, proportional to the amount of policy reduction.

As with universal life, universal variable policies make inefficient term insurance contracts (underfunded policies are not economical). The additional expenses incurred in setting up these contracts are higher than set-up costs for a term policy. Don't even purchase one if you don't intend to be an investor and to keep it beyond the back-end load period. Once this problem is resolved, there's still the potential for ordinary income tax liability when you terminate your policy in some way other than by dying. To the extent that the contract has been successful and the policy account values exceed your total premium contributions, the amount of gain will be subject to ordinary income tax in the year of surrender. If you intend to hold the policy at least beyond the period in which a back-end load is charged, it will be preferable to a front-end load in most circumstances. Front loads reduce your investment, while back-end loads make those funds available to earn an investment return.

The back-end load is an expense you pay when you terminate your contract. It could go on forever, meaning there could always be a surrender charge no matter how long you own your policy. More typically, you will find a contingent deferred sales charge. This is applicable *if* you terminate or reduce your policy within a certain period of time, but not charged otherwise. It's *contingent* upon how long you have owned your contract.

Deferred Sales Charges

Low	Normal	High
None	For 10–15 years Decreasing	A percentage of your account value

|⎵——————————————|⎵——————————————|⎵|

Deferred sales charges go to pay sales-people. The insurance company advances a commission at the time of the sale and will not recover this unless your policy stays on the books long enough for the company to profit by it. Surrender charges or contingent deferred sales charges are frequently defined as a percent of *target premium*.

TARGET PREMIUM

The basic target premium for New York-state-licensed insurance companies is the premium level on which commissions are calculated on flexible premium contracts as determined by the Commissioner of the State of New York. Normally, the commission payable on these types of policies is about 50 percent of the target premium plus 4 percent of payments in excess of the target premium. Renewal commissions based upon your continued investment into your policy for years 2 through 10 average approximately 4 percent of premium paid, and for the 11th year and thereafter, 2 percent. The 2 percent is a transferable service fee payable to the agent providing the policy-owner with service and is currently applicable only to new money being paid into the contract. These commissions are paid out of the expenses you pay to the insurance company. You will note that what the insurance company deducts from what you pay into your policy is insufficient, so it advances the commissions and then amortizes those expenses out of what they earn in future years. Commissions are also paid to the agent when the policy-holder requests an increase in the face amount of the policy.

Target premium is a premium dollar amount you will find referred to over and over again as you examine sales loads and surrender charges. The salesperson is also interested in this number because it is that number upon which commissions are based, e.g., 40 percent of target premium. There has been, and continues to be, pressure to downsize sales commissions. There are those who think that a movement away from high first-year and low renewal commissions toward more level commissions and charges based upon assets under management would be better in the long run for sales-people, the insurance company, and you. With these policies, the help of a knowledgeable agent to manage your policy profitably can be invaluable. You want continued long-term interest in you and your contract, and the commission system of today is not conducive to that. The agents can't do what they are not paid for in the long run.

Your target premium is determined when your policy is issued. It is based upon your age, sex, smoker (non-smoker) status, and your policy face amount. The insurance company will give you this all important number. Target premium generally is approximately 75 percent of a typical whole-life annual premium. This means that you will want to read your contract or prospectus to find the limitations on various expenses based upon target premium so that you can calculate the dollar amount of those costs and determine how they will affect the performance of your policy.

ADMINISTRATION FEES

First-year administration fees are typically higher than ongoing administration fees. The higher first-year fee covers the costs of setting up the policy and those incurred in determining if you are healthy, wealthy, and cautious enough to buy a policy. The average first-year cost is between $300 and $400 with a high of around $600 or $700.

Administration Fees

Low	Average	High
$200	$300 to $400	$700

ONGOING MONTHLY ADMINISTRATION FEE

This fee enables the insurance company to provide continuing services such as mailing your confirmation notices, giving you periodic reports, providing telephone-reporting, the prospectus and annual reports. It can run $4 to $15 a month with $5 to $7 being typical.

The company will tell you what it is currently charging and the maximum it can charge by contract.

Continuing Administration Fees

Low	Average	High
$4/mo.	$5–$7/mo.	$15/mo.

Examples of Calculations

Target premium equals $_____.

Commissions are ____% of target premium = $_____.

Sales charges may stop at _____% of target premiums $_____.

Maximum surrender charges are _____% of target premiums $_____.

Reduced surrender charges are applicable over time.

Determine the dollar amount of your contingent surrender charges from the information provided in your policy and prospectus.

Commissions are _____% above target premium = $_____.

FEES FOR SERVICES

Moving Your Investments within Your Policy

Your universal variable policy will give you the right to move your existing investments among the mutual funds within your policy but may limit the number of moves you may make per year and/or charge for the moves. Your objective is to have the freedom to move as often as possible at the least amount of cost.

Most companies make no charge for four moves per year and thereafter reserve the right to charge up to $25 per move.

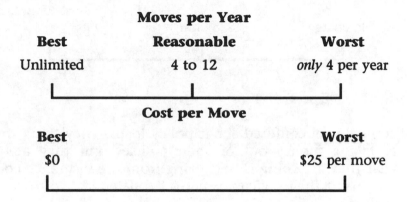

Moves per Year

Best	Reasonable	Worst
Unlimited	4 to 12	*only* 4 per year

Cost per Move

Best	Worst
$0	$25 per move

POLICY LOANS AND WITHDRAWALS

The provisions relating to policy loans and withdrawals are important to examine. They tell you what it takes to get your money out of the policy without terminating it. They determine the liquidity of your universal variable life investment. When you ask for information about loans and withdrawals, the insurance company will give it to you in terms of *cash surrender value*. Let's define terms so that you don't get confused.

   Policy account value (gross value of money in policy)

   – Surrender Charge

   = Cash Surrender Value (CSV).

Typically you will be able to borrow 90 percent of the cash surrender value. You can expect to be charged $25 to process a withdrawal.

Withdrawals (typical)

Best	Typical	Worst
$100% CSV	90% CSV	Cannot withdraw
No charge	$25 charge	

|_____|_____|

What Is "Spread!"?

People do get confused about policy loans. They think they are taking money out of their policies, but they aren't. What they are doing is borrowing from the insurance company, using their policies as perfect collateral.

Policy Loans

Best	Typical	Worst
100% CSV	90% CSV	75% CSV
Zero spread loan	1–2% spread	4% spread

|_____|_____|

If you don't pay off your loan, some day the insurance company will take the money from your policy or the death benefit. The company takes an amount equal to what you have borrowed and moves it into the loan guarantee fund. This fund then earns interest for you. So you are paying interest to the company for money you borrowed and the company is paying you interest on the amount in the loan guarantee fund. The difference between the two is called the "spread." Typically you will find the company crediting you 2 percent less than you are paying it. The spread at best could be zero whereby you would be paying each other the same interest, or at worst, up to 4 percent in excess of what the company is paying you.

Loan Interest Spread

Best	Average	High
0%	2%	4%

LOAN OR WITHDRAWAL?

Management Tip

> *Mike and Karen call. They need some money*
> *from their policy for a down payment on a*
> *home. They like their policy, need the insurance,*
> *and have determined that the expenses and*
> *insurance costs are fair. They like the investment*
> *results within their policy, so their intention is to*
> *"fill the policy back up" as soon as their*
> *finances allow. Should they borrow on the policy*
> *or simply make a withdrawal?*

The answer depends upon the loan interest spread. What is the difference between the interest they pay for the loan and the interest the insurance company pays them on the collateralized portion of the policy? They found that the spread was 1 percent. The company credits the collateral portion of their policy account with 1 percent less than it charges them for the loan.

How about new money coming into the policy? What does it cost to get new money in? They find that there is a 2-percent state premium tax and a 4-percent front sales load. The cost to get new money in is 6 percent, 5 percent more than the 1-percent spread.

Answer

Borrow the money! The cost is 1 percent, and they can pay back that loan without paying the 2-percent state premium tax or the 4 percent front load. They can fill their policy back up faster and with less cost (1 percent vs. 6 percent) than if they withdrew the money and put it back in as new money.

If they decided to make a partial withdrawal, it should be contractually available from the company. However, the Tax Reform Act of 1986, Section 7702, may have made such policy withdrawals impractical from an income-tax standpoint. Withdrawals can create ordinary income-tax liabilities within the first 15 years of the policy's life. It is important to know your rights under the partial withdrawal provision. In some cases there may be a minimum, such as $500, and fees may be assessed for making such withdrawals, such as $25 each time. There also may be a limit on the amount that may be withdrawn, and, from a practical standpoint, it would not be wise to so diminish the account that the policy could fail (lapse) for lack of sufficient cash to continue. Failed policies create income-tax consequences.

EXPENSES AT THE INVESTMENT ACCOUNT LEVEL

Monthly Expenses/Cost of Insurance

This is the cost of the life insurance provided by your policy. Good questions in evaluating these costs are:

1. Do I need/want the life insurance?   Yes/No

(a) If I die will someone experience an
economic loss?   Yes/No

(b) Do I care?   Yes/No

(Three Nos and you're out of here. You don't need to pay
mortality costs that will reduce your investment returns.
You don't "*need*" life insurance.)

If you made it through, your next question is:

2. Are the mortality charges fair and competitive?

As you go about answering this question, you will be
amazed at how expensive any mortality costs look if you
are young, healthy and still enjoying that immortal phase
of life during which death occurs to others but not to you!
But how minor these costs become as life chooses ways
(heart attack, death of a contemporary, using your reserve
chute on a parachute jump) to suggest that your time here,
too, is temporary.

Your monthly cost for life insurance will vary initially based
upon your age, sex, health, use or non-use of any nicotine
products (smoker/non-smoker), and your occupation and
avocations. Once your initial status is determined through a
process the insurance companies call underwriting, your
status should be set for the life of the policy. A future
change in health, smoking habits, avocations, etc., cannot
increase your rates. However, should your situation change
for the better, do ask the company to consider reducing
your rates. If, for example, you have given up all nicotine

products for a period in excess of 12 months, get that smoker's rate removed!

Your cost of insurance will increase nevertheless, as you age. Understand that this is true with every insurance policy. In spite of the fact that this inevitably increasing cost may be masked and unseen in fixed-premium, fixed-face amount offerings, it exists!

ARE MY COSTS OF LIFE INSURANCE FAIR AND COMPETITIVE?

Look around! How much would it cost you to buy term insurance? If the company you are considering just issued you term insurance without the possibility of investing how much would it charge? Is the cost you are looking at a low bid or a cost determined after you have been underwritten to determine *your real status?* That is important. Fictional, unobtainable rates by low bidders do not count!

Once I determine that the costs for insurance are fair, does that mean I can quit looking at them? Will they always be fair?

The company will increase your cost of life insurance as you get older. It can also change the cost based upon its actual experience. So the answer is a double no. You should watch the cost of life insurance within your policy to make sure it doesn't get out of line with the competition. There will be services to help you with this in the future and currently there are people working to keep these costs in line right now.

1. Salespeople want the costs within products they sell to remain competitive because they know you won't buy them and keep them in force otherwise. Salespeople are your allies, and your voice coupled with theirs will be heard by companies that charge unjustifiably high mortality costs because together you vote with your money and your feet. You both can go to other companies that make reasonable charges, fair for you and company purposes. You don't want a company issuing policies that are unprofitable. In spite of the fact that the separate accounts are not attachable by the creditors, you do not need a disappearing company!

2. Your life insurance contract will contain a page that lists the guaranteed maximum cost of insurance rates based on state insurance regulations. The maximum rates will be based on the *Commissioner's 1980 Standard Ordinary Male and Female Smoker and Non-Smoker Mortality Tables*. For the maximums applicable to you, see the appropriate page in a policy issued for you.

MORTALITY CHARGE/COST OF INSURANCE MANAGEMENT TIP

Show me a life insurance policy that has no cost of life insurance and I'll show you a policy with no net amount at risk, no life insurance.

A diagram of a typical fixed-premium, fixed-face-amount whole life policy would look like this:

Conventional Whole Life Insurance Face Amount

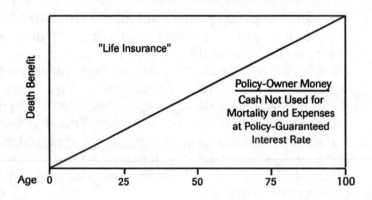

A diagram of a typical fixed-premium, fixed-face-amount *variable* whole life policy would look similar to this, with more ups and downs in the diagonal line, depending upon investment performance.

You can ask your insurance company to make your universal variable life insurance policy look just like the variable whole life as long as it complies with the definition of life insurance in Internal Revenue Code Section 7702. You need to understand the implications of your decision and select what is commonly referred to as Death Benefit Option A (or Option I).

If selecting Option A (Option I):

1. The amount of life insurance will go down as your account value goes up. The insurance company will have less net amount at risk since it will be providing you with less life insurance as your policy account value increases. The bigger the account value, the smaller the net amount at risk. Each month the

company calculates the number of thousands-of-dollars of net amount at risk and multiplies that by the cost per $1,000 of life insurance to determine the total monthly amount to be charged against your policy account. Less life insurance results in less cost for life insurance.

2. The insurance company gets to eliminate the amount it has at risk. Do you want this to happen, or do you want the life insurance (insurance company money) in the event of your death?

If you would prefer to maintain the amount of insurance company money at a constant level rather than reducing its amount at risk with each dollar you pay in, then ask for Option B/II.

DEATH BENEFIT OPTION B (OPTION II)

A diagram of the Option B/II death benefit in comparison to Option A/I would look like the Exhibit on the following page.

With Option B/II, at your death the policy would pay the original face amount *plus* your policy account value. *The New Life Insurance Investment Advisor* usually recommends that you start off using Option B during your account-building days. Then, when you see that you have enough, or are no longer adding capital to your policy, switch to Option A. You can ask the company to reduce your face amount (being careful to avoid partial surrender charges or income taxes) to eliminate unneeded life insurance and mortality charges.

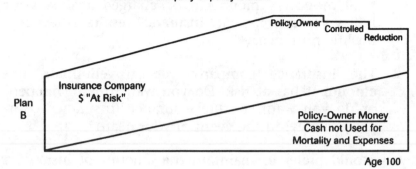

Death Benefit Options

Issue: Who controls $ "at risk" . . .
Insurance company or policy-owner?

Source: Ben G. Baldwin 1993

GUARANTEED INTEREST ACCOUNT

The charges against a guaranteed interest account, should you have one within your policy, are taken prior to the company's quote on your guaranteed interest rate for the period. They quote you the "NET" interest rate. This account is a part of the general account of the insurance company and, as such, is not subject to the Securities Act of 1933 or the Investment Company Act of 1940. You will not see the expenses considered as the company determines its gross expected rate of return on your money within the guaranteed interest division, nor will you see how it arrived at the net interest it is willing to pay you.

You will want to know whether the guaranteed interest account is guaranteed for both principal and interest, how the current interest is credited, and for how long a period the interest is guaranteed.

Shortest	Guarantee Periods	Longest
1 month	1 year	10 years

For the separate accounts, you will see charges listed in the prospectus. You should investigate whether the mutual fund account management team has been consistent in meeting the stated fund investment objectives. You also will want to know how long the company has been in the business of managing variable life separate accounts and the historical performance of those accounts.

EXPENSES AT THE SEPARATE ACCOUNT/ MUTUAL FUND LEVEL

The distinction between the expenses at the investment account level and those itemized in your policy reports is that the former are charged against and reduce the return of your investment accounts. Your mutual fund investment return is reported NET of these charges.

Since your investment accounts are reported to you net of these charges they are not readily seen, but you will find them reported in detail within your policy prospectus and annual reports. Morningstar, an independent rating service, also reports these costs in its *Variable Annuity/Life Annual Sourcebook.*

There is a tendency in each of us to look at the net rate of return, whether it be from the guaranteed interest account or from the various separate accounts offered, and, finding it competitive, we decide not to worry about what the insurance company deducts for itself. The problem is that over the long term, high expenses at the investment account level will affect your return. You want to make sure that what you are paying *is competitive* with the other universal variable life policies available.

MORTALITY AND EXPENSE (M&E) CHARGES (M&E RISK)

Your insurance company provides a number of guarantees within your policy and charges you for them. The guarantees provided are:

- Continuing Lifetime Service

- Maximum Monthly Administrative Charges

- Maximum Monthly Cost of Life Insurance Charges

- Guaranteed Annuity Factors Within the Contract

Mortality and Expense Charges

Lowest	Average	Highest
0.40%	0.82%	1.30%

Keep in mind that these charges are made against your account prior to report of your rate of return. Can they be important? You bet! How would you like to be in a money market account with a 1.3 percent charge against it?

INVESTMENT MANAGEMENT AND FEE ADVISORY

This is the fee charged for the overall management of the underlying mutual funds, what you pay for the professional management of your money. It is taken daily from the underlying mutual funds' daily net assets, and may go down as the size of the funds under management grows (e.g., 0.50 percent on the first $350M down to 0.45 percent on amounts over $750M). It also will vary with the different mutual funds in the family of funds within your policy based upon the differing management required for a money market fund (40 percent) as opposed to a global or asset allocation account (55 percent).

Investment Management/Advisory Fee

Low	Average	High
0.40%	0.80%	2.8%

UNIVERSAL VARIABLE EXPENSE SUMMARY

From What You Pay into the Policy

	Low	Average	High
Sales Charges	0%	4%	8%
State Premium Taxes	0.75%	2%	5%
First-Year Expense	$200	$300–$400	$700

From Your Policy Account (Itemized Charges)
Ongoing Administration Fees

	Low	Average	High
	$4/mo	$5–$7/mo	$15/mo

Fees for Services:

Moves	$0	limited number free	$25/move
Moves/year	Unlimited		4/year

Policy Loans:

	100% CSV 0% spread	90% CSV 1–2% spread	75% CSV 4% spread
Withdrawals	100% CSV No charge	90% CSV $25/charge	cannot withdraw

Surrender Charges:

	none	10 to 15-year/ disappearing	%/acct. value Account Value

FUNDING TO PAY EXPENSES

An important policy investment objective should be to earn sufficient return each year on the capital invested to pay for the expenses and term insurance costs for that particular year. If this is accomplished, you will have paid for your life insurance costs with the pre-tax earnings on your investments. This is the least expensive way to cover these costs.

This means that a specific amount of capital within your policy is used to meet an important near-term objective, i.e., to pay the costs charged against your policy each month. You'll want that amount of capital sufficient to generate the monthly earnings to cover these costs in a relatively conservative account that has a high likelihood of generating the required income. The accounts most certain to accomplish this objective may be those accounts that guarantee both principal and interest or those that can be depended upon to generate income. One strategy would be to put enough into that account to generate the income required to cover all mortality and expense charges. For example, if policy expenses were $100 per month and the guaranteed interest account was earning 5 percent, you would want $24,000 ($1,200 ÷ 5%) in that account.

FUNDING FOR OTHER OBJECTIVES

Additional capital placed in the universal variable contract would be used to accomplish your other investment objectives. In so doing, you have the advantage of 1) *no* current income taxes being assessed against your investment earnings and 2) changes of investment allocation within the family of funds offered under the insurance contract being made without creating income-tax liabilities or transaction costs.

WHAT ELSE CAN YOU BUY WITH YOUR ACCOUNTS EARNINGS?

In addition to the above, there often are additional beneficial purchases. There are riders such as disability premium waiver, accidental death benefit, children's term insurance, other-insured and spouse term insurance, guaranteed insurability riders on yourself or others, cost-of-living increase options, automatic increase options, and survivor insurability provisions. The desirability of any of these is unique to each policy-owner. The advantage of purchasing these riders within the policy is the ability to do so with pre-tax dollars.

EXCHANGE PRIVILEGE

The exchange privilege allows you to change insureds. You can take a policy on your life that you no longer need and have it insure the life of another individual who might need it. In family situations and those involving key employee life insurance, this privilege can be very valuable because you can make one policy provide for a succession of insureds. Policy charges are adjusted based upon the new insured's age, sex, and insurability status, but start-up charges are eliminated. Look for this important feature in your policy. Since first generation universal variable policies often were more favorable to the consumer than the "new improved models," when you no longer want your policy, find someone who does!

CONCLUSION

You have the ability to manage flexible-premium variable life insurance and adapt it to your changing needs and economic situations. This is its advantage. Its disadvantage is the same. You have to actively manage it, and the help you get from the agents/intermediaries often will increase your profits. Keep in touch with them, making sure they know what you are trying to accomplish. They work with these policies every day, and they have learned from policy-owners and through continuing education how to make them perform best for you. It is good for their business to have you *very very* happy with your policy.

CHAPTER 8

How to Invest in
Universal Variable

DEALING WITH UNCERTAINTY

We are concerned here with economic uncertainty. The *will I have enough*? question. Look at the economic lifeline of each of us shown in Exhibit 8.1.

We all come into this world as an economic negative, dependent upon others. As our feet get larger and the cost of education increases, we become greater economic negatives to our parents. At some time, we cross the line. We become economic positives and our parents, in most cases, breathe an economic sigh of relief.

But, some day our ability to earn a living by our personal efforts will deteriorate or cease, and we will again become

Exhibit 8.1 The Economic Life Cycle

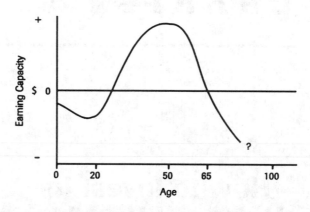

economic negatives. Hopefully we will have chopped off a large enough a piece of those earnings during our productive years and built ourselves an income-generator. We need a pool of capital that, properly invested, will generate *enough* ever-replaceable income to provide for our lifetime economic needs. We need to transfer purchasing power from our productive years to provide for us in our less productive years. Aren't you thankful your folks did that and are not dependent upon you, or if they didn't, don't you wish they had? You can bet that your kids, if you have them, or other potential care-givers are hoping you have provided for yourself economically so they can provide the care you need without suffering economically themselves.

Once you have decided to transfer purchasing power from the present to the future, the next question is, *Where should I store that purchasing power?* The PASS System offers suggestions on how to allocate investment and capital within your policy (see page 152).

Exhibit 8.2 Economic Gravity

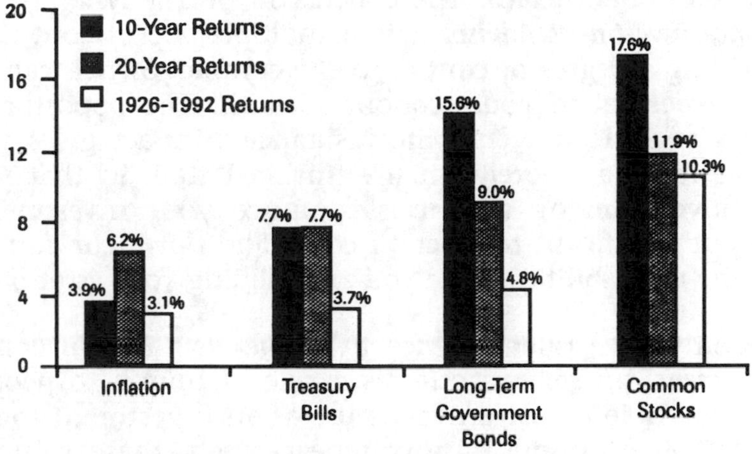

Bar chart legend:
- 10-Year Returns
- 20-Year Returns
- 1926-1992 Returns

Inflation: 3.9%, 6.2%, 3.1%
Treasury Bills: 7.7%, 7.7%, 3.7%
Long-Term Government Bonds: 15.6%, 9.0%, 4.8%
Common Stocks: 17.6%, 11.9%, 10.3%

Source: Ibbotson Associates Inc., Chicago

ECONOMIC GRAVITY

Exhibit 8.2 tells us what various investments have done for the past 66 years. You could assume that these investments will tend to track these norms in the future, or you could say that because history has changed, these investment results likewise will change. Which takes greater courage or arrogance? We will assume that the various investment classes will do as they have in the past.

Asset allocation studies, the PASS System results, and the effects of *economic gravity* as shown in Exhibit 8.2 suggest that we should not invest in only one asset class or *anything that inflexibly dictates and provides only one class for long-term investment.*

The conclusion of *The New Life Insurance Investment Advisor* is that investment in single-pocket insurance contracts (providing only one investment alternative) is hazardous to your economic health. The conclusion of *The New Life Insurance Investment Advisor* is that multiple-pocket contracts, providing a degree of control to the contract-owner, can be very beneficial to your economic health. The opportunity that a variable universal life insurance contract gives you makes it an absolutely unique financial tool, in that you can invest among asset classes, move your investments without significant transaction costs, and not incur current income-tax liabilities while you are building your asset base.

The only investment advice that *The New Life Insurance Investment Advisor* can offer as a rule of thumb to people buying whole life or universal life as an investment today is *don't*! If economic history repeats itself, these vehicles cannot provide an inflation-adjusted rate of return. Life insurance policies are rate-of-return-driven. Expenses and mortality charges are most significant in policies that can't generate investment returns significant enough to pay those costs and help you get ahead.

> *But, I'm still afraid of stocks. Won't the guarantees like the guaranteed cash value and the guaranteed minimum interest rate in universal life be enough so I don't have to worry about diversifying my investments within a policy?*

GUARANTEES?

In spite of, and maybe because of the fact that life is uncertain, we look to guarantees. What we often fail to do is to examine the *guarantor*, the strength behind the guarantee and what is being guaranteed.

If you are going to depend on guarantees, you may want to shop for the company with the best guarantee, the highest guaranteed cash value, and the highest guaranteed interest rate. Acting on that, you may well find yourself buying from a company doomed to disappear first. If general interest rates drop below the company's guaranteed rate and the company's general account becomes unable to earn what its guarantee promises to pay, the company's surplus will be diminished as it delivers its promise to you and continues to pay you more than it is earning. Today's regulatory environment requires companies to own higher-quality and lower-yielding investments in their general accounts. It also dictates that state insurance commissioners take over companies whose surpluses fall below certain levels. In this environment, companies that could have survived economic aberrations in the past will find it more difficult to do so in the future. *Conclusion*: when minimum guarantees become important to you, your guarantor is heading for trouble. The security you seek within the guarantee is weakening. Flexibility, asset allocations, and maximum investing are *more important* than *guarantees*.

How do you buy guarantees in life insurance policies?

By promising to pay a contractually fixed premium! Guaranteed cash value occurs only when policy-owners provide the fixed-premium payments required by the contract. You violate the pay-in provisions, and you lose your guarantee!

Guaranteed death benefits are purchased the same way. You must agree to invest some minimum amount, and if you don't, you lose your guarantee. But, so-and-so (latest financial guru who spouts platitudes rather than useful information) wrote that in universal variable there is no guaranteed cash value and often no guaranteed death benefit, and if you invest unwisely in your policy it could self-destruct!

Like the persistent lawyer interrogating the expert witness, the witness must acknowledge that a universal variable policy could fail. You, the jury, go away concluding that this makes it riskier than a policy with guarantees. This is in spite of the fact that the risk of failure also exists within the policy with the guarantees (if the company mismanages it) and in a universal variable policy if *you* mismanage it. You can control the risk in a universal variable policy; you cannot control the risks in a policy with guarantees.

How can I mismanage a life insurance policy?

There are two primary ways in which you can mismanage a universal variable policy: by investing too little in your policy and by not using common sense and diversification in investing your capital within the policy. If you fund a universal variable policy with the same level of investment required with a comparable whole life policy, and use reasonable care and diversification within your policy investments, the chances of the policy self-destructing are between slim and none.

The way to get rich with universal variable is to invest as much in your policy as you can and the law allows and still retain *all* of the income-tax benefits unique to the life insurance policy investment. The old concepts of whole life—*paid up* at age "?", *short pay*, *vanishing premium*, or whatever other label implies that you no longer have to pay in—are obsolete. They became obsolete the day the investment returns available within the contract were able to compete favorably with your taxable investment portfolio, the day variable universal life became available to you.

To enjoy maximum investment results within your universal variable policy, you will want to maximize your investment. To enjoy maximum income-tax benefits in your policy, maximize your investment. Your question is no longer *how little can I put into this policy* but *how much!*

However, the advantage to this policy is that it is flexible. You will be, at times, a maximum-funder of your life insurance policy and at other times, a minimum-funder. Let's address the subject of universal variable funding levels.

Exhibit 8.3 Funding Worksheet for Universal Variable Life

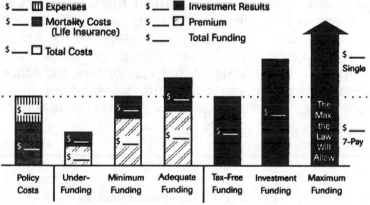

Source: Ben G. Baldwin 1991

FUNDING LEVELS IN UNIVERSAL/ VARIABLE POLICIES

Once you have made the decision to buy life insurance with pre-tax dollars earned on an investment account, you still have to decide *how much* to invest and *where* to invest. If you have decided on conventional whole life and its long-term bonds and mortgages, or the interest-sensitive variety and its short-term money-market types of investments, both the *amount to invest* and the *where to invest* decisions have been made. The company tells you how much to pay based upon the face amount and the type of policy in which you invest. There is little flexibility of premium payment after that. Similarly, with variable whole life, you agree, at contract inception, to set a premium and face amount, but retain management control and flexibility over where the money is to be invested in the contract. On the other hand, if you have purchased a universal life contract, your level of funding is important not only on the day you decide on a specific face amount of life insurance and put the policy in force but also throughout the life of the contract. The ability to vary payments gives you important investment opportunities. To take advantage, it may help you to think of your funding strategy as one of the following: under-funding, minimum-funding, adequate-funding, tax-free funding, investment-funding, or maximum-funding. A description of each follows.

Exhibit 8.4 Tax-Free Funding

Current Investment
Results

"Equal"

Expenses Plus
Mortality Charges

Tax-Free Funding Level

The primary objective of the life insurance policy is to provide life insurance protection in the amount you consider necessary. You may want to pay for this insurance with income-tax-free earnings on an investment account. The tax-free funding point is reached when the amount of capital invested inside the policy will earn enough non-taxable return in the year in question to pay all of the mortality and expense charges within the policy in that year. Such a strategy assures that you will be paying for your life insurance with the pre-tax earnings on the after-tax capital you have invested. As long as the mortality and expense charges are fair and competitive, you will have accomplished your objective.

To determine the tax-free cost-funding level, you need to know the amount of the expenses and mortality charges within your policy for the year. This information is readily available for universal and universal variable policies. For whole life and variable whole life policies, however, the cost amounts are not divulged. These funding levels are determined by dividing the amount of the expenses and mortality charges for the year by the return expected or guaranteed for that year. If your mortality and expenses are to be $400 this year and your expected return is 5 percent, then you will need $8,000 in your policy to reach the optimum funding level. Your $8,000 earning 5 percent will generate $400 of pre-tax interest, which is sufficient to cover $400 in expenses and mortality charges.

Suppose that you are a 45-year-old buying a $250,000 straight term insurance policy with an annual premium of $430 in the first year. To generate the $430 after taxes, you would have to earn $614 [$430 ÷ (1 minus a marginal tax bracket) $430/.70]. Alternatively, you could have elected to pay $571 inside a universal variable policy. You have the option of investing enough after-tax capital in the policy so that the untaxed earnings are sufficient to pay the $571. You would save $43 ($614 − $571) in the year in question if the tax-free return on $11,420 of capital ($571 ÷ 5%) in the policy is competitive with alternative investment opportunities.

On the other hand, if the same $11,420 was invested elsewhere, it would have to earn 5.4 percent to guarantee the $614 of taxable earnings required to service a $430 straight term premium. If the policy-owner can obtain either a 5 percent tax-free return or a near 5.4 percent taxable return outside the policy, the choice between buying straight term or paying for term insurance inside universal or universal variable becomes a toss-up. The returns offered within variable universal policies typically are very competitive, provide for diversification, and offer generally lower risks. Also, future term rates are often lower than those available elsewhere. This is aside from the fact that they also provide opportunity for greater investment.

The next decision you have to make concerns where to invest the capital, given the choices offered within the policy. The first investment objective will be to service the policy's expense and mortality charges. The need is for monthly income to cover monthly costs, so you'll want to look at the guaranteed interest account, a money market account, a bond account or some other account that generates dependable monthly income.

Adequate-Funding

We have defined tax-free funding as a strategy whereby investment proceeds in the policy generate enough investment return to pay all mortality and expense charges incurred in the policy in the year in question. Adequate-funding is a strategy for you if you do not have or do not wish to invest sufficient capital within a policy to reach the tax-free funding level immediately. It provides for a level of payments that allows you to arrive at tax-free funding at some future date.

Exhibit 8.5 Adequate-Funding

Current Premium
Plus
Investment Results

"Exceed"

Expenses Plus
Mortality Charges

Periodically and at least yearly, check your policy to see how it is progressing and adjust the funding level to your current situation and investment objectives.

Under-Funding

If the mortality and expense charges exceed the combined total of the investment earnings in the policy and the current year's payment into the policy, your universal variable policy is under-funded—and in trouble! For example, you look at the annual report on your universal variable life policy and find that your expenses for the year were $500. Upon further examination, you find that your policy interest earnings amounted to only $100 and that you have paid only $100 into the policy during the year. Your contribution and the interest earnings totaled $200, whereas expenses totaled $500. To cover the $500 due in expenses, a $300 bite was taken out of principal, the capital previously accumulated in the policy. At the end of the year, you will find $300 less capital in the policy than you had when you began the year. If you ignore this process, you will find in the coming year that you have less capital to earn interest. If you don't increase your contributions, you'll find at the end of that year another decrease in capital exceeding that of the previous year. The situation gets worse as the mortality charges in the policy increase as you get older. The expense charges also may be increased to some contractual maximum, and the interest earnings in the policy could be decreased because of changes in the prevailing level of interest rates. If all four events occur simultaneously (capital down, interest rates down, expenses up, mortality costs up), your policy costs will consume your principal at a rapid pace. As the capital base in your policy approaches depletion, the insurance company will warn you that the contract will terminate unless you start making payments into that contract. Under-funded policies eat up principal at an ever-increasing rate. Don't let this happen to you!

When universal life policies first appeared in 1979 and 1980, interest rates were high. Funding levels were chosen assuming that those inordinately high rates were going to stay there. Many of these policies are under-funded and indeed many of them have actually been involuntarily terminated. Angry policy-owners don't understand, which has resulted in consumer complaints to state insurance commissioners.

In many cases, even insurance salespeople who were selling these policies were not sure what they were selling. In competitive situations, an agent could sell you the same amount of coverage at a cheaper rate. This smaller premium represented a lower investment and lower investment returns.

Exhibit 8.6 Under-Funding

Current Premium
        Plus
Investment Results

                "Is Less Than"

                                Expenses Plus
                                Mortality Charges

Lower investment returns meant lower tax-free interest and thus a less efficient policy. Under-funding is the poorest of strategies with a universal or universal variable life policy. It is wiser to buy a yearly renewable and convertible term policy with after-tax dollars. Minimum-funding should be the lowest funding level considered.

Minimum-Funding Level

The minimum-funding level for these types of policies should be the level at which the policy interest earnings and your contributions to the policy are no less than the amount of the mortality and expense charges in that particular year. This will assure that the capital accumulated within your contract stays at a constant level for the year and is not depleted by policy costs. You can adjust what you put into it back to that of a straight term policy during times when you have no extra money to invest.

Exhibit 8.7 Minimum-Funding

Current Premium
Plus
Investment Results

"Is Equal to"

Expenses Plus
Mortality Charges

This feature can be a great benefit and comfort if you suddenly find yourself out of work. Your life insurance continues uninterrupted at minimal outlay.

Investment-Funding

If you have reached the tax-free funding level and policy earnings are sufficient to cover all policy expenses, why would you choose to invest even more capital? Let's assume that you have purchased a universal variable life policy and have started out with a strategy of adequate-funding. This strategy, though interspersed (in times of stress) with years of minimum-funding, has helped you attain efficient-funding, the point at which expenses and mortality charges are entirely covered by policy earnings. You have been utilizing the guaranteed-principal, guaranteed-interest account to hold the monies that represent the tax-free funding level, and you still have the family of mutual funds available for your use. These funds differ from commercially available funds because the earnings, capital gains, dividends, and interest earnings within them create no current income-tax liability. You have enjoyed tax-free compounding in your IRAs and qualified retirement plans, and this now is available to you within your life insurance policy as well!

Many of you participate in successful mutual funds and use them to build family wealth. Being outside the life insurance policy, they entail taxes each year on any earnings and capital gains. Just look at Schedule B in last year's income tax returns to see the investment earnings on which you paid taxes. If you decide to sell one of the mutual funds and reinvest the money in a different mutual fund, the transaction will result in current taxation on the capital gains realized. Yes, even if you sell your investment in one of the family funds and reposition those assets in another of that family's funds, you are still subject to taxation on any capital gains realized from the sale.

Exhibit 8.8 Investment-Funding

Current Investment
Results

"Exceed"

Expenses Plus
Mortality Charges

The funds in your universal variable will treat you more generously, and you won't have to share your gains with Uncle Sam. The gains may be reinvested intact within the funds in your policy, and taxation will be either deferred until some future time, or eliminated entirely if the policy pays off as a death benefit. If you own a universal variable policy, taxable mutual funds are a poor investment for you until that policy has reached its maximum-funding level.

Maximum-Funding

The maximum-funding level is based upon the policy death benefit. The death benefit dictates the point at which no additional funds can be added to the policy based upon the controlling income tax provisions in Internal Revenue Code Section 7702. According to the tax code, a policy funded above this level ceases to be a life insurance policy, resulting in immediate taxation of all deferred earnings. Your insurance company should not, and in all likelihood will not, accept money that would cause your policy to go above maximum-funding. To determine if a maximum-funding strategy would be advantageous, you have to determine exactly what additional expenses, if any, will be incurred when you send in additional investment dollars. For one thing, these dollars will be diminished by state premium taxes. The taxes are charged by your state of residence on every premium paid into a life insurance policy and typically run about 2 percent. You may also have to pay a front-end sales load which averages about 4 percent.

Exhibit 7.4 lists the state premium taxes as charged by the individual states. If you live in New York, you will find that only about nine-tenths of one percent of your investment goes to state premium tax. A $100 premium would incur only a 92-cent tax. If the insurance company makes no additional charges against your investment, $99.00 would go to work for you in your accumulation account. In this case, this charge will probably be lower than most low-load mutual funds.

On the other hand, a resident of the Virgin Islands has a state premium tax of 5 percent. This means that $100 going into a universal variable policy will be diminished by $5—only $95 will be invested. In either case, you probably can find investments within your policy advantageous to you because the income-tax savings involved and the tax-free compounding you can enjoy far outweigh these one-time charges. Determine these costs before you buy a policy.

Exhibit 8.9 Income Tax Benefits of Life Insurance

1. The total death benefit received by the beneficiary from a life insurance contract is excluded from the beneficiary's income. This total death benefit includes not only the net amount at risk but also the total amount of the policy-owner's equity accumulated within the contract and the earnings on that equity over the years.

2. The annual increases in value (inside build-up) and the accumulated increases in value, be they interest or investment appreciation, are not subject to current taxation and will escape taxation entirely if they are eventually delivered as a death benefit. Transactions among the mutual funds within the policy are not subject to current taxation.

3. Policy *"cost basis"* includes funds spent on the expenses and mortality cost within a policy, making such expenditures *tax-free* whether a policy terminates as a death benefit or is otherwise terminated.

4. With the significant exception as of June 20, 1988, of policies that exceed the seven-pay threshold and are modified endowment policies, policy values can generally be accessed via policy loans, collateralizations, or withdrawals without the imposition of current taxation or 10-percent penalties. Note the difference between life insurance and annuities.

Death Benefits—Tax-Free

The primary advantage of life insurance is that if you contribute a small sum when the life insurance hat is passed, the whole hat will be given to your beneficiary when you subsequently die. This is good for not only you and your beneficiaries, but for all of us too. Your beneficiaries do not become economically dependent upon us. This is the reason that death benefits of life insurance policies have been exempted from income taxation. It doesn't matter whether the death benefit comes from net amount at risk, the policy-owner's investment in the contract, or positive investment results. It is *all* tax-free income under Section 101 of the Internal Revenue Code. This, the first income-tax benefit of life insurance, is enjoyed by all life insurance policyholders. However, there are ways you may mismanage your policy, (such as selling it to another for valuable consideration), that result in the death benefit becoming taxable income. Don't make any such changes without considering them carefully with your tax advisor.

Current Earnings and Gains Not Currently Taxed

The second advantage of life insurance is that during your lifetime and while the policy is still in force, all interest earned, dividends earned, and/or capital gains realized on the policy investments are not subject to current income tax. You can even take your gains from a very profitable policy fund and move them to another fund within the contract, without being subject to current taxation, capital gains taxes, and often transaction costs. The taxation is deferred until you take gains from the policy. All investment life insurance policies provide for tax-deferral on this inside build-up and the possibility of total tax-exemption on investment returns when the proceeds are disbursed as death benefits.

Tax Basis Includes Payments for Life Insurance Expenses

The third income-tax benefit of life insurance containing investment capital is the amount of money you recover tax-free when you surrender your policy and have a gain. Your tax basis includes all the life insurance costs the policy has incurred during the time the policy has been in force. In this situation, the costs *increase your basis* and thus are recovered tax-free.

Tax-Free Use of Untaxed Earnings and Gains

The fourth income-tax benefit is that you can use the values accumulated within the life insurance policy while it is still in force, and still 1) withdraw, 2) borrow against them, or 3) pledge the policy as collateral for a loan (e.g., borrow from a bank). If you withdraw an amount exceeding your investment in the contract, the amount withdrawn above your cost is subject to ordinary income tax. As a result, you normally would withdraw no more than what you put into a policy. If you want additional funds, you could make a loan against the policy or collateralize the policy to get at those funds without being currently taxed on them. Prior to June 21st, 1988, this could be done on almost any policy without paying income tax on any accumulated gain within the contract. However, as of that date Uncle Sam limited the amount you could invest in a policy and still get at the money without income taxation and 10 percent, pre-age 59-1/2 penalties.

MODIFIED ENDOWMENT INSURANCE—
TAMRA 88

Single-premium life policies are the most investment-oriented. In effect, they become maximum-funded policies with the first and only premium. Prior to June 21, 1988, they combined 1) high returns (because of relatively high interest rates available at that time) with 2) a deferral (no tax on those returns) and 3) the ability to access those returns without current taxation. In 1988, Congress decided this was too much of a good thing. The result was that in November of 1988, the Technical and Miscellaneous Revenue Act of 1988 (TAMRA) was signed into law. This new law defined modified endowment policies, a new class of life insurance policies that Uncle Sam considered too investment-oriented. It removed tax-free accessibility to the cash in them. Any policy issued after June 20, 1988, classified as a modified endowment policy contract (MEC) cannot provide the policy-owner with the privilege of withdrawing from, borrowing from, or collateralizing the values accrued within the policy without incurring immediate taxation on policy gains. Indeed, if you're under 59-1/2, not only do income taxes become due on the amount of gain accessed in the contract, but you also are subject to a 10 percent penalty on the amount included in gross income as a result of the withdrawal, borrowing or collateralization. The only exceptions to this penalty are if the funds are withdrawn as a result of disability or over a period related to the policy-owner's lifetime (annuitized).

How to Avoid Modified Endowment Status

We'll assume that you, the policy-owner, want all four income-tax benefits. In particular, you want the ability to make withdrawals up to your basis or loans on your policy without being exposed to ordinary income tax or penalties. To accomplish this with a policy issued after June 20, 1988, you may invest no more during the first seven policy years than an amount determined by the government-mandated test called the seven-pay test. The seven-pay test has nothing to do with your paying seven premiums; it only limits the amount that you can pay into your policy within the first seven years of its existence. For example, if the insurance company offering you a policy informs you (and it *should*) that the seven-pay test allows no more than $1,000 per policy year, you could put up to, but no more than, $1,000 into the policy in the first year. You could pay up to, but not more than, a total $2,000 by the end of the second year. For the first seven policy years, the cumulative maximum you could contribute would be $7,000. At that point, your policy would have completed the testing period, would not be a modified endowment contract, and your accessibility to policy values by way of loans and withdrawals up to basis should not incur taxation or penalties. The amount of your contributions to your policy is also controlled by the other provisions of Internal Revenue Code (IRC) Section 7702. Indeed, often you will find these more restrictive in the fifth through seventh policy years than the seven-pay test restrictions, and you will not be able to contribute even as much as the seven-pay test indicates. Your insurance company should inform you if your contributions have exceeded both those allowed by the provisions of IRC Section 7702 and the seven-pay test limits and refund any excess to you. Most insurance companies do offer tracking assistance. Find out how your company does it.

Material Change to a Pre-TAMRA Policy

The TAMRA 1988 provisions also put restrictions on any policy issued prior to June 21, 1988, if it is subject to a *material change.* Almost any change in a policy is likely to be deemed a material change, other than death benefit and future policy-value increases resulting naturally from the payment of premiums that comply with the seven-pay test in the first seven contract years and benefit increases resulting from investment and/or interest earnings on those premiums. A material change will result in the policy being considered a *new* contract entered into after June 20, 1988, and subject to the seven-pay test as of the date the material change takes effect. The policy then must be tested under the 1988 rules. If it fails the test at any time in the following seven years, it becomes a modified endowment contract. Policies that can pass the seven-pay test are *not* modified endowments and retain *all* the tax benefits of life insurance. Be careful in making changes to your currently grandfathered policies.

When to Ignore Seven-Pay Test Limits

If you wish, you can still buy a single-premium investment-oriented policy, the policy referred to by Uncle Sam as a modified endowment contract. These policies still pay the tax-free death benefit of the total proceeds and the tax deferral on the inside build-up or earnings within the policy as a result of interest, dividends, and/or capital gains. What's new for these policies is that now (post-June 20, 1988) if you borrow, withdraw from, or collateralize this policy, you will have to pay income taxes to the extent that you have gain in your policy as well as a 10-percent penalty on any amount included in income as a result of withdrawing, borrowing, or collateralizing if you're under age 59 1/2 (the exceptions being disability or annuity pay-outs). If the inability to access the money within your policy without current taxation is *not* important to you, then the 1988 change in the law is irrelevant and you may continue to use these policies to accomplish your objectives. In the past, less than 10 percent of purchasers of single-premium policies have borrowed from them. If you don't intend to use this money during your lifetime, the new rules will have no impact.

If you are not sure whether or not it will be necessary to access the money in the future, we recommend that you comply with the seven-pay test regulations. Make sure that your policy is not deemed a modified endowment contract so that you may keep the fourth advantage of life insurance available to you—tax-free and penalty-free access to your cash.

In short, the rule of thumb in determining how much to invest in universal variable is *as much as you can* while still retaining *all* the income-tax benefits. The next consideration is how and where to put your investment.

CHAPTER 9

Getting Rich Using Universal Variable

The author expresses his particular thanks to Dr. William G. Droms, CFA, Powers Professor of Finance and International Business at Georgetown University, for the use of his Portfolio Allocation Scoring System (PASS) and for his careful review of this chapter and many beneficial suggestions.

When you assess the available investment options within your universal variable policy, you must make what investment experts refer to as the *asset allocation decision*. That is, you must select the kinds of investments accounts to be used and determine the percentage of money to be allocated to each. A simple asset allocation model called the Portfolio Allocation Scoring System (PASS), developed by Professor William G. Droms of Georgetown University, serves as a tool to assist you.

The PASS system has been extensively tested and implemented by major insurance companies and used successfully to plan investment portfolios for literally thousands of clients. The system has also been used by a number of banks and CPA firms, has been published in the *Journal of Accountancy*,[1] and is included in the American Institute of Certified Public Accountants' *Personal Financial Planning Practice Management Handbook*.

The system is easy to use and is based on your unique risk/reward preferences. Successfully implementing it requires that you understand the asset allocation process, the risk constraints you should impose on your portfolio, and the return opportunities available from the various investment alternatives offered to you. PASS brings all of these factors together in a simple system you can use to guide your investment selections.

ASSET ALLOCATION AS A STRATEGIC DECISION

Asset allocation is a process of distributing portfolio investments among the various available categories of investment assets, such as money-market instruments, bonds, and stocks. *Selection of the asset mix is the single most important determinant of long-term investment performance.* In a widely diversified portfolio, for example, the selection of specific

---

[1] William G. Droms, "Investment Asset Allocation *for PFP Clients.*" *Journal of Accountancy*, April 1987, pp. 114–118.

Exhibit 9.1 Determinants of Portfolio Performance

Security
Selection 6%   Market-Timing 2%
Other Factors 1%

Asset Allocation
Policy 91%

Source: Brinson, Singer, and Beebower. "Determinants of Portfolio Performance," *Financial Analysts Journal,* May–June 1991.

stocks to hold within the equity portion of the portfolio
normally has much less impact on total portfolio performance than does determination of the percentage of the total
portfolio that will be allocated to equity investments, such
as common stocks (See Exhibit 9.1).

Asset allocation is the key strategic decision to be made in
planning your investment portfolio. Once the strategic decision of how much of each asset category to hold is made,
tactical decisions can be made to implement the overall investment strategy. Tactical decisions involve selections
made from the mutual funds available within your policy.

Making strategic asset-allocation decisions requires consideration of your return objectives as well as the constraints
on these objectives. Constraints would include such factors
as the degree and types of risk to which you submit your
portfolio along with your liquidity requirements, income
needs, long-term growth expectations, tax situation, and in-

vestment time horizon. For most of us, return objectives and planning constraints tend to be extremely broad and highly qualitative in nature, making the asset allocation problem more difficult for individuals than it is for institutions.

Exhibit 9.1 is taken from a study by Brinson, Singer, and Beebower presented in their article "Determinants of Portfolio Performance," published in the May-June 1991 issue of the *Financial Analysts Journal*. Its message is that determining how much of your portfolio to invest in equities is by far the most important decision you make (91% impact). Over the long term, your portfolio performance is affected relatively little by how hot a stock-picker you are (security selection 6% impact) or how great a market-timer you think you can be (market-timing 2% impact).

Exhibit 9.2 shows the effect of your asset allocation decision on your expected return and risk.

Exhibit 9.2 Asset Allocation Strategies (And What You Can Expect from Them)

Average Annual Returns 1926-1991

Portfolio	1926-1991 Average	Range of One-Year Returns Realized Two-Thirds of the Time 1926-1991 High	Low
100% Stock/0% Bond	10.4%	31.0%	(6.2%)
90% Stock/10% Bond	10.0%	28.7%	(8.7%)
70% Stock/30% Bond	9.2%	24.2%	(5.8%)
50% Stock/50% Bond	8.1%	19.8%	(3.6%)
30% Stock/70% Bond	6.9%	16.1%	(2.3%)
10% Stock/90% Bond	5.5%	13.8%	(2.8%)
0% Stock/100% Bond	4.8%	13.4%	(3.8%)

As you examine it, you will note that downside losses were less in the past when people owned at least 30 percent stock (–2.3%) and actually greater when they owned 100 percent bonds (–3.8%). The point is that diversifying a portfolio away from 100 percent bonds and going to 30 percent stock and 70 percent bonds creates a *less* risky portfolio.

ASSET CATEGORIES FOR INDIVIDUALS

From the virtually unlimited array of possible investments, the asset allocation framework (PASS) proposed here focuses on three generic investment classes: money-market funds, bond funds, and equity investments in common stock mutual funds. This classification scheme is adopted because these investment options are now commonly available in insurance policies, and reliable long-term risk and return data are available on the investment performance of these asset categories. This approach does not imply that other types of investments, such as real estate, precious metals, commodity options or venture capital, may not be appropriate for some other portions of your portfolio. It is merely adopted as a means of simplifying the conceptual process and as a method that reflects the asset allocation choices made by most individuals and available within universal variable policies. The three generic categories are characterized by different types of investment risk/return trade-off patterns and meet different investor needs and objectives.

Money-market instruments, such as Treasury bills, short-term bank certificates of deposit, bankers' acceptances, and bond repurchase agreements, are generally purchased by individuals in the form of money-market mutual funds or through bank money-market deposit accounts. Such investments offer a high degree of safety of principal, immediate liquidity, and a rate of return commensurate with inflation.

Fixed-income mutual funds such as corporate or government bond funds and mortgage-backed funds generally offer a high degree of current yield, moderate liquidity (from virtually instantaneous marketability for bonds to lesser degrees of liquidity for mortgages) and, if of high quality, excellent protection of principal. Additionally, high-quality, long-term bonds offer an excellent hedge against deflation. In times of falling prices and interest rates, *bonds are king* because they increase in principal value as interest rates fall. In increasing-interest-rate environments, the opposite is true. Bond values typically decrease as interest rates go up.

Equity investments, such as common stock mutual funds, offer the best opportunity for long-term capital appreciation, but do have the potential for loss and fluctuation in principal values. Common stock/equity investments are the classic hedges against inflation in that they generally increase in value over long periods of time as the economy expands.

INVESTMENT RISKS AND RETURN

It is not too much of an exaggeration to note that in planning our individual investment portfolios many of us know exactly what we want in an investment: something that will double in six months with no risk. It is critical that we assess our attitudes toward risk before designating objectives for return.

It is important to understand that there is no such thing as a risk-free investment. We cannot avoid risk with our investment capital. The choice of *doing nothing* or *leaving it in the bank* is extremely important in terms of the impact on our wealth. Risk is commonly measured quantitatively in terms of standard deviation about the mean total annual return. This measure of total risk can be applied to virtually any investment. Standard deviation measures dispersion about the mean of the distribution of total annual returns; the higher the standard deviation of return relative to the mean level of return, the greater the risk. Exhibit 9.3 shows the long-term historical returns and risks for a number of asset classes. The standard deviation essentially tells you the range about the mean return within which security returns can be expected to fall most of the time (approximately 70 percent of the time). The standard deviation for common stock is 20.5 percent (the difference between the mean and the high and the mean and the low 70 percent of the time). Thus, for example, common stock returns in any single year have a 70 percent probability of falling between –10.3 percent and +30.8 percent. Over long periods of time, the average return is 10.3 percent for common stocks.

Exhibit 9.3 Total Annual Returns on Securities (1926–93)

Investment	Average Mean Annual Compound Return (%)	Standard Deviation of return (%)
Consumer Prices	3.1%	4.6%
United States Treasury Bills	3.7%	3.3%
Long-Term Government Bonds	5.0%	8.7%
Long-Term Corporate Bonds	5.6%	8.4%
Commons Stocks	10.3%	20.5%
Small Stocks	12.4%	34.8%

Source: Stocks, Bonds, Bills and Inflation 1994 Yearbook. Published by Ibbotson Associates, Capital Market Research Center, Chicago, Illinois.

Treasury bills, by comparison, average a 3.7 percent return. Their standard deviation of return is much lower, 3.3 percent compared to 20.5 percent for common stocks.

In short, you pick an investment with a relatively low average return, 3.7 percent Treasury Bills, and 70 percent of the time the return ends up within ± 3.3 percent of the 3.7 percent average. Whereas, when you pick an investment with a higher average rate of return, 10.3 percent common stocks, your return 70 percent of the time will end up within 20.5 percent of that average. You can see why risk is sometimes equated with standard deviation. More risk is more deviation from the average or mean return. Now take that to your next cocktail party!

Individual investors also are concerned with other aspects of risk that may not be captured by the standard deviation of total return. Liquidity risk (inability to liquidate promptly without loss of principal) and the risk of incurring a loss within a particular investment-holding period are chief among these risk factors. The latter risk is especially important to investors in the stock market because while historical experience shows that stocks provide higher returns in the long run than do fixed-income instruments, they do so at the price of incurring losses during some years. The PASS asset-allocation model attempts to capture all these risk concerns and balance them against return objectives.

A PORTFOLIO ALLOCATION SCORING SYSTEM (PASS)

Modern portfolio theory provides the formal theoretical framework for most quantitatively-based asset allocation models used by institutional portfolios, such as pension funds and endowment funds. Portfolio theory assumes that investors base their portfolio decision on only two considerations: the expected return from an investment and its riskiness as measured by standard deviation of expected return. Investors are assumed to attempt investment in *efficient portfolios*, defined as those portfolios that provide the greatest return at a given risk level or, alternatively and equivalently, the least risk for a given return objective.

For individual investors, risk is a more complex and subtle concept than the simple standard deviation of expected future return. However, we should not abandon the lessons of modern portfolio theory altogether. In particular, two central lessons should guide any asset allocation system. First, the risk/return trade-off hypothesized by portfolio theory does in fact exist, and we must recognize that attempts to earn higher rates of return necessitate accepting greater volatility in our annual returns. Secondly, portfolio theory concludes that portfolio diversification reduces risk (volatility of return). Rational investment management dictates that portfolios must be diversified among asset classes as well as among individual securities within asset classes. Developing an appropriate asset allocation strategy requires that you make a realistic assessment of the type and magnitude of the risk you are willing to accept, commensurate with the rate of return you desire to earn. Exhibit 9.4 presents the PASS system for determining an appropriate portfolio allocation scheme. PASS is designed to provide a rough outline of an action strategy for an individual investor.

PASS requires that you score yourself on a 1-to-5 scale of important return and risk objectives. The more points you score, the more your portfolio will be oriented toward equity investments. Conversely, a low score would orient your portfolio more toward fixed-income investments. As a result, the PASS system demonstrates that in order to earn

Exhibit 9.4 Portfolio Allocation Scoring System

	Strongly Agree	Agree	Neutral	Disagree	Strongly Disagree
1. Earning a high long-term return that will allow my capital to grow faster than the inflation rate is one of my most important investment objectives.	5	4	3	2	1
2. I would like an investment that allows me to defer taxation of capital gains and/or interest to future years.	5	4	3	2	1
3. I do not require a high level of current income from my investments.	5	4	3	2	1
4. My major investment goals are relatively long-term.	5	4	3	2	1
5. I am willing to tolerate sharp up and down swings in the return on my investments in order to seek a higher return than would normally be expected from more stable investments.	5	4	3	2	1
6. I am willing to risk short-term losses in return for a potentially higher long-run rate of return.	5	4	3	2	1
7. I am financially able to accept a low level of liquidity in my investment portfolio.	5	4	3	2	1

Portfolio Allocation Models

Total Score	Money Market Instruments	Fixed-Income Securities	Equity Investments
30–35	10%	10%	80%
22–29	20	20	60
14–21	30	30	40
7–13	40	40	20

Source: William G. Droms, "Investment Asset Allocation for PFP Clients," *Journal of Accountancy* (April 1987).

higher returns you would be accepting greater risks, and one way to mitigate these risks is to diversify.

To use PASS, simply circle the number under the column that best describes the importance of each investment objective to you. After responding to each statement, add up the total value of all the numbers you circled and use this score to determine your diversification guidelines, given in the lower section. The PASS system statements are structured to award 5 points for a response of "strongly agree" and 1 point for a response of "strongly disagree." A "neutral" response scores 3 points.

The first three statements measure return objectives. Strong agreement with the statement that you need to earn a high long-term total return so your capital will grow faster than the inflation rate results in a score of 5. If this objective is not at all important to you, you would strongly disagree with the statement and score 1 point. Remember that this is not an exam; a high score is best only if it most closely matches your attitudes toward risk and return. It is important that you answer these questions carefully and thoughtfully.

The second statement deals with the importance of deferring taxation on capital gains and/or interest; opportunities to defer taxes are generally associated with equity investments. The third statement assesses the extent to which you need the portfolio to generate current income. A lower current income requirement allows you to orient the portfolio toward more aggressive long-term capital gains.

The last four statements on the PASS survey deal with your time horizon, fluctuations in total return, the probability of realizing losses in some years, and liquidity needs. These statements measure four different aspects of your risk-tolerance. More willingness to tolerate these kinds of risk are reflected in a higher PASS score, suggesting a stronger port-folio orientation toward equities.

The highest possible PASS score of 35 means that you strongly agreed with all of the statements on the form. This indicates a set of risk and return objectives best met by allo-cating nearly all of your capital to equity investments such as common stocks or common stock mutual funds. Even with a PASS score of 35, your portfolio should combine 10 percent of money-market instruments and 10 percent of fixed-income securities with the high 80-percent-proportion of common stock.

The lowest possible PASS score of 7 would result if you strongly disagreed with all of the statements about your in-vestment return and risk objectives. With this score, PASS suggests that you invest only 20 percent of your assets in equity investments, allocating 40 percent of your remaining capital to money-market instruments and 40 percent to fixed-income securities. A PASS score between the extremes suggests that you allocate your portfolio among the three asset classes in some intermediate proportion.

Obviously, the PASS system provides only a rough guideline for portfolio allocation. It is not meant to be a fail-safe, mechanical system to meet all of your planning needs. The PASS score does, however, provide an approximation of your optimal portfolio, based upon which you can begin to turn your personal return and risk objectives into an action strategy. The system also forces you to recognize the trade-off between risk and return and come to grips with your own *risk-return preferences* and income needs.

Risk-return preference: The amount of risk
volatility an investor is willing to accept in
pursuit of increasing investment returns.

APPLYING YOUR PASS RESULTS TO
A UNIVERSAL VARIABLE POLICY

Suppose your PASS system results suggested that a 60 percent equity 40 percent debt (20 percent fixed income, 20 percent money market) asset allocation would be appropriate for you. Your next question may be, which separate accounts do I use for what?

First we have to define how much you intend to invest and how often? If your answer is not much and not often, we would probably recommend that you *don't use universal variable if you are not, or will not be, an investor.* Just buy term insurance until you learn to be an investor. On the other hand, if you are going to invest a great deal, are utilizing a tax-free exchange to move money from an old life insurance policy, or are planning on maximum-funding of your policy up to its modified endowment limits, then we need to select the separate account investments with care, knowing the nature of each investment alternative.

There will be all sorts of ways to invest for those of you that fall between these two extremes.

The reason universal variable has been referred to as *the Swiss army knife of financial products* and *the financial product of this century* is because it gives a vast majority of people a low-hassle, convenient and economical way to invest. For example, look at the allocation of a $100 deposit in Katie Leipprandt's universal variable life insurance policy on June 15, 1987. Where else could a 25-year-old newlywed carve up a $100 bill and take advantage of so many and varied investments, knowing it would have no reflection on her tax return?

CHAPTER 9

Allocation Percentages

Investment Division	Allocation Percentages
Guaranteed Interest/Money Market	10%
Common Stock	30%
Aggressive Stock	20%
Balanced	20%
High Yield	20%

Investment Division Activity
(Effective Date: June 15, 1987)

Transaction Investment Divisions	No. of Units	Unit Value	Amount
Gross Premium			$100.00
State Premium Taxes			–(2.00)
Guaranteed Int.			9.80
Common Stock	.195	$150.396	29.40
Aggressive Stock	.111	$175.850	19.60
Balanced	.128	$152.068	19.60
High Yield	.193	$202.114	19.60

This got her started on a lifetime of investing. A more recent review of the unit values shows the following:

Unit Values

	1987	1993	% Increases
Common stock	150.396	289.33	92%
Aggressive Stock	175.850	462.89	163%
Balanced	152.068	265.72	75%
High Yield	101.117	191.25	89%

You will note that this asset allocation is 60 percent equity (common stock, aggressive stock and one-half of the balanced fund) and 40 percent fixed-income (guaranteed interest, high yield and one-half of the balanced fund). She concluded that she should invest in this way because she strongly agreed on PASS questions 1 and 2, generating 10 points, and was neutral on questions 3 through 7 because some investment account income was needed to pay her monthly policy expenses and life insurance costs, and at that point in her life she really wasn't sure what the answers were. Her PASS score of 22 led her to the 60% equity 40% fixed-income split she used when choosing among funds available within her policy. She might otherwise easily have chosen to try shot-gun investing, firing $100 per month into lots of accounts to see what happened. Would that have been thoughtless? No. It would have been investing in her investment education with a relatively small amount of money, and the education would have paid a lifetime of investment benefits.

HOW TO CHOOSE AMONG SEPARATE ACCOUNTS

It is the nature of the beast. Go to the basic makeup of the investment, know what that type of investment has done in the past. Do not ask your investments to do something other than what they have done in the past. No! They cannot leap tall buildings in a single bound! The past does not predict the future . . . but it is the best indicator.

Exhibit 9.5 Economic Gravity

Stocks, Bonds, Bills, and Inflation
(For Various Holding Periods)

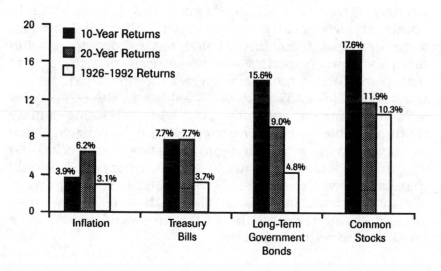

Source: Ibbotson Associates Inc., Chicago

Katie's conclusion, after reviewing the economic gravity chart, was that stocks have tended to provide a better inflation-adjusted rate of return than bonds or fixed-income investments.

The latter do better than stocks in providing the monthly income necessary to cover her monthly policy costs.

Let's diagram what the investment alternatives available within a typical policy might do.

Exhibit 9.6 Variable Universal Separate Accounts
What to Expect

Performance Expectation

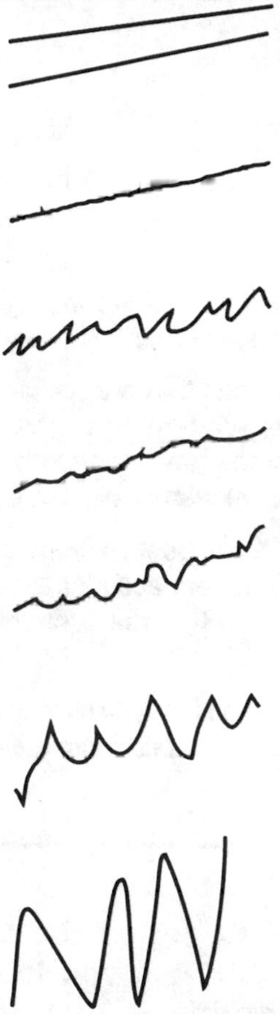

Money	Money Market Guaranteed Interest (General Account Investment)	
Market	Intermediate Term Government Bonds	
Fixed	Long-Term Bonds	
Income	Government/Corporation	
	High-Yield Bonds	
Combination	Balanced Total Return Growth and Income Asset Allocation	
Equity	Index Fund Common Stock Growth Global Aggressive Growth	

Exhibit 9.7

Investment Objective	Accounts to Use
Pay policy costs	Guaranteed Interest
	Intermediate-Term Bond (when interest rates are inordinately low)
	Longer-Term High-Yield Bonds (when interest rates are inordinately high)
	Any of the above if interest rates are staying constant (but who can tell?)
Funds that are *important* for a purpose within five years	Same as above
Funds that are for growth and purposes beyond five years based upon how much volatility Katie thinks she can stand	Balanced growth and income Common stock Global Aggressive
Dollar Cost-Averaging (a) From account to account within the contract	Source account: non-volatile accounts Target account: the most volatile ones!
(b) Monthly/quarterly investments for dollar cost-averaging	Most volatile Most growth-oriented accounts Diversity

Katie feared the loss of her principal just as you probably do. But if you look at the generic categories in which you can invest, that risk of loss of principal can really be viewed as a risk of volatility. Historically, although these investments were periodically in the dumper, all eventually provided positive returns.

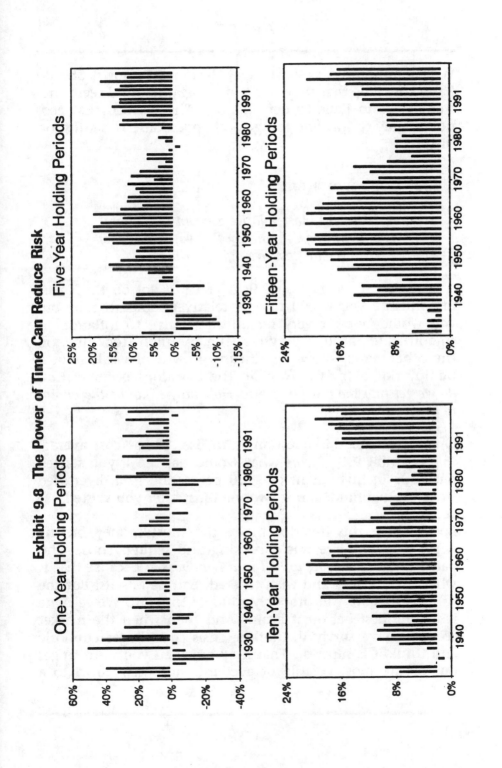

Exhibit 9.8 The Power of Time Can Reduce Risk

Will common stocks do it again? Nobody knows! Should
Katie conclude that they won't do it again? It did seem pre-
sumptuous to Katie to defy history. She decided that economic gravity was not going to change. Katie is betting on
history.

Dollar Cost-Averaging

*"Why the most volatile account for dollar
cost-averaging . . . and by the way, what does
dollar cost-averaging mean?"*

As you can see in Exhibit 9.9, if you just got on the Treas-
ury-bill line you would have a relatively smooth ride, but
you would not get very far ahead relative to inflation. A
smooth ride but little progress. The common stock line, on
the other hand, shows significant growth of wealth but a
bumpy ride along the way. So the questions become: *How
do we get into the fast lane?* and *How do we handle the bumps
in the road?*

One answer to this question is to use "dollar cost averaging." Exhibit 9.10 shows what would happen if you started
out with an investment of $100 per period in a diversified
stock mutual fund, and it swooned just after you started.

Look where this investor made the most money buying
while everyone else was panicking and selling. Those who
panic say *we are going to hell in a handbasket!* because that is
what they believe and wish to read. Bad news sells! But the
truth is that we will probably muddle through. We've done
it before, best bet on it again. And then when the market
sees we have survived another crisis, it will get euphoric
and think it is superior. That may be when you want to get
out of the most volatile of accounts and step down to a

Exhibit 9.9 Wealth Indices of Investments in the U.S. Capital Markets 1925–1993

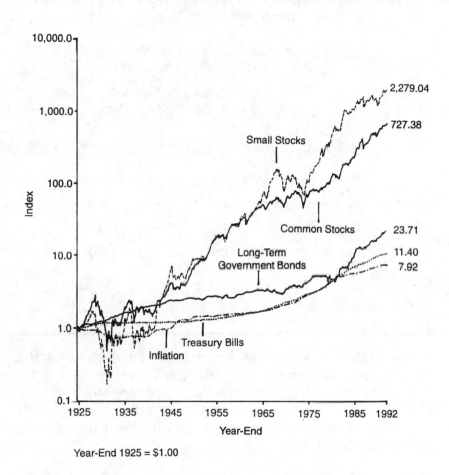

Year-End 1925 = $1.00

Exhibit 9.10 Dollar Cost Averageing

Invest Constant Dollar Amounts at Equal Intervals Over Long Periods of Time

	Period One	Period Two	Period Three	Period Four	Period Five	Totals
Investment	$100	$100	$100	$100	$100	= $500
Unit Market Value	$100	$50	$25	$50	$100	
Units Purchased	1	2	4	2	1	= 10 Units

Period Five Unit Market Value	=	$100
Number of Accumulated Units	=	× 10
Total Market Value	=	$1,000
Total Investment All Periods	=	$500
Gain	=	$500

Source: Ben G. Baldwin 1990

milder ride with your now larger base of *important* capital, so you can rest more easily. But don't give up that dollar cost-averaging into your volatile common stock mutual fund investments. Maybe now you can also use the earnings on your accumulated investment to dollar cost-average into equity accounts.

This is an excellent strategy to help you cope with uncertainty and volatility in investing, and it makes it easy to become lifetime successful investors. The worst thing financial advisors can do is to put too much of a person's investments into volatile accounts, causing them to panic and vow never to touch the stock market again. That too-hot-to-handle reaction is likely to engender a lifelong aversion, making it almost impossible for them to overcome the eroding effect of inflation on their long-term investments. But aren't all those investment transactions going to create income taxes and transaction costs? Normally this would be true, but here you are inside your universal variable life policy—no income-tax hassle and probably no transaction costs. These savings are likely to far exceed the costs in your policy.

The well-constructed universal variable life policy is second only to your income-tax-deductible IRA, 401(k), and other qualified retirement plans as a wealth-accumulator. Use them all!

SUMMARY

Everyone who is insurable or owns a life insurance policy today can do this type of investing. If you already are insured, you are paying part of the costs associated with a universal variable policy, but into your existing contract. The possibility of a 1035 tax-free exchange is certainly one to be explored with your advisors.

If you are paying for a term life insurance policy, you are paying for a tax-shelter *sack* (the expenses and cost of life insurance), but not putting anything into it—not investing. When the original *Life Insurance Investment Advisor* was published in early 1988, there were very few universal variable life policies on the market and very few people who understood what they could do. Today the universal variable market is exploding, and there is no reason not to explore how this very important family-wealth-builder would work for you. If your financial advisor is not up to speed yet, suggest that he or she read this book.

CHAPTER 10

Financial Analysis of
Life Insurance

In 1975, the Institute of Life Insurance and the Life Insurance Marketing and Research Association prepared a joint study of life insurance consumers. The results of the survey showed that 54 percent of the group surveyed erroneously equated a policy's premium with policy cost, 61 percent indicated that they had experienced difficulty in determining whether their policies were cost efficient, and 73 percent said they had trouble understanding their policies.

The statistics probably would not improve if the same survey was taken today. The variations and alternatives available in life insurance have increased significantly since 1975, but the industry still is unable to clearly communicate the costs and benefits of life insurance policies to the public.

Over the years, a number of systems have been developed and presented to assist in the financial analysis of a life insurance policy. Some of the approaches are:

1. Traditional net cost method

2. Net present value method

3. Retention method

4. Interest-adjusted indices
   Interest-adjusted *net payment* cost index
   Interest-adjusted *surrender* cost index

5. Linton Yield method

6. Joseph M. Belth Method

Each method has been built upon the previous one, seeking to eliminate the perceived inaccuracies. Understanding the tools that have been used to evaluate life insurance will provide a basis for a system of financial evaluation that has validity not only with the traditional forms of life insurance but also with all new types including universal, variable, and universal variable products.

NET COST METHOD

The first of the six methods is the traditional net cost method. It adds up the total premiums as of a particular date. The total cash available to the policy-owner as of that date (also referred to as cash value plus dividends if available, account value or policy-owner equity) is subtracted from that summation of premiums paid to that date to determine the policy-owner's net position. This is defined as *net cost*. In short, what you have paid, minus what you could realize, equals what it costs. The advantage of this traditional net cost system is that it is simple, quick, and easy to understand.

Problems associated with it arise from its practical application. It includes inaccurate assumptions and does not take the time value of money into consideration. For example, if you put $20,000 in total premium payments into a policy, terminated the policy after 20 years and $20,000 was returned to you, you could inaccurately conclude that the insurance cost you nothing. An amount equal to the premiums paid was returned to you. The error is that you have not accounted for interest earnings. You have forfeited the use of the $20,000 for the 20-year period. The insurance company retained the interest that it earned on the money to pay for the life insurance, expenses, and profits.

You might also conclude erroneously that two policies that have the same bottom line—$20,000 in and $20,000 out—cost the same. This would not be true if one of the policies required payment of the full $20,000 immediately and the other required that the $20,000 be paid in equal annual installments of $1,000 each. The former would obviously be far more expensive when you consider the time value of money.

You look at the ledger statement or policy illustration provided by the life insurance company as the source of the information for the traditional net cost method. The ledger statement figures regarding face amount, premium, and guaranteed cash value can be relied upon as accurate.

Face amount, premium and guaranteed cash value are *guaranteed* in the whole life insurance contract as of the date of issue. The columns referring to dividends are not guaranteed and become less credible each year that the policy is in force. This is because the insurance company figures are less likely to be accurate as they attempt to project farther into the future.

You might be inclined to use these policy illustrations as if they were accurate predictions. You would lay the illustrations side by side in a decision-making situation and make your purchase decision based upon which statement looked the best. The most optimistic prognostication wins! The facts are that actual dividends will differ from projected dividends, that insurance companies may change the ways they credit dividends for different policies, and that companies do not make such changes on a consistent or predictable basis. The only thing you can be sure of when it comes to dividend projections is that whatever is presented in the policy illustration will not occur. Future dividends will either be more or less than what was predicted.

Dividends are paid from (1) excess investment earnings over and above what is expected on the insurance company's invested capital, (2) mortality savings (fewer people die than were expected to die), and (3) savings and expenses that end up lower than projected. Until about 1975, the dividend projections provided by insurance companies had a higher degree of credibility than they do today. The business environment was relatively stable. The investment portfolios of all companies were relatively similar as a result of both regulation and the business practices of the day. Earnings on those investments and taxation on those earnings were fairly predictable. The expenses of operating an insurance company were also predictable and consistent. Old conservative mortality tables were being used during a period of improving mortality. In addition, there was not the intense competition of many new companies seeking a share of the market.

Today we have a highly competitive environment with many new companies seeking market share. These companies have underlying portfolios with varying degrees of risk and reward, aggressively low current mortality charges, and the challenges accompanying the threat of AIDS to deal with. Company expenses are increasing rapidly due to the requirements for sophisticated technology and the cost of distributing the product. Consequently, the companies are aggressively seeking alternative means of distribution and ways to cut expenses which backfire, in some instances, as short-run expense-cutting efforts call for even higher expenditures to correct the mistakes made. All of these factors make dividend-forecasting likely to be less accurate than in the past.

Policy illustrations are generated for universal life, variable life and universal variable life, but forecasting the long-term results is even more prone to error than the ledger statements for whole life policies. In fact, in his *Insurance Forum* publication of January 1987, Joseph M. Belth states, "In my opinion, life insurance sales illustrations are out of control."

The lack of credibility involved was recognized formally by insurance professionals with introduction of the *Illustration Questionnaire* (IQ) distributed by the American Society of CLU & ChFC in 1993. The questionnaire invites companies to answer a set of 25 questions revealing the assumptions used in developing their illustrations. It is intended to help educate intermediaries on the methodology used to generate life insurance proposals, sales illustrations, and/or ledger statements, as they are variously called. As the IQ states, ". . . it is safe to say that the sales illustrations will never accurately portray the policy's actual performance."

The IQ asks for answers in five different areas:

1. *General.* Do non-guaranteed factors illustrated differ from current experience? Do you treat new and existing policy-holders consistently? If not, describe.

2. *Mortality.* Are mortality rates in the illustration consistent with current experience? Are mortality improvements assumed in the illustration? Do the mortality rates (cost of insurance) include some expense charge? Do the mortality charges vary by product? When are the mortality rates the same by attained age?

3. *Interest or Crediting Rates.* Describe the basis of the interest rate used—gross, net, etc. Does this interest rate or crediting-rate exceed what the company currently is earning? Is there a different rate for existing vs. new policies?

4. *Expenses.* Do expense charges reflect actual experience? Are they different in new vs. existing policies? Are they adequate to cover actual expenses? Increased mortality charges? If not, where/how are they covered?

5. *Persistency.* If the actual experience is better than that assumed, would that negatively impact illustrated values? Does the illustration include non-guaranteed persistency bonuses?

The purpose of the IQ is disclosure of non-guaranteed risk elements. It is intended as an educational tool.

You can order the *Illustration Questionnaires (IQ)* directly from:

The American Society of CLU and ChFC
Attention: Customer Service
270 S. Bryn Mawr Avenue
Bryn Mawr, PA 19010-2195
Toll Free: 1-800-392-6900 *FAX: 215-527-1499

The ledger illustrations on *interest-sensitive* and *investment-sensitive* whole life, universal life and variable life policies are less reliable than those of whole life policies because there is a rapid flow-through of investment results and mortality and expense charges. With the whole life products, a change is not felt by the policy-owner until the insurance company changes its dividend scales. There is lag time which cushions the impact. With new contracts, expense and mortality charges may be charged immediately, and investment changes are recorded immediately. In short, they are contracts which respond rapidly to the current economic environment.

It is highly unlikely that the ledger statements generated for these products will resemble reality in any way. The accounting profession might describe 40- or 50-year policy illustrations as "affirmatively misleading minutia", i.e., they report amounts with such detail that they give an unrealistic impression of accuracy.

Appropriate use of long-term policy illustrations with the new products lies in determination of the point at which the policy could fail (lapse without value), using worst-case assumptions such as maximum contractual mortality charges, maximum expense charges, and very conservative interest-earnings assumptions. The monthly illustrations for universal life types of policies show both current monthly expenses and mortality charges. These illustrations can be of great value for comparison purposes during the first few years of the policy's life. The problem with each of the first six methods of policy valuation cited at the beginning of this chapter is that they use illustration numbers typically for year 20 in their calculations, which dooms them to failure. Annual reports on existing policies show actual expenses and life insurance charges and can be depended upon! In-force illustrations on your existing policies can be requested from your company for use in short-term planning.

NET PRESENT VALUE METHODS

The net present value method of comparing policies improves on the traditional net cost method by applying the time value of money to the numbers provided in a ledger statement. This method requires that you take the ledger statement of a traditional whole life policy, determine the premium flow needed to support the policy over some predetermined period of time, and discount that flow at an assumed interest rate, usually between 5 and 8 percent, to determine the present value of the premium flow required. You would thereby answer the question, "How much money would I need today to provide the required premium payments for 20 years?" For example, assuming a $1,000-per-year premium for a policy with $100,000 face value, 5-percent interest, and a 20-year time period, the net present value of this cash flow would be $12,462.21. Thus, you would need $12,462.21 in today's dollars to fund the minimum payments for the next 20 years.

The next question is, "What will be the policy's reported total asset value on that date 20 years in the future?" Using our example, suppose that the policy illustrations indicated a total value on the ledger statement for the 20th year of $25,000. Traditional net cost calculation would indicate that the policy-owner had earned a profit of $5,000

($20,000 paid in, $25,000 to be paid out). However, when the $25,000 figure to be delivered 20 years hence is discounted at 5-percent to its present value, we find that it has a present value of $9,422.24. The present value of the benefits expected from the policy is $9,422.24. Subtracting this from the present value of the payments that must be paid to receive these benefits ($12,462.21 – $9,422.24) shows that the cost of the policy is $3,039.97, at a 5-percent discount rate.

Net Present Value Method

	Net Cost Method	# of Years	Discount Factor	Present Value
Premium Flow $1,000	($20,000)	20	5%	($12,462.21)
Future Value $25,000	$25,000	20	5%	$ 9,422.24
Net Gain	$ 5,000	**Net Present Value Policy Cost**		($ 3,039.97)

This method makes an adjustment for the time value of money and also allows you to compare policies with dissimilar premiums and values. However, it continues to rely on numbers provided by the policy illustration. If this method is used to compare life insurance contracts with the objective of choosing the most efficient, the following assumptions are made, all of which are *wrong*.

1. The numbers presented in the ledger are accurate and comparable.

2. Current dividend scales will continue unchanged for each of the competing companies for the 20-year period.

3. The companies use similar assumptions in developing their dividends and setting dividend policy.

4. If there are future changes in dividend scales, it will affect all companies under consideration in an equal manner.

5. The contracts will be terminated at the end of the chosen period of time.

6. Death benefits are equal.

7. All other policy provisions are identical.

The results of this method must be used with a great deal of caution. It is not recommended as a final selection technique.

RETENTION METHOD

An alternative to the present value method is the retention method, which asks how much of the future value of the premium stream, at an assumed interest rate, is retained by the insurance company upon termination of the contract.

To continue our example, suppose that you want to know the future value of this premium stream of $1,000 per year at the beginning of each year for the next 20 years if it is in an account earning 5-percent interest. You would find the future value of that premium stream to be $33,065.95. If the insurance company returned $25,000 to you in the 20th year when you terminated your policy, you would determine that the insurance company had retained $8,065.95 to pay mortality charges and expenses and take profits on your policy. Using this form, this best means of policy selection would be to select the one with the lowest retention level. Since this method uses the same invalid assumptions as the present value method, and also utilizes projected numbers from policy illustrations, you can expect it to provide the same unusable results.

INTEREST-ADJUSTED INDICES

The regulators have responded to the difficulties involved in comparing life insurance policies and their cost-effectiveness by recommending the interest-adjusted indices. The Joint Special Committee on Life Insurance Costs met and in 1970 recommended an alternative cost-comparison method known as the *Interest-Adjusted Method* which considers the time value of money. In 1976, the National Association of Insurance Commissioners (NAIC) adopted a life-insurance-solicitation model regulation which it recommended to the various states for their adoption. Approximately 38 states have adopted the model regulation which requires insurers to provide buyers with an interest-adjusted surrender cost index and an interest-adjusted net payment cost index for the 10th and 20th policy years, using a 5-percent interest assumption.

The inputs required for the interest-adjusted methods are:

1. The annual level premiums accumulated at 5 percent.

2. The face amount.

3. The time period over which the analysis is to be made. (The model regulation requires it for 10 and 20 years.)

4. The interest rate. The NAIC chose 5-percent net after-tax as an acceptable long-term interest rate from personal investments of comparable security and stability.

5. Dividends are to be accumulated at 5-percent interest, if dividends are available in the contract.

6. The cash surrender value.

The NAIC requires that we use two indices. The interest-adjusted *net payment* cost index assumes that the policy is continuing in force, and therefore only the dividend values plus 5-percent interest earnings (if the policy in question pays dividends) are available to the policy-owner to reduce cost. The cash surrender value is not available and, therefore, not included in the interest-adjusted net payment cost index. The interest-adjusted *surrender* cost index assumes the policy is terminated; thus the cash value is available to reduce cost and is included in the calculation of the surrender cost index.

INTEREST-ADJUSTED NET PAYMENT COST INDEX

The interest-adjusted net payment cost index builds an index based upon the continuation of a policy. Since the policy is continuing in force, it assumes that the cash value of the policy is not available to the policy-owner. Dividends, and 5-percent interest on those dividends, are assumed to be available to the policy-owner in participating policies.

Accumulate the annual dividends, if available, plus the 5-percent interest earnings on those dividends for the period of time in question. In order to convert those dividend credits and their interest earnings to a level annual amount for the period of time in question, the dividend amounts are divided by the future value of $1 at 5 percent for the period. The payment of $1 per year, assuming a 5-percent interest and a 20-year time period, results in a future value of $34.72. That is, if you deposit $1 each year at the beginning of the year in a 5-percent account, you will accumulate $34.72 in 20 years. By dividing the insurance-company-provided future dividend value by this 20-year divisor, you will find the number of dollars that would have been required annually to arrive at this amount. The 10-year divisor is $13.21; that is, $1 per year deposited at the beginning of the year in an account earning 5 percent would accumulate to $13.21 in 10 years.

The adjusted premium is the level annual premium accumulated at 5 percent. For example, a $1,000 annual premium accumulated at 5 percent for 20 years would total $34,719.30. If the 20th-year accumulation of dividends was $12,000, you would calculate the 5-percent-interest-adjusted dividend value by dividing the $12,000 by 20 years ($600) and then determine the future value of that average annual dividend of $600 compounded at 5 percent for 20 years, arriving at an adjusted dividend value of $20,831.60. The difference between the interest-adjusted premium ($34,719.30) and the interest-adjusted dividend ($20,831.60), which amounts to $13,887.70, is the interest-adjusted cost for this $100,000 policy. To calculate what this $13,887.70 total cost is as an equivalent to a 20-year interest-adjusted annual premium you may use your calculator or the 20-year factor of 34.72 just described. The $13,887.70 divided by 34.72 is $400. Dividing this by 100 gives us the per-$1,000 interest-adjusted net payment cost index of $4 per $1,000 per year.

INTEREST-ADJUSTED SURRENDER COST INDEX

The interest-adjusted *surrender* cost index assumes that the cash surrender value of the policy *and* any termination dividend available at policy termination will be available, along with the dividends and their interest earnings.

If in the preceding example the total cash available upon surrender amounted to $10,000, you would subtract the $10,000 from the $13,887.70 and arrive at $3,887.70 for the $100,000 policy. Dividing that by the 20-year 5-percent factor of 34.72 results in the amount of $112, and dividing this by 100 gives you the per-$1,000 interest-adjusted surrender cost index of $1.12. This, they say, can then be used to compare the policy to others of comparable size and type.

According to the Report of the Joint Special Committee on Life Insurance Costs,[1] the advantages of these two interest-adjusted methods are as follows.

1. They take the time value of money into account.

---

[1] Report to American Life Convention, Institute of Life Insurance, and Life Insurance Association of America (New York: Institute of Life Insurance, May 4, 1970), page 6

2. They are easy to understand.

3. They do not require recourse to advanced mathematics.

4. They do not suggest a degree of accuracy that is beyond that justified by the circumstances.

5. They are significantly similar to the traditional methods, so that transition could be accomplished with a minimum of confusion.

Although these indices do take the time value of money into consideration, not you, or I, or many insurance agents have found them easy to understand or to communicate. Unfortunately, these indices are regarded by the public as having a degree of accuracy beyond that which is justified.

The public press and the regulators still attribute a great deal of credibility to the 10- and 20-year interest-adjusted indices, in spite of the fact that the numbers are developed from policy illustrations quite probably unreliable. The insurance company that designs its illustration most aggressively for 10- and 20-year values will be rewarded with low cost indices even though its figures are less likely to be met than the company that presents a ledger statement based on more conservative assumptions.

Although the interest-adjusted indices do take the time value of money into consideration, they fail because you cannot rely on assumed policy values 10 and 20 years hence. Strict reliance on the indices provides for potential misuse which may mislead rather than help the consumer. Keep in mind these numbers: 48 insurance companies were seized by state insurance commissioners in 1989, 33 in

1990, 40 in 1991, and 19 in 1992. All of them generated great-looking illustrations with competitive and attractive indices.

The ledger statements from which the indices are derived are becoming less and less accurate as a result of today's volatile economy and the many changes in the industry. To the degree that illustrations do not reflect what is going to happen within the policies, the indices become an inappropriate tool for comparing insurance products. Over-reliance on the indices should be avoided.

LINTON YIELD METHOD

The Linton yield method is named after an actuary who, in 1919, demonstrated that a whole life or an endowment life insurance policy could be mathematically analyzed as equivalent to a combination of decreasing term insurance and a savings fund. The method consists of subtracting the *cost of protection* from each year's policy premium, net of dividends, and treating the remainder as a savings deposit.

Linton decided that life insurance was a product that could be divided into component parts of protection and savings and analyzed on the basis of the value provided by each. The *Linton Yield* would be the average interest rate on the invested amount over the selected period.

The method operates in this manner. The policy's savings or cash value portion is subtracted from the face amount, giving you the amount at risk or amount considered term insurance. This term insurance can be given a value based on the age, sex and health of the insured, that is, on what it would cost the insured to replace this net amount at risk by purchasing retail term insurance. This amount, the value of the protection, is then subtracted from the annual premium for the policy as a whole, along with whatever current dividend the policy is generating, resulting in a net amount which is going into a savings portion of the contract. Annual premium, minus dividend minus cost of protection, equals savings.

The amount going into the savings portion is the investment element. The Linton yield is that average rate of return on the savings over the selected time period.

The problems associated with various published Linton Yields are:

1. The term life insurance costs that go into calculating the yields are composite numbers, not necessarily accurate in any individual case.

2. The assumption is made that a policy is terminated at the end of the chosen period for which the Linton Yield is calculated.

3. The Linton Yield implies that the yield calculated is constant over the period of time chosen.

4. The Linton Yield takes its future value assumptions from the same illustrations we have found lacking in accuracy.

Published Linton Yields, then, are homogenizations of assumptions. The numbers are of value for rough comparison purposes only. They are invalid on an individual policy basis.

JOSEPH M. BELTH METHODS

Joseph M. Belth, Ph.D., professor of insurance at Indiana University, is noted for his work in determining the costs of life insurance policies.

His level price approach was based on the premise that the protection provided by a policy was not the full face amount of the policy but rather the face amount minus its cash surrender value. Belth used the level cost method to attempt to measure the average cost of this amount at risk to policy-owners. He developed a price-per-thousand for each age, for this net amount of protection. He then converted these yearly prices into amounts that represented a level price-per-thousand per net amount of protection provided by the policy for a particular time period. He has referred to them as benchmark life insurance costs that represent a base value of the protection provided by a policy.

In the June and October of 1982 issues of *The Insurance Forum*, Belth published a method of determining costs and/or rates of return within policies that was more easily adapted by an individual to determine the cost-efficiency of an individual policy.

Belth's inputs for his calculations are these.

1. Death benefit (F).

2. Policy cash surrender value as of the last previous anniversary date (CVP).

3. Policy cash surrender value as of the current anniversary date (CSV).

4. Most recent annual premium (P).

5. Most recent annual dividend (D).

6. Insured's insurance age.

7. Assumed alternative use of funds interest rate (i). (The rate of interest that the policy-owner feels could be earned in an investment with equivalent safety and liquidity as that within a life insurance policy.)

8. Benchmark rates per $1,000 of life insurance (net amount at risk).

You will note that seven of the eight items are specific to the policy-owner; that is, you have to enter your own personal information into the calculation. The information is of value personally rather than just generally. This is a vast improvement over all previous methods when you are attempting to make personal life insurance decisions.

The eighth item in Professor Belth's formula, the cost of term insurance for the policy-owner, is derived as he describes in *The Insurance Forum* of June 1982, Volume 9, Number 6:

... The benchmarks were derived from certain United States population death rates. The benchmark figure for each 5-year age bracket is slightly above the death rate per $1,000 at the highest age in that bracket. What we are saying is that, if the price of your life insurance protection per $1,000 is in the vicinity of the 'raw material cost' (that is the amount needed just to pay death claims based on population death rates), your life insurance protection is reasonably priced. (p.168)

Exhibit 10.1 Joseph Belth's Benchmark and Formula

Belth's Benchmarks:

Age	Price
Under 30	$1.50
30–34	2.00
35–39	3.00
40–44	4.00
45–49	6.50
50–54	10.00
55–59	15.00
60–64	25.00
65–69	35.00
70–74	50.00
75–79	80.00
80–84	125.00

Belth's Formula is as follows:

$$\frac{(P + CVP)\,(1 + i) - (CSV + D)}{(F - CSV)\,(.001)} = \text{Cost per } \$1,000$$

P = Premium
CVP = Cash Surrender Value Previous Year
i = Alternate Use of Funds Interest Rate (net after taxes)
CSV = Cash Surrender Value This Year
D = Dividend
F = Death Benefit

Belth's formula may be described in the following manner. The cash value for the previous year and this year's premium input are considered the investment in the contract. To determine the amount to which that investment should have appreciated on your behalf in the year in question, Belth multiplies that amount by one plus the after-tax yield obtainable on a comparable investment. This determines what you *should have received*. From this amount, he subtracts the total current cash surrender value plus the dividend credited to the policy in the current year. This determines what you *actually did receive*.

You could say "This is what I should have had: contract investment multiplied by 1 plus after-tax yield," and then subtract what you actually did get. The difference between what you should have received and what you did receive is the net cost for the year.

Once the current year's cost has been determined, you divide it by the net amount at risk in thousands of dollars provided by this particular policy. This divisor is calculated by taking the death benefit, subtracting the current cash surrender value, and then multiplying by .001 to reduce that down to the number of thousands of dollars of coverage of net amount at risk in the policy.

Compare this calculated life insurance cost per $1,000 per year with Belth's benchmarks. His rules of thumb are that if the policy cost per thousand is less than the benchmark, no replacement would be appropriate; if the policy cost per $1,000 is more than the benchmark but less than twice the benchmark, probably no change is indicated; but, if the policy cost per $1,000 is more than twice the benchmark, replacement should be considered.

Belth's system has the advantage of being more client specific and fairly easy to understand. It has been the most credible system of evaluating the cost of life insurance to date.

However, some of the inputs to Belth's system need to be examined.

1. *The benchmarks.* Consider the term insurance costs. Do they reflect what an individual actually pays for life insurance? For example, Belth's benchmark for a 50-year-old is $10. We find that a 50-year-old male non-smoker can buy term insurance for from as low as $2.25 per thousand to as high as $6.71 per thousand. Belth's benchmarks are generalizations which appear to be higher than today's costs. To make an informed decision, you need to know your actual retail cost of term insurance based on your age, sex, and risk category.

2. *Policy loans.* Belth's formula, like the preceding methods discussed, does not take policy loans into consideration. Policy loans do affect the amount of investment within the policy and therefore have a substantial effect on rate of return.

3. *Policy loan interest rate.* The interest rate paid on the policy loans will be either more or less than the reinvestment rate for the funds outside the policy. If the rate charged is higher, the policy cannot be leveraged profitably; if lower, it may be. To determine the net result, the net after-tax cost of the interest paid must be subtracted from the net after-tax gain realized by reinvesting the loan proceeds outside the policy.

4. *Policy loans affect policy dividends.* Currently, insurance companies pay you higher dividends on your whole life policies if you do not borrow and/or if you accept higher loan or variable loan interest charges.

5. *Marginal tax bracket, state and federal.* Earnings within a life insurance policy are not subject to current income taxation. Interest charged on policy loans is not deductible.

The rate of return within a life insurance policy is more valuable to a high-bracket taxpayer. By inserting marginal tax bracket into the formula, we will be able to indicate the equivalent net after-tax rate of return required outside the policy to match the rate of return inside.

THE BALDWIN SYSTEM

This step-by-step method proceeds as follows.

STEP 1   Determine how much life insurance is provided by the policy.

Total Death Benefit _____

less Total Current Asset Value _____

equals Life Insurance _____

Total Death Benefit

Total death benefit is the policy face amount plus any policy provisions that increase the death benefit in the event of a natural death, e.g., term insurance riders or paid-up additional life insurance as a result of dividends being left in your policy or account value being added to the policy face amount, etc.

Total Current Asset Value

Total current asset value is the capital at work in the policy on which you are earning a return. The objective of this calculation is to determine how much of the total death benefit is your money and how much is company money or life insurance.

STEP 2 Determine what you have paid to maintain the life insurance in force this year.

Premium _____

plus Loan Interest Cost _____

Total Current Year's Cost _____

Premium

The premium is what you have paid into the policy in the current year. It is the billed gross premium for a fixed-premium policy or what you have chosen to pay if the policy is a type of universal life without a stated premium.

Policy Loan Costs

Most companies have offered enhancements to their participating whole life insurance policies. If policy-owners will accept an arrangement whereby higher interest may be charged on policy loans, they are rewarded with higher dividends. Conversely, if policy-owners refuse the enhancement in order to maintain a low policy loan interest rate, they receive lower dividends.

This dividend credit differential between borrowers and non-borrowers is effectively an increase in the cost of policy loans. The precise dividend differential and loan interest rate alternatives offered to an individual policy-owner in an enhancement or upgrade can be used to determine the impact on a specific policy and must be obtained directly from the issuing company.

Leveraging life insurance through borrowing to pay premium— minimum deposit plans—is obsolete today. Loan interest has to be paid. Loans reduce dividends. As stated in *Forbes,* June 29, 1987, "If you own a minimum deposit life insurance policy, condolences are in order." The strategy was based upon the fact that non-competitive rates of return were paid on investments within life insurance policies in the past; so it made no sense to leave the money in the policy. This is no longer a fact. Investments in variable policies are very competitive.

Economic conditions have made it difficult to borrow from a policy, pay loan interest, and profitably reinvest the money to earn an easy profit. The increased costs for policy loan interest, along with reduced dividends for policies that retained their low interest rate on policy loans, combined with the lower interest rates available on alternative safe investments altogether provided little opportunity for gain.

STEP 3   Determine the cash you received as a result of maintaining the policy in force for the current year.

Current Year's Increase in Cash Value,
Account Value or Asset Value _____

plus Current Year's Dividend if any _____

equals Total Policy-owner Credit _____

Critics will find weaknesses and advocates will find strengths in this particular section of this system for the financial analysis of life insurance. The critics will say that you are looking at the policy for only one particular year. They will question whether the financial results for any particular year are an accurate report of what has happened in the past or a predictor of what will happen in the future. The criticism is valid because the policy, under analysis could be a variable life insurance policy with its investment in a common stock account in a year when the common stock fund has taken a substantial beating. Given that case, current year return could easily be negative. If you concluded that one year's negative return meant that you should get rid of the policy, that would certainly be an erroneous conclusion. You should perform further evaluation by re-entering your numbers in the formula, using the average annual increase in account value and the average annual dividend received since the policy's inception as the credits received as a result of maintaining the policy in force. For input into the policy, you could use average annual premium, average policy loan costs, and the average net after-tax costs for maintaining cash within the policy. This would give you an indication of average return from policy inception. From the standpoint trying to make a *Where do I go from here?* decision, the current year's actual return compared to the average return provides information that will help in determining how you can expect the policy to perform in the future.

If you are considering an upgrade or enhancement offer, you can use the formula by entering assumptions such as the elimination of the policy loan and the acceptance of the higher dividend yields to determine the impact of the offer.

STEP 4 Determine your investment in the contract.

Total Asset Value _____

less Loan Outstanding _____

equals Investment Remaining in Contract _____

The investment capital in the contract is extremely important as it is that upon which you are going to calculate your investment return. You may want to refine this figure bringing it closer to your average investment in the contract during the year in question. That is, you could calculate your investment in the contract at the beginning and at the end of the year, add the two (2) together, subtract any policy loan, and divide by two to come up with the average investment in the contract for that year. In our computerized calculations (Lotus spread-sheet), we show rate of return based upon both equity at the beginning of the year and average equity during the year.

When entering the figure for the outstanding policy loan, the unpaid outstanding interest on the loan at the time of the evaluation should be added to the policy loan amount.

STEP 5 Determine the dollar amount of return you have earned in the current policy year.

From Step 3, take your increased value for the current policy year and subtract your current input into the contract for the current year, shown in Step 2.

Policy-Owner Credit (Step 3) _____

minus Policy-Owner Costs (Step 2) _____

equals Policy-Owner Net Gain (Loss): _____

STEP 6 Determine your cash-on-cash return for the current year.

To determine your cash-on-cash annual percentage rate of return for the current year, take the amount of the credit from Step 5 and divide it by the investment remaining in the contract from Step 4.

Amount of Credit (Step 5) _____

divided by Amount Invested (Step 4) _____

equals % of Cash-On-Cash Return _____

STEP 7 Determine your equivalent taxable return.

The cash-on-cash return varies in value for high-bracket and low-bracket taxpayers. This step helps to calculate how much of taxable return you would have to earn in order to net the cash-on-cash rate of return. Take your tax-free rate of return as calculated in Step 6 and divide it by one (1) minus your tax bracket.

Policy-Owner's Untaxed Cash-on-Cash
Rate of Return (Step 6) _____

divide (1 minus tax bracket) _____

equals Equivalent Taxable Return: _____ %

STEP 8 Determine the value of your life insurance.

This is a very important point of departure. If you are not in need of protection and place no value on the life insurance protection provided by the contract, then you need go no further. Step 7, focused on the cash-on-cash return, is all that matters, and the viability of the contract as an investment depends upon the competitiveness of this cash-on-cash return with other investment alternatives available. Cash-on-cash return is a return net of all costs, including life insurance costs.

Various individuals will place varying degrees of value on the protection provided by the contract. The young non-smoker who has an opportunity to purchase term insurance at discounted rates through some association, an employer, or another advantageous source might see value to some extent in his preferred status. An individual who is older, has a great personal need for life insurance, and has just had a heart attack—making existing insurance irreplaceable—would value the net amount at risk far more highly. In some cases the insurance protection will be of so much value to the policy-owner that the cash-on-cash return or investment return of the policy is irrelevant. The death benefit represents the entire value of the contract.

Life insurance does have value, and that value has to be individually determined. The most accurate cost-per-thousand to be entered in this section of the formula would be the figure you obtained as a result of applying for an equivalent amount of term life insurance, submitting to medical examination, and receiving an offer at a contractually-guaranteed rate. All other entries are estimates, and the financial analysis is only as good as that estimate is accurate.

Once the equivalent retail value of $1,000 of term life insurance is determined, it is multiplied by the amount of life insurance protection provided by the contract (face amount minus asset value of the policy as determined in Step 1) to calculate the value of the life insurance within the contract.

You could argue that your retail cost of the term insurance divided by one (1) minus your current marginal tax bracket is the figure that should be entered. This figure would represent the amount you would have to *earn* in total to service a retail term insurance policy. For example, if you are in the 30-percent marginal state and federal tax bracket, you would have to earn $142.86 for every $100 you paid for term insurance (100 divided by [1 − .30] = $142.857).

This method of valuing the cost of retail term insurance would be accurate if the untaxed earnings on an investment within the life insurance policy were entirely sufficient to cover all mortality and expense charges within the policy. We have taken the more conservative approach using just the equivalent retail cost of term insurance for the policy-owner.

Value of Life Insurance

Life Insurance in Thousands (Step 1) _____

× Policy-Owner's Cost per $1000 _____

equals Value of Life Insurance: _____

STEP 9 Determine the total value you receive as a result of continuing this life insurance contract.

The total value you receive as a result of continuing the life insurance contract is the cash-on-cash return plus the value you put on the life insurance protection. Add the life insurance value determined in Step 8 to the cash return of Step 5 to come up with the total dollar amount of benefit you receive from the contract.

Policy-Owner Net Gain (Loss) (Step 5) _____

plus Life Insurance Value (Step 8) _____

equals Total Benefit Received: _____

STEP 10 Determine the percentage return on the contract when the cash-on-cash return is added to the life insurance value.

Value Received (Step 9) *divided by* Amount Invested (Step 10) =
_____% Rate of Return

STEP 11 Determine the equivalent taxable return that you must earn to match this tax-deferred/tax-free return from the life insurance contract.

Percent Rate of Return (Step 10) *divided by* (1 Minus Tax Bracket) = _____ %

CONCLUSION

The Baldwin System may be used with all types of life insurance: term, whole life, single premium life, universal life, variable life and universal variable life. In testing and evaluating the system, a computer program was developed.[2] The program gives simultaneous results of Belth's system of evaluating the cost-effectiveness of life insurance policies, the cash-on-cash rate of return, and cash and life insurance value rate of return.

The Baldwin System has proved to be valuable in making individual decisions regarding existing life insurance and potential purchases. Although it takes a bit of effort to understand, it is easily computerized and therefore accessible to all at reasonable cost. Since you can understand the data that is used to come up with the conclusions, you are in a good position to evaluate the results.

---

2 A Lotus template is available for $25.00. To order a template, write Baldwin Financial Systems, Inc., 5 Revere Drive, Suite 400, Northbrook, Illinois 60062.

Exhibit 10.2 The Baldwin System of Determining
Rate of Return on Cash Invested in a Life Insurance Policy

STEP 1 - Life Insurance Provided:
        Total Death Benefit
        - Total Current Value

                    Life Insurance _____

STEP 2 - What Was Paid In:
        Annual Premium
        + Loan Interest (Net of Tax Savings, if any) _____

              Total Current Cost:

STEP 3 - What Benefit Was Received:
        Increase in Cash Value/Account Value
        (This Year's Value—Last Year's Value)
        + Current Year's Dividend _____

          Total Cash Benefit Received:

STEP 4 - Policy-Owner's Investment inPolicy
        Total Asset Value
        - Loan Outstanding _____

           Policy-Owner's Investment:

STEP 5 - Determine Dollar Amount of This Year's Gain or (Loss)
        Policy-Owner's Credits   (Step 3)
        - Policy-Owner's Costs   (Step 2) _____

          Policy-Owner's Net Gain (Loss):

STEP 6 - Cash on Cash Return
        Amount of Gain   (Step 5)
        ÷ Amount of Investment   (Step 4) _____

             Cash on Cash Return: _____ %

CHAPTER 10

Exhibit 10.2 Continued

STEP 7 - Policy Owners Equivalent Taxable Return
Cash on Cash Return (Step 6)
÷ (1 – Marginal Tax Bracket)

Equivalent Taxable Return: %

STEP 8 - Value of Life Insurance
Life Insurance in Thousands (Step 1)
× Policy Owner's Cost per $1,000 of
Term Life Insurance

Life Insurance Value:

STEP 9 - Determine Total Value of Benefit Received
This Year's Gain (Loss) (Step 5)
+ Life Insurance Value (Step 8)

Total Benefit Received:

STEP 10 - Determine Cash on Cash and Life Insurance Rate of Return
Total Benefit Received (Step 9)
÷ Policy-Owner's Investment (Step 4)

Total Return on Policy: %

STEP 11 - Determine Equivalent Taxable Rate of Return to
Match Policy's Total Return
Total Return on Policy (Step 10)
÷ (1 – Marginal Tax Bracket)

Equivalent Taxable Return: %

CHAPTER 11

Life Insurance Strategies

The Swiss Army Knife Approach

Throughout this book, we refer to monies going into life insurance company products, over and above that spent for mortality and expense charges, as investment. People who put money into these products expect a return. Certainly the allocation of one's cash to buy term life insurance protection for a year, and then terminate without value, is more like a retail purchase of a consumable than an investment. Should the insured die, however, the family surely would consider that allocation of assets one of its finest investments.

To cover as many investment opportunities and insurance company products as possible, let us consider the situation as a life cycle investment/insurance/accumulation/distribution decision. Your needs, attitudes, and opportunities change as you pass through the life cycle, and as they change, your use of insurance company products and competitive alternatives will change also.

In the following pages, we will consider young adults, young singles, young married couples, the middle-aged, and advanced-mature as those in the general stages of the life cycle. In considering each stage, we will try to address the typical problems and opportunities that relate to life insurance and annuities, including some typical business situations. At each stage, we also will illustrate how to evaluate each situation. For example, a youth might ask, "Why do I want or need life insurance or annuities? Or an IRA? It's eons before I'll retire. Why now?" We will look at the many opportunities that may be offered to you through employment during middle age, such as bonus plans, key employee life insurance, salary continuation, deferred compensation, corporate and personal minimum deposit plans (and how to extricate yourself), split-dollar plans (conventional and reverse), and 1035 exchanges.

When we arrive at maturity, we will discuss various ways to enjoy the income you have managed to accumulate and how to protect the assets, if you wish, for the next generation. As we do this, we will describe how two marrieds have elected to use their life-cycle policy to serve their various needs and how they adjust it to their needs. We also will explain the quantitative analysis that led them to their decisions.

YOUNG ADULTHOOD STRATEGIES

Young and Single (The "Wow" Years)

During the young and single phase of your life-cycle, it is hard to be concerned with anything but improving career opportunities and making yourself more valuable to society. Your long-term security objective will be to build sufficient net worth so that one day you can work for fun rather than for money. Your best and primary investment at this stage of the life-cycle is your education. That will probably continue to be your very best investment throughout your lifetime. What insurance products are generally appropriate for consideration by the young and single?

The primary function of life insurance is to provide protection, *life insurance* or *net amount at risk*, in return for which you accept the loss of relatively small sums (policy costs) so that in the event of your death relatively large sums can be provided to your beneficiary. The means to accomplish this is entirely unique to life insurance.

During this phase of your life, there probably is not anyone economically dependent upon you and your ability to continue to earn a living. If this is the case, paying for term insurance is an unnecessary expenditure. Why then do so many people do it? Life insurance costs less if you are in good health. It is often wise to purchase it while you are healthy, assuring availability at preferred health rates when it is needed in the future. In addition, since *investasurance* (life insurance supported by investment) becomes more self-supporting as it accumulates more investment capital, you can justify starting a policy at this stage of life. You can accumulate some capital within the contract during these relatively low-expense years so that you can suspend payments during the coming more expensive years of marriage and child-rearing.

It is highly likely that as a young single you will have some death benefits provided through an employer's group insurance. You need not report that expenditure of funds on your behalf as taxable income. The employer may purchase up to $50,000 of life insurance per employee, deduct the cost, and not report any of these expenditures as taxable income to you as an employee as long as the plan is not deemed to be discriminatory. Amounts in excess of $50,000 are subject to income tax based upon the imputed income value of the benefit provided. This is calculated by dividing by $1,000 the amount of life insurance you have in excess of $50,000, and then multiplying by the Uniform Premium Table 1 premiums shown in Exhibit 11.1.

Exhibit 11.1 Uniform Premiums per $1,000 Group Term Life Insurance Protection

Table 1

Five-Year Age Bracket	Cost per $1,000 of Protection for 1-Month Period
Under 30	8 cents
30 to 34	9 cents
35 to 39	11 cents
40 to 44	17 cents
45 to 49	29 cents
50 to 54	48 cents
55 to 59	75 cents
60 to 64	$1.17
65 to 69	2.10
70 and over	3.76

The cost of taxable life insurance is calculated on a month-by-month basis. An example follows.

1. Enter the uniform premium (commonly referred to as Table 1 rate) at the individual insured's attained age on the last day of the taxable year.

2. Multiply this *cost per $1,000 Table 1 rate* by the number of thousands of taxable life benefit (amount in excess of $50,000).

3. Subtract monthly employee contributions, if any.

4. Add together each month's calculations to determine the total reportable amount for the tax year, which is referred to as *inputed income.*

If you contribute to your life insurance through payroll deduction, your employer will deduct what you pay from the amount that is reported to you as taxable income. You have to pay tax on only that which you receive (life insurance over $50,000) and have not paid for. There are exceptions to this for business-owners, officers, and highly compensated and key employees who may be taxed on the actual cost of the coverage or the Table 1 rates, whichever is greater.

Investasurance

What about paying more into the life insurance policy than is required simply to have the insurance protection? This is a viable alternative if you decide that there is a personal need for life insurance. If there is no need, then the costs associated with the insurance protection and the expenses of maintaining the policy diminish the value of your investment return. However, if you decide that the expenditure for the insurance protection is justified because of present or future needs and/or wants, the question becomes, "What is the best way to pay for this insurance protection, not only presently but in the future?"

There are a number of things you should keep in mind when you begin making investments into a life insurance policy. First, if you put extra cash into a policy, you can get at some of it. While some will be expended for life insurance and expenses or held for surrender charges, you will want to know exactly how much remains accessible. It should be readily available either through loans or withdrawals from the policy (assuming you wish to keep the policy in force) or by cancelling the policy and recovering your equity (which can have income-tax consequences). Second, today you can choose to control where the company invests your money. Third, you do not have to pay income taxes or penalty taxes when you borrow on your policy as long as you do not invest in excess of the seven-pay limits. Fourth, you do not have to pay current taxes on interest, dividends, or capital gains earned within your policy. Fifth, it can offer a comfortable, convenient accumulation device with broad diversification at a relatively low investment level. In short, it works.

Some people will choose a stream of investments into a family of mutual funds. By choosing taxable mutual funds, you lose the tax shelter and death benefit of the life insurance contract. You will pay taxes each year on interest, dividends and capital gains. There are taxes when you switch from one fund to another within the family of taxable mutual funds. The difference between taxable mutual funds and mutual funds inside life insurance is that taxable mutual funds don't carry the costs associated with life insurance. With lower expenses come higher taxes. Look at

Schedule B of your income tax return. You paid taxes on the positive results shown there. The life insurance policy provides you with the income-tax-free death benefit as well as tax shelter for the build up within the policy.

YOUNG MARRIEDS

Are you a *DINK* (Dual Income—No Kids)? At this stage in life, you still are two relatively economically independent individuals, with neither yet dependent upon the continued income of the other. Your economic interdependence may increase as you take on a home mortgage and have children. As this economic interdependence increases, your need for life insurance will increase and insurance company products will become more attractive.

Non-qualified annuities are as attractive to DINKs as they are to young singles, meaning, not very. The expenses, pre-59-1/2 tax penalties, and tax liability of taking money out of annuities makes them inappropriate in most cases because of their lack of liquidity.

On the other hand, the qualified annuity, (one that is part of a qualified retirement plan) is more important to DINKs than to young singles. Both partners are advised to make maximum contributions to the deductible retirement plans. At this stage, you should avoid the tendency to become dependent upon the continuation of *both* incomes for your standard of living. This is a time in your life for maximum accumulation of net worth. The basic conclusion is that qualified plans are certainly an appropriate investment, in spite of the fact that the young are penalized should they wish to invade such plans prior to age 59-1/2. The lack of liquidity is certainly important and should be considered.

However, every time you complete a financial statement in order to borrow money, your habits of the past will be an important consideration to the lender. The more you show the lender you have been able to accumulate, the more interest there will be in lending to you.

What life insurance products serve the needs of the young couple? As is always the case, available resources are the first consideration. You have needs for adequate medical, disability income insurance and life insurance. Once funds are available to cover these basic needs, the question of additional investments can be addressed.

Emergency Funds

For instance, where should the emergency fund (three to six months of gross income) be invested? What you require here is (1) liquidity (ready access to your cash without loss) and (2) a reasonable rate of return.

Let's use an example. We have a male non-smoker, age 30, and a female non-smoker, age 28. They each have purchased retail term insurance policies in the amount of $200,000. Their purchase decisions were made on the basis of wants and needs, and the contracts will cost them in total about $500 in the current year. They are in the 30-percent marginal income tax bracket, so it takes gross family earnings of about $714 ($500 ÷ .70) to service these two policies. They send $214 to Uncle Sam, which leaves $500 to send to the insurance company.

They have a good start on their emergency fund. They have accumulated it in a certificate of deposit (CD). It is now up for its six-month renewal at current interest rates. The question is, where should they put that $10,000? Should it go into a life insurance policy? Should they leave it in the CD (earning a net after-tax amount of about 70 percent of the interest quoted) or should they put it someplace that provides the features they require of an emergency fund (liquidity and a reasonable rate of return)? The only way to find the answer is to look at the facts. If left in the CD, the $10,000 would have to earn $714 or 7.14 percent to cover the cost of the life insurance with the taxable earnings from the CD, providing $214 for income taxes and $500 for life insurance. Demand to know from the insurance company exactly what would happen if you each deposited $5,000 within a universal variable life insurance product providing $200,000 of protection.

If the expenses were comparable to the term insurance, then the policy would be acceptable from a cost standpoint. Let's look at the investment side. You have $4,000 per policy because $2,000 was eaten up in policy expenses in the first year. So that's $8,000 at work in your policy accounts. Each $4,000 would have to earn about 6.25 percent (6.25% × $8,000 = $500) to get you to the point at which the *tax-free* earnings on the insurance investments could pay for life insurance without Uncle Sam receiving anything, a savings of about $214 in taxes. When you pay extra money into your policy for investment, it will be subject to front-end costs to get it into the policy; but once inside, it does *not* change the insurance costs.

In the first year, it would not be surprising to find that the account values within your policies totaled about $4,000 of the $5,000 you put into each policy. You might also find that only $3,000 per policy was liquid or could be borrowed out because of contingent deferred sales charges. To some this will seem expensive, but to those used to whole life policies that have no value in the early years, it will look good. In the second year, you would look at the total policy expenses to see if they were approximately equal to what you would pay for term insurance. If acceptable, then *maximum-fund* your policies. *Burp* them, as we like to say. Put in as much as you can up to the seven-pay maximum. (The insurance company will often return or burp back what you send in excess of the limit.) After all, someday you could face . . .

Single Income with Kids (The *Oh My* Years)

Additional cash accumulation needs will arise as you get older. College educations may be a major expense in the future. Let's take these policies and use them to fund two college educations, based on the premise that you decided to put the $10,000 into the two universal variable life insurance policies for your emergency fund, adding in what you had been paying for term life insurance. The policies have reasonable and competitive rates of return, acceptable mortality and expense charges for life insurance, and the advantage of deferral on taxation. You have even considered the disadvantage of having to pay $25 if you wished to make a withdrawal or to pay a market rate of interest that would, in all likelihood, not be deductible should you choose to borrow on your policies rather than withdraw cash.

You understand that when you borrow, you have not removed monies but rather collateralized the policy accounts held by the insurance company. The insurance company continues to pay you interest on the collateralized money while you pay it interest on the borrowed money. You will pay the company usually 1 to 2 percent more than it pays you. A spread of 1 percent to 2 percent is what it costs you to get at your policy monies via policy loans.

You have decided that you wish to accumulate college education funds at a rate of $400 a month, the maximum you feel you can allocate at the present time. Yes, push yourself . . . you won't be sorry. Should you establish separate accounts, one for each child? Should you put it in accounts under the Uniform Gift to Minors Act or some other minor's trust fund rather than into your insurance policies? These strategies are not the best alternatives. TRA-86 requires that a child's investment earnings over $1,200 per year be taxed at the parent's tax rate until the child attains the age of 14. In addition, under the Uniform Gift to Minors Act, gifts are passed to the child in an outright fashion. You may find that at age 18 your child chooses to use the funds for some purpose other than education. Consider what you might have done had you found yourself with a lot of cash at age 18.

What investment alternatives are available within universal variable life policies? You can dollar-cost-average into the investment accounts. This offers a relatively conservative means of investing in the stock market. Let's assume that in the third year the policies are in force, you start making monthly contributions of $400 (in addition to the term insurance premiums) and continue with those contributions for the next 15 years. We also will assume current expense charges, current mortality charges, and an 8-percent return. What will be available to your family when college educations start 15 years hence? We are now in the fantasy-land of assumptions, compound returns, and policy illustrations. The most important function of such illustrations is to show you how *projected* expenses may impact investment return.

Let's evaluate whether it makes sense to put $400 per month into your life insurance policies to help you accumulate for the children's educations. If you contribute $400 per month for the next 15 years and earn a net 8 percent, you will have accumulated $120,000 or more at the end of that time.

If you concluded that the expenses being charged within the policies were fair and less than what you projected paying on the outside for just term life insurance, you would proceed. If you liked the tax shelter and the idea of dollar-cost-averaging into some of the stock accounts for at least the first 10 years (hoping to do better than the 8 percent), you probably would decide to go ahead. The life insurance plan offers a strategy (equity investment), convenience (monthly deposits), performance (diversification), and freedom from current taxation that probably appeal to you.

The strategy during the college years would be to discontinue deposits and withdraw (or borrow) $12,000 a year to cover expenses. Understanding that all numbers within the projections will have changed significantly, ask to see what the projections would look like using the $12,000 withdrawals. In reviewing the printout, you may find that the $12,000 withdrawals at the beginning of each of six education years will reduce your policy accounts less significantly than you expected. The continued earnings within the policies may be able to support them nicely.

MIDDLE-AGE STRATEGIES

It's Time to Get Serious about *Us* Years

Middle age is a time to accumulate for financial independence day (or if you prefer, retirement). The college educations are behind you. What a great day! A major effort in life, child-rearing, has been completed as well as possible. It is now time for *you*. Often, people will say that life insurance needs diminish at this stage in life. In some cases, this may be true; however, in most cases it is not. You buy the second home in Florida or Arizona with a mortgage. You decide that the family homestead is not what you want now, so you go out and buy a new home with an even bigger mortgage. You get concerned because your spouse won't get all of your pension if you die. The only thing that may have changed about your insurance requirements is your reason for needing it.

For purposes of example, we will assume that you as a couple decide to start accumulating for retirement by saving $1,000 per month. You will do this by dollar-cost-averaging into the common stock accounts of your universal variable policies. You are now ages 53 and 51.

The effect on your policies if you add to them at this rate for seven years, until the older of you attains age 60, can be dramatic. At that time, you might like to consider retirement, or at least be in an economic situation where continued work is for the love of it and not of necessity.

At the end of the 30th policy year, assuming 8-percent return and current expenses, you could find that if you were to withdraw $12,000 per year from the policies to supplement your retirement income, it would take until age 70 to withdraw your non-taxable cost basis (what you had invested). Thereafter, if the tax laws are as they are today, you could make your withdrawals by way of policy loans so that the $12,000 per year would not be subject to income tax. You could also find that your policy accounts have grown to over $600,000 and that, assuming 8 percent, the policies are still providing about $800,000 of life insurance and still increasing in value. That being the case, you could even increase your rate of withdrawal.

In addition to what you are doing for yourself, at some time during your mature career years your employer may well come up with some individually-designed employee benefit opportunities using variable universal life insurance products as a means of accumulating assets or providing death or disability benefits. The 1986 Tax Reform Act pretty much did away with corporate-owned, non-qualified tax deferred *annuities* as accumulation vehicles. It requires current income taxation on the earnings of any annuities begun, or contributed to, after February 28th, 1986. However, the use of universal variable life insurance allows you to avoid current taxation. As a result, it has become even more popular, particularly in an increasing-income-tax environment.

BUSINESS LIFE INSURANCE FOR PROTECTION AND WEALTH ACCUMULATION

There are potentially four scenarios for business life insurance. The first is life insurance purchased for employees by corporate employers within non-discriminatory plans of group life insurance. These plans can provide up to $50,000 of group term life insurance for the employee, with the premium being deducted by the employer and not recognized as income by the employee. The only other ways an employer can purchase life insurance for an employee and deduct the premium are if it is purchased within a qualified retirement plan or if the premium is deductible as a part of the reasonable compensation of the employee.

The reason that the premium is deductible in the qualified retirement plan is that it is part of the employer's deductible contribution to the qualified plan. The trustees of the qualified plan purchase the life insurance on the employee's behalf.

A plan in which the premium is deductible as compensation is referred to as a Section 162 plan. The employer pays the premium for the employee, deducts it as employee compensation, and the employee picks up the premium as a fully taxable bonus.

The employing firm may also purchase insurance on the life of an employee to indemnify itself for a loss. Key employee life insurance, as it is called, may only be purchased with non-deductible dollars. Internal Revenue Code Section 264(a)(1) expressly prohibits the employer from deducting any premiums paid on life insurance if the employer is directly or indirectly the beneficiary of the policy. The offsetting benefit is that the death proceeds generally are received income-tax-free by the corporate beneficiary under Code Section 101.

The Tax Reform Act of 1986 created the possibility of corporate beneficiaries being subject to tax on the death benefits of life insurance. This act made the difference between a company's book and taxable incomes subject to an alternative minimum tax (AMT). Don't let the name fool you; the tax is neither *alternative* (it is mandatory) nor is it *minimum* (you pay the maximum). For corporations, this brings insurance policy gains in excess of premium and death benefits in excess of cash value, into the web of the corporate AMT (mandatory maximum tax) since these gains are added to a corporation's book income.

The third and fourth ways in which life insurance is used in an employer/employee relationship are as a tool of compensation or as a stock buy-back vehicle to maintain the continuity of ownership that the principal shareholders determine is appropriate. When life insurance is used in these scenarios, contractual promises and/or liabilities may be created for the corporation by its promises to employees or shareholders. Then the employer will use key employee life insurance as the vehicle to ensure that the funds required by the promises are available when the liabilities created must be paid.

Key Employee Life Insurance

Exhibit 11.2 Key Person Insurance

Objectives:
- Pay Employer for Death or Disability of Key Person
- Provide Tax-Free Cash to Pay Employer and Family
- Allows Employer to Make Commitments to the Employee and Family

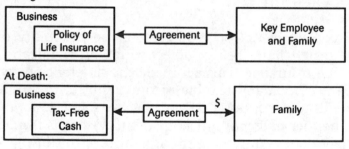

The primary function of key employee life insurance, as of all life insurance, is to offset the economic loss associated with the death of an individual. It may be purchased on the life of an employee whose services constitute a substantial asset to the company. The loss of that employee's services could result in substantial costs to replace the talent and additional costs to replace business that the company may lose as a result of the employee's death. Key employee life insurance may also enhance the credit-standing of the business and may serve as a source of collateral if it is the type of policy that accumulates asset value and/or serves as a reserve-funding vehicle to pay promised death, disability, or supplemental retirement benefits. It can provide funds to the business through death benefits that can be used to assist the survivors. The business should be legally set up to survive, i.e., the business may use the funds to redeem a partial owner's interest so that the remaining owner-operators may continue the business knowing that they can purchase inherited stock for cash from inactive survivors. Such plans assist and maintain business continuity. If an owner/operator lives to retirement, the reserve built up in the key employee life policy can be used to provide for systematic buy out of the retiring shareholder's interest, conveniently coordinated with other retirement sources of income.

One basic common denominator in *key employee life insurance* is that the business entity owns the policy. Under such circumstances, the business entity should also be the beneficiary of the policy, although this is not always the case.

If the employee's spouse or some personal beneficiary is named on a corporate-owned policy, the IRS could claim that the policy is providing personal benefits. As a result, the premium could be construed as compensation subject to income taxes or, even worse, as a corporate divided non-deductible to the corporation and as taxable income to the shareholder-employee. A more critical situation would arise in the event of a death of a shareholder-employee when the corporate-owned-policy death proceeds were paid directly to that shareholder-employee's spouse. In this case, the total death benefit could be construed as a non-deductible dividend, fully taxable as ordinary income to the beneficiary.

In one recent case, a personally owned policy had a split beneficiary, with part going to the insured's corporation and part to the insured's spouse. Part was intended for buy/sell agreement purposes; however, no buy/sell agreement was ever put in force. In the event the insured had died, the corporation and the spouse would have received money. The surviving, non-working spouse would have become an equal shareholder with the surviving, professional-working shareholder in a professional service company. Murphy's law implies that if it can be done wrong, it will be; and if it is done wrong, litigation and business failures are likely to follow. Always check ownership and beneficiary provisions.

Deferred Compensation Plans

The principal difference between a *salary-continuation* plan and a *deferred-compensation* plan is who initiates it. If an employee requests that the employer defer partial compensation until some future date, we have a true employee-motivated *deferred-compensation* plan. This request must be made before such compensation is earned. In this case, the two obligations of the corporation, should it agree to such a plan, would be to pay corporate income taxes on the compensation not paid and to pay the compensation deferred at the agreed-upon future date. To avoid current taxation to the employee, the employee's status would have to be that of a general creditor of the corporation. Assets could *not* be set aside by the corporation so as to prevent the allocated assets from being accessible by the corporation's general creditors. This does not mean that the employer is not free to *informally* fund such an arrangement (reserve for it) as long as any reserve so established is still available to satisfy the claims of the general creditors.

In these days of mergers and acquisitions, it is difficult for employees to accept the fact that their deferred compensation or salary continuation could also be subject to the whims of new management. Employees usually prefer to see informal funding rather than hope for *pay as you go* deferred compensation. That assumes that the employer will pay your retirement benefits out of current earnings when you retire. With informal funding at least there is a corporate asset there to fund a recognized liability of the employer. The more closely the asset is identified with the employee, the more secure the employee is likely to feel. Recently, some employers have established what are referred to as *rabbi trusts*. Assets are placed in an irrevocable trust established by the employer for the employee to fulfill the liabilities stated within the trust agreement. The existence of the trust makes it highly unlikely that either current or new management will revise the terms of the trust; however, the trust assets are specifically made available to the creditors of the corporation in the event of a corporate bankruptcy. Favorable IRS revenue rulings have been issued regarding these trusts.

It is also highly likely that the employee would like some return on that deferred compensation. In some instances, this may be done on a straight book basis and, for example, some corporations make book-entry of paying the current prime rate of interest on such funds. With smaller employers, reserve of the actual cash may be preferable and, if such is the case, the employer will look to put the cash in a place that will not create income-tax problems for the company. Any investments that generate taxable interest, taxable dividends, or capital gains create an extra asset to be tracked by the corporation, along with corporate income-tax liabilities. Until February 28, 1986, the annuity contract was the investment vehicle of choice for many deferred-compensation plans. Prior to that, the inside build-up of interest, dividends, or capital gains of an annuity was not subject to tax. Since then, contributions that result in inside build-up for corporately-owned annuity contracts are subject to income tax. Now, with annuities owned by corporations losing the income tax shelter, variable universal life insurance has become the preferred investment vehicle. The contract has retained its tax shelter on the inside build-up and the corporation can use the income-tax-free (AMT excepted) death benefit to meet corporate obligations.

Salary-Continuation Plans

Employer-motivated salary-continuation plans usually use life insurance as an investment vehicle because employers promise employees not only supplemental employee retirement benefits (SERBs) or *private pensions*, but also benefits in the event of the employee's premature death or disability. In the event of the employee's death, the life insurance proceeds provide the corporate asset necessary to fulfill and pay corporate liability under the salary-continuation plan. In the event of employee disability, individual disability income contracts, the disability premium waiver on the life insurance contract, and the assets built up in the insurance policy would be available to provide the cash necessary. Retirement benefits would be paid from the reserve built up in the asset value of the life insurance policy. Today's universal variable life policies make the design of such plans very easy, efficient and flexible.

Regardless of whether the non-qualified plan was a deferred-compensation or a salary-continuation plan, in most cases the life insurance policy would be established as a regular key employee life-insurance contract. The company would be the owner and beneficiary of the contract without

reference to the legal agreement established between employer and employee that laid out the payment schedules in
the event of the employee's death, disability, or retirement.

Buy-Sell Agreements/Cross-Purchase Agreements

Exhibit 11.3 Buy/Sell
Cross-Purchase Plan (Individual Buy-Out)

Objectives:
- Provide a Market for Business
- Establish Value of Business
- Life Insurance Assures Cash Is Available
- Survivor Buys and Increases Basis in Business
- Control of Ownership

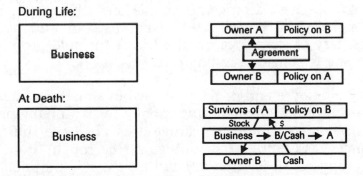

Business-owners who do not arrange for the continuation
of their businesses in the event of death are likely to have
their survivors realize little or nothing from their business
interests.

Sole Proprietors

The problem of the sole proprietor is to identify who would
be interested in buying out the business and continuing it

in the event of the proprietor's death. The question comes down to transferability of the customer base. Can a new owner expect to retain that base? If so, the business has value and a buy/sell agreement is feasible. The next question for the sole proprietor is who would both retain the business and want it? It could be a competitor, an employee, or another family member. The type of agreement will depend upon the relationship between the sole proprietor and the potential buyer. It is likely to be a one-way arrangement. In the event of the sole proprietor's death, the one chosen to be the new owner will buy the business. However, if the key employee or relative dies, there may be no necessity for the surviving sole proprietor to buy anything. Sole proprietor buy-out agreements are between individuals and may be one-way buy-out contracts or cross-purchase contracts between the two sole proprietors. In cross-purchase arrangements, the one who is obligated to purchase the business will want to own and be the beneficiary of insurance on the life of the sole proprietor he or she is obligated to buy out.

In key employee and/or relative buy-out situations, there is often the difficulty of finding money to pay premiums. If the key employee and/or relative does not have sufficient resources, assistance in so doing will be sought from the sole proprietor. It is often difficult for the sole proprietor to understand why he should pay to help someone else buy out the business interest. Indeed, it may be better for him to just own enough life insurance payable for the benefit of family members and then pass the business to them by will. This way, the beneficiaries may be economically independent of the business. If they can get anything out of it, fine; but if not, they'll be all right anyway. It is important for sole proprietors to understand that they either come up with an equitable buy-out arrangement or their families get what is left when business assets are sold, at possibly forced-sale liquidation values. Once the business-owner understands that *there is indeed a cost for doing nothing*, creative solutions for funding the life insurance, with the assistance of those with the necessary resources, can be found. (See Split-Dollar Life Insurance later in this chapter.)

Partnerships

A partnership is one of the most legally fragile forms in which to do business. In the event of the death of a partner, the partnership is legally terminated, and the surviving partner or partners are bound in a fiduciary capacity to wind up the affairs of the partnership, terminate business, and pay out the remaining assets to the deceased partner's survivors based on their partnership shares. During the process of winding up the business, the deceased partner's survivors have a right to the deceased's distributable share of partnership profits or gains; however, survivors of the deceased partner are not to be charged with any partnership losses. Indeed, even while all partners are alive and well, each is totally liable not only for his or her own acts, but the acts and liabilities of the partnership and all other partners as well. Of all business structures, the partnership is the one most in need of proper liability insurance and legally binding business continuation agreements. Without such arrangements, partnerships can be very hazardous to your economic health.

Cross-Purchase Agreement

In the simple two-person, equal interest business, a legally binding cross-preference buy/sell agreement between the individual owners states that at the death of the first, the surviving partner will buy out the deceased's share for a stipulated sum. This same sum would be the price of a living buy-out under the same agreement, funded by each becoming the owner and beneficiary of a policy on the other's life. This is referred to as a cross-purchase agreement because the *individuals* are the ones bound by the agreement. They are the ones who own the insurance policy and the ones who pay out the proceeds to the deceased's family in completion of the agreement to buy out the business interest. Such an agreement is beneficial to the economic health of both parties. Each knows what the family will realize in the event of death, and each knows that the surviving owner may carry on the business without interruption, continuing to earn a living in the event of the co-owner's death.

This arrangement becomes somewhat more complicated as the number of business-owners involved grows. With six, each would be required to own a life insurance policy on each of the other five lives. We would have five life insurance policies per owner, and 30 policies in all, to maintain and manage in order to carry out the agreement. The advantage of the cross-purchase agreement is that as each survivor buys out a deceased's interest, each of their cost bases in the business increases by the amount of the purchase price, which, upon sale, would reduce gain and therefore taxes. This advantage may be offset by the disadvantages of managing and paying for multiple life insurance policies. Alternatively, we may turn to an entity buy-out agreement.

Entity Buy/Sell Agreement

Under an entity buy/sell agreement, the obligation to purchase would be turned over to the entity. The business itself would own and be the beneficiary of the life insurance. The business would carry out the agreement by paying the

**Exhibit 11.4 Buy/Sell
Stock Redemption Plan (Entity Buy-Out)**

Objectives:
- Provide a Market for Business
- Establish Value of Business
- Life Insurance Assures Cash is Available
- Retire Stock of Decedent
- Control of Ownership

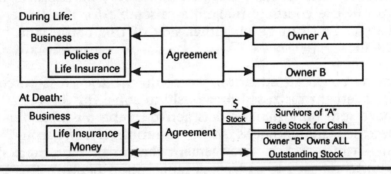

agreed upon amount to the deceased's heirs in order to retire that interest. Using the example just given, we would
now have the entity owning and being the beneficiary of
six life insurance policies, one on each co-owner. In the
event of the death of an owner, the interest of each surviving owner would go from a one-sixth interest to a one-fifth
interest in the business with no *change in cost basis*. This
would mean that higher taxes would be due upon sale because the entity buy-out arrangement would not increase
the survivors' cost bases.

Corporations

The corporation is a less risky way of doing business than is
a partnership. To some extent you are protected from liability by the corporate veil, and you do not pick up additional

liability from fellow stockholders. However, in the closely held business made up of owner-operator shareholders, the death of one can bring about a host of problems for those surviving. Inactive, surviving shareholders with minority interest in the company do not have the same interests as the active shareholder/employees. The inactive will want dividends as a result of their ownership or to be bought out. Although the majority owner-operator shareholders can probably freeze them out, the minority shareholders may turn to the courts to make life miserable for the owner-operators. You can be on either side of this battle, and both sides lose.

In the corporate situation, we could use the cross-purchase arrangement discussed previously to solve this problem and make sure only shareholders active in the business buy the deceased shareholder's stock. Alternatively, we could use the entity purchase arrangement that in the corporate situation is referred to as a stock redemption plan. In this case, the corporate entity purchases the stock of the deceased shareholder, is the owner and beneficiary of insurance on the life of each shareholder, and buys the stock at a shareholder's death.

Such agreements work well for both sides since survivors of the deceased shareholder get cash from sale of their inherited business interest at a fair price and surviving owner-operators can continue the business free of concern for interests of inactive shareholders.

Section 303 Partial Stock Redemptions

Section 303 partial redemptions work well when the issue is *not disposing of the business*. Indeed, the business is to be retained. But in representing over 35 percent of the de-

Exhibit 11.5 Section 303
Partial Stock Redemption

Objectives:
- Provide Liquidity to Pay Death Taxes, Funeral and Administration Expenses
- Qualify Under IRC Section 303 Stock Is a Major Asset (35%+ of AGE)
- Have Company Buy Sufficient Stock to Cover 303 Allowed Taxes and Expenses without Having the Partial Redemption Considered a Corporate Dividend

During Life:

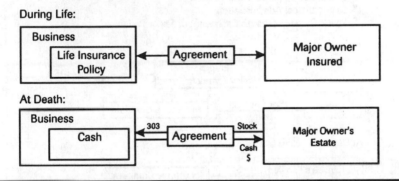

ceased's gross estate, it creates the issue of having enough cash to pay expenses and estate taxes. The 303 solution allows for a partial redemption of stock sufficient to provide the stipulated liquidity needed without having the redemption characterized by the government as a non-deductible dividend for the corporation and ordinary income to the shareholder.

LIFE INSURANCE AS COMPENSATION

Section 162 Bonus Plans

A Section 162 Plan is a bonus plan to an employee. Such a bonus can be used to pay a life insurance policy premium. The cost to the employee is the income tax on the pre-

Exhibit 11.6 Bonus Plan Life Insurance

(Section 162 Plan)
(Stockholders Compensation Plan)
(Supplemental Executive Retirement Plan–Serp)
(Key Employee College Funding Plan)

Objectives:
- Pick and Choose Benefit Plan
- No Government Approvals or Restrictions
- Deductible Employer Contributions
- Easy, No-Cost Administration
- Policy-Owner Access to Cash without Tax or Penalties

During Life:

```
                        Employee          Income Tax
                   Policy-Owner/Insured   On Bonus  → IRS
                                ↑
 Business  → Section 162 →  Insurance Company
               Bonus
```

At Death:

```
 Employee's Family  ←  $  ←  Insurance Company
                    Tax Free
```

mium paid by the employer for the life insurance. These plans are popular because *once paid, the plan belongs to the employee* and is not subject to the creditors of the employer. Further, to the extent that your state shelters life insurance assets from the claims of creditors, it is also protected from the employees' creditors. The employer could limit the plan benefits by a vesting agreement that would stretch out the time before the plan belonged entirely to the employee. These plans can be less expensive to employees because marginal tax brackets *now* may be lower than in the future upon retirement. They are a way for a corporate employer to pay something to employees other than straight compensation. They also complicate things for competitors trying to hire away the employees. Such policies do indicate special consideration by the employer. Today's universal variable contracts can offer attractive benefits to the right employees.

Split-Dollar Life Insurance

Exhibit 11.7 Split-Dollar Life/Disability Insurance

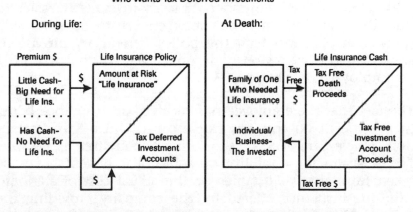

Objectives:
- Divides Amount Put Into Policy
- Divides Amount Paid Out of Policy
- Allows Choice: Who Wants Death Benefit
  Who Wants Tax Deferred Investments

Split-dollar life insurance is an arrangement whereby both a life insurance policy's death benefit and what is paid into a policy are split between two parties, frequently the employer and the employee. In split-dollar arrangements for transparent universal variable policies, the employee can pay the mortality and expense charges and have the right to name the beneficiary of the death benefit. The employer, on the other hand, will pay the *plus* dollars going into the investment account and be the owner of these funds. In the event of the insured's death, the employer can collect an amount equal to what the corporation has contributed, or the policy surrender value, and the balance (the earnings) can belong to the employee.

Split-dollar works because it can provide inexpensive life insurance for the employee and have little impact on earnings for the employer.

There are many ways to design a split-dollar contract. An employee may observe that the initial contribution to the premium is substantial whereas later on contributions become zero. He or she may ask the employer to average these charges over a number of years to make it easier to start the plan. An employer may choose to do a *no split* split-dollar plan in which the policy beneficiary provisions are set up as just previously described but without requiring an employee contribution.

The fact that the employee has received an insurance benefit at little or no cost has not escaped Uncle Sam's attention. Uncle Sam sees an economic benefit that is taxable. The measure for taxability of split-dollar benefits may be taken from the PS-58 tables or the actual cost of standard issue life insurance offered by the company providing the coverage. The PS-58 tables in Exhibit 11.8 show the amount of money on which an employee will have to pay tax as a result of the death benefit payable to beneficiaries. Any amount actually paid by the employee toward the death benefit is deducted from the PS-58 imputed income figure.

The currently popular Second-to-Die or survivorship life policies can also be arranged on split-dollar plans. While both insureds are living, imputed income on these contracts is measured by the US-38 tables. (See Exhibit 11.9) It is essential that plans be made to unwind the split-dollar arrangement at the death of the first because it can cause problems thereafter, e.g., inputed income to non-employee insureds.

Exhibit 11.8 "P.S. No. 58" Rates

The following rates are used in computing the "cost" of pure life insurance protection that is taxable to the employee under qualified pension and profit sharing plans, split-dollar plans, and tax-sheltered annuities. Rev. Rul. 55-747. 1955-2 CB 228: Rev. Rul. 66-110. 1966-1 CB 12.

One Year Term Premiums for $1,000 of Life Insurance Protection

Age	Premium	Age	Premium	Age	Premium
15	$1.27	37	$3.63	59	$19.08
16	1.38	38	3.87	60	20.73
17	1.48	39	4.14	61	22.53
18	1.52	40	4.42	62	24.50
19	1.56	41	4.73	63	26.63
20	1.61	42	5.07	64	28.98
21	1.67	43	5.44	65	31.51
22	1.73	44	5.85	66	34.28
23	1.79	45	6.30	67	37.31
24	1.86	46	6.78	68	40.59
25	1.93	47	7.32	69	44.17
26	2.02	48	7.89	70	48.06
27	2.11	49	8.53	71	52.29
28	2.20	50	9.22	72	56.89
29	2.31	51	9.97	73	61.89
30	2.43	52	10.79	74	67.33
31	2.57	53	11.69	75	73.23
32	2.70	54	12.67	76	79.63
33	2.86	55	13.74	77	86.57
34	3.02	56	14.91	78	94.09
35	3.21	57	16.18	79	102.23
36	3.41	58	17.56	80	111.04
				81	120.57

The rate at insured's attained age is applied to the excess of the amount payable at death over the cash value of the policy at the end of the year.

Exhibit 11.9 Second-to-Die US 38 Rates per $1,000

First Age	Second Age														
	40	41	42	43	44	45	46	47	48	49	50	51	52	53	54
40	0.02	0.02	0.02	0.02	0.03	0.03	0.03	0.03	0.04	0.04	0.04	0.05	0.05	0.05	0.06
41	0.02	0.02	0.02	0.03	0.03	0.03	0.03	0.04	0.04	0.04	0.04	0.05	0.05	0.06	0.06
42	0.02	0.02	0.03	0.03	0.03	0.03	0.04	0.04	0.04	0.04	0.05	0.05	0.06	0.06	0.07
43	0.02	0.03	0.03	0.03	0.03	0.04	0.04	0.04	0.04	0.05	0.05	0.06	0.06	0.07	0.07
44	0.03	0.03	0.03	0.03	0.04	0.04	0.04	0.04	0.05	0.05	0.06	0.06	0.06	0.07	0.08
45	0.03	0.03	0.03	0.04	0.04	0.04	0.04	0.05	0.05	0.06	0.06	0.06	0.07	0.08	0.08
46	0.03	0.03	0.04	0.04	0.04	0.04	0.05	0.05	0.05	0.06	0.06	0.07	0.08	0.08	0.09
47	0.03	0.04	0.04	0.04	0.04	0.05	0.05	0.05	0.06	0.06	0.07	0.07	0.08	0.09	0.09
48	0.04	0.04	0.04	0.04	0.05	0.05	0.05	0.06	0.06	0.07	0.07	0.08	0.09	0.09	0.10
49	0.04	0.04	0.04	0.05	0.05	0.06	0.06	0.06	0.07	0.07	0.08	0.09	0.09	0.10	0.11
50	0.04	0.04	0.05	0.05	0.06	0.06	0.06	0.07	0.07	0.08	0.09	0.09	0.10	0.11	0.12
51	0.05	0.05	0.05	0.06	0.06	0.06	0.07	0.07	0.08	0.09	0.09	0.10	0.11	0.12	0.13
52	0.05	0.05	0.06	0.06	0.06	0.07	0.08	0.08	0.09	0.09	0.10	0.11	0.12	0.13	0.14
53	0.05	0.06	0.06	0.07	0.07	0.08	0.08	0.09	0.09	0.10	0.11	0.12	0.13	0.14	0.15
54	0.06	0.06	0.07	0.07	0.08	0.08	0.09	0.09	0.10	0.11	0.12	0.13	0.14	0.15	0.16
55	0.06	0.07	0.07	0.08	0.08	0.09	0.10	0.10	0.11	0.12	0.13	0.14	0.15	0.16	0.18
56	0.07	0.07	0.08	0.08	0.09	0.10	0.10	0.11	0.12	0.13	0.14	0.15	0.16	0.18	0.19
57	0.07	0.08	0.08	0.09	0.10	0.10	0.11	0.12	0.13	0.14	0.15	0.17	0.18	0.19	0.21
58	0.08	0.09	0.09	0.10	0.11	0.11	0.12	0.13	0.14	0.15	0.17	0.18	0.19	0.21	0.23
59	0.09	0.09	0.10	0.11	0.11	0.12	0.13	0.14	0.15	0.17	0.18	0.19	0.21	0.23	0.25
60	0.09	0.10	0.11	0.12	0.12	0.13	0.14	0.16	0.17	0.18	0.20	0.21	0.23	0.25	0.27
61	0.10	0.11	0.12	0.13	0.14	0.15	0.16	0.17	0.18	0.20	0.21	0.23	0.25	0.27	0.29
62	0.11	0.12	0.13	0.14	0.15	0.16	0.17	0.18	0.20	0.21	0.23	0.25	0.27	0.29	0.32

Exhibit 11.9 Continued

	0.12	0.13	0.14	0.15	0.16	0.17	0.19	0.20	0.22	0.23	0.25	0.27	0.29	0.32	0.35
63	0.12	0.13	0.14	0.15	0.16	0.17	0.19	0.20	0.22	0.23	0.25	0.27	0.29	0.32	0.35
64	0.13	0.14	0.15	0.16	0.17	0.19	0.20	0.22	0.23	0.25	0.27	0.30	0.32	0.35	0.38
65	0.14	0.15	0.16	0.18	0.19	0.20	0.22	0.24	0.25	0.28	0.30	0.32	0.35	0.38	0.41
66	0.16	0.17	0.18	0.19	0.21	0.22	0.24	0.26	0.28	0.30	0.32	0.35	0.38	0.41	0.45
67	0.17	0.18	0.19	0.21	0.22	0.24	0.26	0.28	0.30	0.33	0.35	0.38	0.41	0.45	0.48
68	0.18	0.20	0.21	0.23	0.24	0.26	0.28	0.30	0.33	0.35	0.38	0.41	0.45	0.49	0.53
69	0.20	0.21	0.23	0.25	0.27	0.29	0.31	0.33	0.36	0.39	0.42	0.45	0.49	0.53	0.57
70	0.22	0.23	0.25	0.27	0.29	0.31	0.33	0.36	0.39	0.42	0.45	0.49	0.53	0.58	0.62
71	0.24	0.25	0.27	0.29	0.31	0.34	0.36	0.39	0.42	0.46	0.49	0.53	0.58	0.63	0.68
72	0.26	0.28	0.30	0.32	0.34	0.37	0.40	0.43	0.46	0.50	0.54	0.58	0.63	0.68	0.74
73	0.28	0.30	0.32	0.35	0.37	0.40	0.43	0.46	0.50	0.54	0.58	0.63	0.68	0.74	0.80
74	0.31	0.33	0.35	0.38	0.40	0.43	0.47	0.50	0.54	0.59	0.64	0.69	0.74	0.81	0.87
75	0.33	0.36	0.38	0.41	0.44	0.47	0.51	0.55	0.59	0.64	0.69	0.75	0.81	0.88	0.95
76	0.36	0.39	0.41	0.44	0.48	0.51	0.53	0.60	0.64	0.70	0.75	0.81	0.88	0.95	1.03
77	0.39	0.42	0.45	0.48	0.52	0.56	0.60	0.65	0.70	0.76	0.82	0.88	0.96	1.05	1.12
78	0.43	0.46	0.49	0.53	0.56	0.61	0.65	0.71	0.76	0.82	0.89	0.96	1.04	1.13	1.22
79	0.46	0.50	0.53	0.57	0.61	0.66	0.71	0.77	0.83	0.89	0.97	1.04	1.13	1.22	1.33
80	0.50	0.54	0.58	0.62	0.67	0.72	0.77	0.83	0.90	0.97	1.05	1.13	1.23	1.33	1.44
81	0.55	0.58	0.63	0.67	0.72	0.78	0.84	0.90	0.98	1.05	1.14	1.23	1.33	1.44	1.57
82	0.59	0.63	0.68	0.73	0.79	0.84	0.91	0.98	1.06	1.14	1.24	1.34	1.45	1.57	1.70
83	0.64	0.69	0.74	0.79	0.85	0.92	0.99	1.06	1.15	1.24	1.34	1.45	1.57	1.70	1.84
84	0.70	0.75	0.80	0.86	0.92	0.99	1.07	1.15	1.25	1.35	1.45	1.57	1.70	1.84	2.00
85	0.76	0.81	0.87	0.93	1.00	1.08	1.16	1.25	1.35	1.46	1.58	1.70	1.84	2.00	2.17

Exhibit 11.9 Second-to-die US 38 rates per $1,000 (continued)

	Second Age														
First Age	55	56	57	58	59	60	61	62	63	64	65	66	67	68	69
40	0.06	0.07	0.07	0.08	0.09	0.09	0.10	0.11	0.12	0.13	0.14	0.16	0.17	0.18	2.00
41	0.07	0.07	0.08	0.09	0.09	0.10	0.11	0.12	0.13	0.14	0.15	0.17	0.18	0.20	0.21
42	0.07	0.08	0.08	0.09	0.10	0.11	0.12	0.13	0.14	0.15	0.16	0.18	0.19	0.21	0.23
43	0.08	0.08	0.09	0.10	0.11	0.12	0.13	0.14	0.15	0.16	0.18	0.19	0.21	0.23	0.25
44	0.08	0.09	0.10	0.11	0.11	0.12	0.14	0.15	0.16	0.17	0.19	0.21	0.22	0.24	0.27
45	0.09	0.10	0.10	0.11	0.12	0.13	0.15	0.16	0.17	0.19	0.20	0.22	0.24	0.26	0.29
46	0.10	0.10	0.11	0.12	0.13	0.14	0.16	0.17	0.19	0.20	0.22	0.24	0.26	0.28	0.31
47	0.10	0.11	0.12	0.13	0.14	0.16	0.17	0.18	0.20	0.22	0.24	0.26	0.28	0.30	0.33
48	0.11	0.12	0.13	0.14	0.15	0.17	0.18	0.20	0.22	0.23	0.25	0.28	0.30	0.33	0.36
49	0.12	0.13	0.14	0.15	0.17	0.18	0.20	0.21	0.23	0.25	0.28	0.30	0.33	0.35	0.39
50	0.13	0.14	0.15	0.17	0.18	0.20	0.21	0.23	0.25	0.27	0.30	0.32	0.35	0.38	0.42
51	0.14	0.15	0.17	0.18	0.19	0.21	0.23	0.25	0.27	0.30	0.32	0.35	0.38	0.41	0.45
52	0.15	0.16	0.18	0.19	0.21	0.23	0.25	0.27	0.29	0.32	0.35	0.38	0.41	0.45	0.49
53	0.16	0.18	0.19	0.21	0.23	0.25	0.27	0.29	0.32	0.35	0.38	0.41	0.45	0.49	0.53
54	0.18	0.19	0.21	0.23	0.25	0.27	0.29	0.32	0.35	0.38	0.41	0.45	0.48	0.53	0.57
55	0.19	0.21	0.23	0.25	0.27	0.29	0.32	0.34	0.38	0.41	0.44	0.48	0.53	0.57	0.62
56	0.21	0.23	0.25	0.27	0.29	0.32	0.34	0.37	0.41	0.44	0.48	0.52	0.57	0.62	0.67
57	0.23	0.25	0.27	0.29	0.32	0.34	0.37	0.41	0.44	0.48	0.52	0.57	0.62	0.67	0.73
58	0.25	0.27	0.29	0.32	0.34	0.37	0.41	0.44	0.48	0.52	0.57	0.62	0.67	0.73	0.80
59	0.27	0.29	0.32	0.34	0.37	0.41	0.44	0.48	0.52	0.57	0.62	0.67	0.73	0.79	0.86
60	0.29	0.32	0.34	0.37	0.41	0.44	0.48	0.52	0.57	0.62	0.67	0.73	0.79	0.86	0.94
61	0.33	0.34	0.37	0.41	0.44	0.48	0.52	0.57	0.62	0.67	0.73	0.79	0.86	0.94	1.02
62	0.34	0.37	0.41	0.44	0.48	0.52	0.57	0.62	0.67	0.73	0.79	0.86	0.94	1.02	1.11

Exhibit 11.9 Continued

63	0.38	0.41	0.44	0.48	0.52	0.57	0.62	0.67	0.73	0.79	0.86	0.94	1.02	1.11	1.21
64	0.41	0.44	0.48	0.52	0.57	0.62	0.67	0.73	0.79	0.86	0.94	1.02	1.11	1.21	1.31
65	0.44	0.48	0.52	0.57	0.62	0.67	0.73	0.79	0.86	0.94	1.02	1.11	1.20	1.31	1.43
66	0.48	0.52	0.57	0.62	0.67	0.73	0.79	0.86	0.94	1.02	1.11	1.20	1.31	1.43	1.55
67	0.53	0.57	0.62	0.67	0.73	0.79	0.86	0.94	1.02	1.11	1.20	1.31	1.43	1.55	1.69
68	0.57	0.62	0.67	0.73	0.79	0.86	0.94	1.02	1.11	1.21	1.31	1.43	1.55	1.69	1.84
69	0.62	0.67	0.73	0.80	0.86	0.94	1.02	1.11	1.21	1.31	1.43	1.55	1.69	1.84	2.00
70	0.68	0.73	0.80	0.87	0.94	1.02	1.11	1.21	1.31	1.43	1.55	1.69	1.84	2.00	2.18
71	0.74	0.80	0.87	0.94	1.02	1.11	1.21	1.31	1.43	1.55	1.69	1.84	2.00	2.18	2.37
72	0.80	0.87	0.94	1.02	1.11	1.21	1.31	1.43	1.55	1.69	1.84	2.00	2.18	2.37	2.58
73	0.87	0.95	1.03	1.11	1.21	1.32	1.43	1.55	1.69	1.84	2.00	2.18	2.37	2.57	2.80
74	0.95	1.03	1.12	1.21	1.32	1.43	1.55	1.69	1.84	2.00	2.17	2.37	2.57	2.80	3.05
75	1.03	1.12	1.21	1.32	1.43	1.56	1.69	1.84	2.00	2.17	2.37	2.57	2.80	3.05	3.31
76	1.12	1.22	1.32	1.43	1.56	1.69	1.84	2.00	2.17	2.36	2.57	2.80	3.04	3.31	3.60
77	1.22	1.32	1.44	1.56	1.69	1.84	2.00	2.17	2.36	2.57	2.80	3.04	3.31	3.60	3.92
78	1.32	1.44	1.56	1.69	1.84	2.00	2.17	2.36	2.57	2.79	3.04	3.31	3.60	3.91	4.26
79	1.44	1.56	1.70	1.84	2.00	2.17	2.36	2.57	2.79	3.04	3.30	3.59	3.91	4.25	4.63
80	1.56	1.70	1.84	2.00	2.17	2.36	2.56	2.79	3.03	3.30	3.59	3.90	4.25	4.62	5.03
81	1.70	1.84	2.00	2.17	2.36	2.56	2.78	3.03	3.29	3.58	3.89	4.24	4.61	5.02	5.46
82	1.84	2.00	2.17	2.36	2.56	2.78	3.02	3.29	3.57	3.89	4.23	4.60	5.00	5.44	5.92
83	2.00	2.17	2.35	2.56	2.78	3.02	3.28	3.56	3.88	4.22	4.59	4.99	5.43	5.91	6.43
84	2.17	2.35	2.55	2.77	3.01	3.27	3.55	3.86	4.20	4.57	4.97	5.41	5.88	6.40	6.97
85	2.38	2.55	2.77	3.00	3.26	3.54	3.85	4.19	4.55	4.95	5.39	5.86	6.38	6.94	7.55

Exhibit 11.9 Second-to-die US 38 rates per $1,000 (continued)

First Age	Second Age													
	70	71	72	73	74	75	76	77	78	79	80	81	82	83
40	0.22	0.24	0.26	0.28	0.31	0.33	0.36	0.39	0.43	0.46	0.50	0.55	0.59	0.64
41	0.23	0.25	0.28	0.30	0.33	0.36	0.39	0.42	0.46	0.50	0.54	0.58	0.63	0.69
42	0.25	0.27	0.30	0.32	0.35	0.38	0.41	0.45	0.49	0.53	0.58	0.63	0.68	0.74
43	0.27	0.29	0.32	0.35	0.38	0.41	0.44	0.48	0.53	0.57	0.62	0.67	0.73	0.79
44	0.29	0.31	0.34	0.37	0.40	0.44	0.48	0.52	0.56	0.61	0.67	0.72	0.79	0.85
45	0.31	0.34	0.37	0.40	0.43	0.47	0.51	0.56	0.61	0.66	0.72	0.78	0.84	0.92
46	0.33	0.36	0.40	0.43	0.47	0.51	0.55	0.60	0.65	0.71	0.77	0.84	0.91	0.99
47	0.36	0.39	0.43	0.46	0.50	0.55	0.60	0.65	0.71	0.77	0.83	0.90	0.98	1.06
48	0.39	0.42	0.46	0.50	0.54	0.59	0.64	0.70	0.76	0.83	0.90	0.98	1.06	1.15
49	0.42	0.46	0.50	0.54	0.59	0.64	0.70	0.76	0.82	0.89	0.97	1.05	1.14	1.24
50	0.45	0.49	0.54	0.58	0.64	0.69	0.75	0.82	0.89	0.97	1.05	1.14	1.24	1.34
51	0.49	0.53	0.58	0.63	0.69	0.75	0.81	0.88	0.96	1.04	1.13	1.23	1.34	1.45
52	0.53	0.58	0.63	0.68	0.74	0.81	0.88	0.96	1.04	1.13	1.23	1.33	1.45	1.57
53	0.58	0.63	0.68	0.74	0.81	0.88	0.95	1.04	1.13	1.22	1.33	1.44	1.57	1.70
54	0.62	0.68	0.74	0.80	0.87	0.95	1.03	1.12	1.22	1.33	1.44	1.57	1.70	1.84
55	0.68	0.74	0.80	0.87	0.95	1.03	1.12	1.22	1.32	1.44	1.56	1.70	1.84	2.00
56	0.73	0.80	0.87	0.95	1.03	1.12	1.22	1.32	1.44	1.56	1.70	1.84	2.00	2.17
57	0.80	0.87	0.94	1.03	1.12	1.21	1.32	1.44	1.56	1.70	1.84	2.00	2.17	2.35
58	0.87	0.94	1.02	1.11	1.21	1.32	1.43	1.56	1.69	1.84	2.00	2.17	2.36	2.56
59	0.94	1.02	1.11	1.21	1.32	1.43	1.56	1.69	1.84	2.00	2.17	2.36	2.56	2.78
60	1.02	1.11	1.21	1.32	1.43	1.56	1.69	1.84	2.00	2.17	2.36	2.56	2.78	3.02
61	1.11	1.21	1.31	1.43	1.55	1.69	1.84	2.00	2.17	2.36	2.56	2.78	3.02	3.28
62	1.21	1.31	1.43	1.35	1.69	1.84	2.00	2.17	2.36	2.57	2.79	3.03	3.29	3.56

Exhibit 11.9 Continued

63	1.31	1.43	1.55	1.69	1.84	2.00	2.17	2.36	2.57	2.79	3.03	3.29	3.57	3.88
64	1.43	1.55	1.69	1.84	2.00	2.17	2.36	2.57	2.79	3.04	3.30	3.58	3.89	4.22
65	1.55	1.69	1.84	2.00	2.17	2.37	2.57	2.80	3.04	3.30	3.59	3.89	4.23	4.59
66	1.69	1.84	2.00	2.18	2.37	2.57	2.80	3.04	3.31	3.59	3.90	4.24	4.60	4.99
67	1.84	2.00	2.18	2.37	2.57	2.80	3.04	3.31	3.60	3.91	4.25	4.61	5.00	5.43
68	2.00	2.18	2.37	2.57	2.80	3.05	3.31	3.60	3.91	4.25	4.62	5.02	5.44	5.91
69	2.18	2.37	2.58	2.80	3.05	3.31	3.60	3.92	4.26	4.63	5.03	5.46	5.92	6.43
70	2.37	2.58	2.80	3.05	3.32	3.61	3.92	4.26	4.63	5.04	5.47	5.94	6.45	6.99
71	2.58	2.80	3.05	3.32	3.61	3.92	4.27	4.64	5.04	5.48	5.95	6.46	7.01	7.61
72	2.80	3.05	3.32	3.61	3.93	4.27	4.64	5.05	5.49	5.96	6.48	7.03	7.63	8.28
73	3.05	3.32	3.61	3.93	4.27	4.65	5.05	5.49	5.97	6.49	7.04	7.65	8.30	9.01
74	3.32	3.61	3.93	4.27	4.65	5.05	5.49	5.97	6.49	7.06	7.66	8.32	9.03	9.80
75	3.61	3.92	4.27	4.65	5.05	5.50	5.98	6.50	7.06	7.67	8.33	9.05	9.82	10.65
76	3.92	4.27	4.64	5.05	5.49	5.98	6.50	7.07	7.68	8.34	9.06	9.84	10.68	11.59
77	4.26	4.64	5.05	5.49	5.97	6.50	7.07	7.68	8.35	9.07	9.85	10.70	11.61	12.60
78	4.63	5.04	5.49	5.97	6.49	7.06	7.68	8.35	9.07	9.86	10.71	11.63	12.62	13.69
79	5.04	5.48	5.96	6.49	7.06	7.67	8.34	9.07	9.86	10.71	11.64	12.63	13.71	14.87
80	5.47	5.95	6.48	7.04	7.66	8.33	9.06	9.85	10.71	11.64	12.64	13.72	14.89	16.16
81	5.94	6.46	7.03	7.65	8.32	9.05	9.84	10.70	11.63	12.63	13.72	14.90	16.17	17.54
82	6.45	7.01	7.63	8.30	9.03	9.82	10.68	11.61	12.62	13.71	14.89	16.17	17.55	19.04
83	6.99	7.61	8.28	9.01	9.80	10.65	11.59	12.60	13.69	14.87	16.16	17.54	19.04	20.65
84	7.58	8.25	8.98	9.76	10.62	11.55	12.56	13.66	14.84	16.13	17.52	19.02	20.64	22.39
85	8.21	8.94	9.72	10.58	11.51	12.52	13.61	14.80	16.08	17.48	18.98	20.61	22.37	24.27

Reverse Split-Dollar

Another twist to split-dollar is to change who typically gets and pays for the account value of the policy. What if your objective as an employee was not a substantial amount of life insurance, but rather a substantial build-up of assets? Why not reverse the normal split-dollar situation? Why not have the corporation pay the expenses and mortality costs of a policy and turn the investment account over to you? The employer would take the death benefit and you would take the cash or account value. The employer gets key employee life insurance, and you get the tax-free build-up of the insurance policy without the normally associated expenses. You could even do this in a family situation where one party wants life insurance and the other wants an annuity without pre-59-1/2 penalties or income taxes.

With the typical whole life insurance policies of the past, reverse split-dollar did not work very well. There was no excitement about the investment value in spite of the fact that, in many cases, it offered a reasonable rate of return in relation to the risk entailed. The reason for current excitement regarding reverse split-dollar plans is the new universal variable life insurance policies with their array of different investment accounts offering diversification, the opportunity to dollar-cost-average, and the opportunity to shift among these accounts without current income taxation or transaction costs. These policies give you the ability to manage investments, earn dividends, earn interest and take capital gains when desired, without concern for any income-tax liability. If the expenses and management fees associated with the policy are reasonable, and the investment performance of the accounts is competitive, it can offer an attractive arrangement. Universal variable life insurance is the foundation of today's private pension plans.

How could we make it more attractive? The corporation gets the death benefit in this case, so the corporation is supposed to pay for the life insurance. The question is how to charge the corporation for the term insurance. The government-sanctioned PS-58 cost seems a logical choice. After all, the corporation is receiving the economic benefit and consequently is responsible for paying the PS-58 rates as set forth in revenue ruling 64-328. Let's take a look at a typical $200,000 universal variable policy and determine the impact of this decision. The relatively conservative funding level within such a policy would be approximately $4,000 per year for a non-smoking, 50-year-old male. Of this amount, we would ask the corporation to pay the PS-58 costs for the executive which are $9.22 per $1,000 for the year that the executive is age 50. A $200,000 policy would require a payment by the corporation of 200 times the PS-58 cost ($9.22) or $1,844 annually. This leaves the employee paying the balance of approximately $2,156 per year. In examining the $200,000 policy, we might find that the total expenses amount to only $1,200, for which the corporation pays $1,844. The extra money ends up in the employee's investment account. This is wealth-shifting without current taxation. It falls into the category of *it sounds too good to be true* and probably is; but for the present time it *is* true, and seems to be a justifiable procedure. Uncle Sam typically is not a giver of generous gifts, so when you set up your split-dollar plan, set it up knowing it can be a good deal without the additional benefit of the PS-58 tables. For the present, talk to your attorney and accountant and see if you can enjoy this great deal until it is snuffed out.

There will be those who want all the investment features offered by the policy and accessibility to the cash without taxes or penalties, while still objecting to the cost of the life insurance. If the individuals have any charitable inclinations, we suggest that they establish a reverse split-dollar plan with charitable organizations of their choice and assign the death benefit of the policy to those charities.

THE 1035 TAX-FREE EXCHANGE

What do you do with your under-achievers—those policies that are no longer paying acceptable dividends or excess interest? Let's say you computed the rate of return within your insurance product using the system described in this book and have decided that the performance of one of your old contracts is not what you want it to be and feel you can get elsewhere. You run a new product being offered through the same evaluation, balance the risks and rewards, and decide that you would rather acquire the new than retain the old. The most economical alternative is a 1035 tax-free exchange from your old contract into the new one.

Internal Revenue Code Section 1035 allows a policy-owner to exchange one life insurance contract for another on a tax-free basis. It provides that no gain or loss shall be recognized on the exchange of:

1. A contract of life insurance for another contract of life insurance.

2. A contract of endowment insurance for another contract of endowment insurance that provides for the regular payments beginning at a date not later than the date payments would have begun under the contract exchanged, or for an annuity contract.

3. An annuity contract for an annuity contract.

4. A contract of life insurance for an annuity contract.

Section 1031 (b) provides that gains from exchanges not solely in kind can create tax liabilities. When a life insurance policy subject to an existing loan is exchanged for a new life insurance policy without a policy loan, the exchanger has received what is referred to as *net debt relief*. As far as Uncle Sam is concerned, if you are relieved of a debt, it is exactly the same as being paid, so you will be taxed at ordinary income-tax rates to the extent of your net debt relief and the untaxed gain in your contract.

The IRS stated in Revenue Ruling 72-353 that an exchange qualified as a tax-free exchange under 1035 (a) because the new policy would be issued in exchange for the old policy. With no money received by the taxpayer, the basis in the new policy would be the same as the basis in the old policy. The underlying principle justifying the non-recognition of gain in the tax-free exchange situation, according to the IRS, is that "the property received in the exchange is substantially a continuation of the old investment still unliquidated." Tax-free exchanges for both life insurance and annuity contracts offer the opportunity to turn under-performing contracts into better-performing contracts without incurring tax liabilities. Binding exchange assignment agreements should be executed by the policy-owner and the insurance company, and *all* of the old policy proceeds should be rolled over into the new contract. Funds may need to be transferred to balance the arrangement or pay off policy loans to ensure that there is no net debt relief as the funds flow between the two insurers. The paper trail is important; it will enable you to show Uncle Sam exactly what was intended as you went about the exchange process.

You may exchange policies with your present insurance company if it has a new contract that can outperform the one you now own. Your present company may charge less in expenses for the change, and, in some cases, you may not have to pass a physical or go through any underwriting requirements to obtain the new policy.

Moving to a new company is not difficult. The process is simple even though it takes a bit of paperwork. First, you apply for and make sure you can get a satisfactory new policy from the new company. At the time of filling out the new application, you indicate on it that this is to be a 1035 tax-free exchange from policies X, Y, and Z to the new contract, when it is issued on a basis acceptable to you. You execute forms assigning your old policies to the new company when you know you have an acceptable policy issue. The new company now owns your old policies. You instruct the new company to send them in for surrender, collect the surrender proceeds, and deposit them into your new policy. That completes the process.

ADVANCED MATURITY

Advanced maturity, or whatever you wish to call it, is that stage in life during which career and work are for *fun* and not for economic necessity. If you want to retire you do; if you don't want to retire, you do what you like to do. Unless your assets are illiquid (such as invested in real estate or your own closely held business), your need for life insurance will be based upon how you want your estate handled for the next generation. You will have insured that your spouse can afford to live in the manner to which the two of you have been accustomed. You currently are receiving mandatory (over 70-1/2) income from your IRA accounts, pension plans, profit-sharing plans, 401(k) plans, thrift plans, SEP plans, Keogh plans, and deferred-compensation contracts. You have determined that your asset base is large enough for your surviving spouse, or you may have chosen joint and survivor arrangements on your various plans. Alternatively, you may have chosen life income only and have provided sufficient death benefits in life insurance to accomplish the same objective—sufficient income for the surviving spouse.

Life Insurance to Pay Federal Estate Taxes

You may need life insurance at this time, not to build an asset base for your surviving spouse, but to provide cash for your offspring so that they can pay estate taxes from life insurance proceeds, rather than by selling the real estate or closely held business in your estate. You know that everything *over* $600,000 that you and over $600,000 that your spouse pass to your children will create an estate-tax liability. The tax rate at $600,000 is 37 percent, a $37,000 tax liability for the first $100,000 over the $600,000 breakpoint. The rate is 37 percent for the first $150,000, 39 percent for the next $250,000, 41 percent for the next $250,000, and so on, up to a maximum rate of 55 percent on amounts for transfer over $3 million. In short, the two of you can plan to pass $1,200,000 of assets to your children without an estate-tax liability. Your estate should have ready cash to pay these expenses either from cash within the estate or proceeds from life insurance. If it does not, then assets will have to be sold to pay the bill which is due nine months after the death that created the liability.

The Unified Transfer Tax System establishes a means of taxing everything that you or I own and pass to others. There are limited non-taxable transfers of assets during lifetime and at our death. The general rule regarding these gifts is that if you own it and transfer that ownership, the transfer is a taxable event. This holds true with these exceptions.

1. Except if the recipient is your spouse (spousal gifts and marital deduction).

2. Except if it is a present interest gift of $10,000 or less per year, per individual recipient (joint with spouse gifts, $20,000).

3. Except if the total of all the gifts, not counting the $10,000-per-year gifts, totaled less than $600,000 in your whole lifetime, including the total of all you passed by inheritance at your death.

The way to alleviate high estate taxes is to reduce the size of your estate, and a gift of life insurance can result in a substantial estate reduction. Life insurance will be taxed in the estate of the policy-owner. If the policy-owner and the insured are one and the same individual, it will be the death benefit of the life insurance that will be included within that estate. If that is an unsatisfactory arrangement, the solution is to give it away. If you give it away to your spouse, you will accomplish nothing—the full face amount of the life insurance policy still will be included in the estate of the second-to-die, regardless of whether you or your spouse owns the policy. If your spouse dies first and you are the insured, the cash value of the policy is a part of the spouse's estate, not the face amount. If special provisions were made to ensure that the policy passes to a new owner other than you, they prevent inclusion of the life insurance face amount in your estate as the survivoring spouse, for estate-tax purposes.

A better way to get life insurance outside of your estate is to have it owned by someone other than you or your spouse.

1994 Federal Estate and Gift Tax Rates

If the Tax Base Is—		The Tentative Tax Is—		
Over	But not over	Flat amount	+ %	Of excess over
$ 0	$ 10,000	$ 0	18%	$ 0
10,000	20,000	1,800	20%	10,000
20,000	40,000	3,800	22%	20,000
40,000	60,000	8,200	24%	40,000
60,000	80,000	13,000	26%	60,000
80,000	100,000	18,200	28%	80,000
100,000	150,000	23,800	30%	100,000
150,000	250,000	38,800	32%	150,000
250,000	500,000	70,800	34%	250,000
500,000	750,000	155,800	37%	500,000
750,000	1,000,000	248,300	39%	750,000
1,000,000	1,250,000	345,800	41%	1,000,000
1,250,000	1,500,000	448,300	43%	1,250,000
1,500,000	2,000,000	555,800	45%	1,500,000
2,000,000	2,500,000	780,800	49%	2,000,000
2,500,000	3,000,000	1,025,800	53%	2,500,000
3,000,000	. . . .	1,290,800	55%	3,000,000

These rates apply to gifts made and estates of persons dying in 1994.

The tax base is the sum of the taxable estate and any adjusted taxable gifts made during life.

The unified estate and gift tax credit is set at $192,800. This credit exempts the estate from tax if the tax base is $600,000 or less.

That person can buy life insurance on either or both of your lives and be the policy owner and beneficiary. In this case you, the insureds, would have no ownership rights and no control rights over any part of the policies, and would never have had such rights; consequently, the policies would not be included within your estates.

From an estate-tax standpoint, difficulties arise in trying to get rid of existing life insurance currently owned by spouses on their own or each other's lives. These policies may be necessary to accomplish certain estate-owner objectives such as paying estate taxes at eventual death. The objective is to have the policies serve their required purposes and also be excluded from the estate-owner's gross estate for estate-tax purposes. The irrevocable life insurance trust offers a solution.

LIFE INSURANCE: IRREVOCABLE LIVING TRUSTS

You will need a good estate attorney to draft the irrevocable trust. Community property states have unique planning problems and opportunities that you will want to discuss. Internal Revenue Code sections 2035 and 2042 are pertinent to this area of planning. Section 2035 says that a decedent's estate includes life insurance transferred within three years of death. This means that you will need to be cautious of transferral of the policy itself and future premium payments. Section 2042 says that a decedent's estate includes the proceeds of life insurance if the decedent had any incidence of policy ownership. You will need to make sure that the estate-owner, from whose estate we are trying to eliminate the policy, does not retain any incidence of ownership or control over the particular policy. This requires special consideration in community property states to avoid having the policy treated as community property.

The assets that flow into an irrevocable trust, such as a family trust owned and controlled by the children can then be used to buy illiquid assets from the decedent's estate. This accomplishes transferral of the liquid assets or life insurance proceeds from the irrevocable trust for the benefit of the family, while providing cash to the decedent's estate to pay estate taxes.

The concept of an irrevocable trust is frightening to some because *irrevocable* sounds like a very long time. Most people are reluctant to give up the control, use, and enjoyment of assets in substantial amounts during their lifetimes. However, if the irrevocable trust can be established as a family trust (assuming good family relationships), many of the objections to an irrevocable trust can be overcome. For example, the assets of the trust could be used prior to the insured's death to accomplish trust beneficiary objectives (such as advanced education), and the trust could be established so as to self-destruct in the event that it no longer served family needs. Funding such trusts with today's universal variable life insurance policies allows the trustees to raise and lower payments into the policy, increase and decrease face amounts, and maintain strategic control over the investment of the assets within the life insurance contract. The irrevocable trust used in this way does not have to be as inflexible as it sounds. If at any time the trust is deemed to no longer be serving family purposes, payments into the trust may be terminated, assets removed from the policy and distributed to beneficiaries, and the policy allowed to implode, that is, use itself up and terminate. Yes, this may result in the trust or its beneficiaries being subject to an ordinary income-tax liability on the gain in the policy in excess of the trustee policy-owner's basis; however, a policy that uses up all accrued gains in term insurance costs and expenses will not leave taxable gain.

MULTIPLE LIFE LIFE INSURANCE CONTRACTS

Popular for the Wrong Reason

Survivor life insurance, joint and last survivor life insurance, and second-to-die and first-to-die joint life are all forms of providing life insurance on two lives, with the death benefit paid out at *one* of the deaths. The death benefit is paid at the death of the second insured with survivor, joint and last survivor, and second-to-die insurance, but at the death of the first insured in a first-to-die contract (tricky names—did they give you a clue?). These policies are receiving much publicity because they require less premium than standard life policies on a single insured. They are purported to be *cheaper*. This myth has led to use of them without careful thought about how well they provide for specific and long-term needs.

FIRST-TO-DIE

In the case of first-to-die joint life, the policies are perceived as inexpensive when compared to two separate single life policies. They do cost less because the insurance company needs to pay off only at the death of the first, leaving the survivor uninsured. If lack of insurance is a problem and the survivor is now uninsurable, or if resources are not available to pay for what now will be a standard single life policy, then using the first-to-die contract will not have been cheap, rather improperly used and costing dearly.

SECOND-TO-DIE

Second-to-die policies, even more popular than first-to-die, are perceived as inexpensive because people feel they have a lot of insurance at a premium much less than that for two individual life policies. But again, the company needs to pay off only at one death, the last of the two insureds to die. This dramatically delays the time and chance that the company will be called upon to pay a death benefit. Therefore, it follows that the mortality costs for life insurance within the policy are much lower than with a conventional single life policy. The *other shoe* in these policies is what happens when the first of the two insureds dies. The survivor may not receive any death benefit payments from this contract and now may have to pay the premium on what is essentially a standard single life policy. Does the survivor have the resources and want to use them to service the ongoing premium requirements of a policy that is not personally beneficial? Also, what is to be the disposition of the policy if one of the insureds should no longer *be* one of the insureds, such as in a divorce situation, the termination of a key employee, or the break-up of a business arrangement?

The bottom line is that these policies should not be thought of as bargains but rather as merely policies that meet the needs of a particular situation very efficiently. Keep in mind that the very efficiency with which they provide for the *particular* situation is likely to make them quite inefficient should the situation change.

Let's take a look at some of the situations to which these policies are particularly well suited and then give some reasons why the *cheaper* approach may backfire.

SITUATION: HUSBAND AND WIFE

The need is cash to pay federal estate tax at the second death. This is the most popular use of the second-to-die policy. It hits the nail on the head. A husband and wife first plan their estate with their attorney, accountant, and other appropriate professionals. This assures that the estate passes to whom they wish with a minimum of cost, delay, and complication. Having determined the most efficient method of passing their property and minimizing the costs involved, they make an informed decision *not* to pay any estate taxes until the second death. After estimating the inflation-adjusted amount of the taxes and expenses to be paid, they buy a second-to-die policy sufficient to pay the estimated costs. The cash from the policy death benefit will arrive as a result of the same event that causes the taxes and expenses to become due. What could be more perfect? What could possibly make this a less than perfect decision? After all, the premium is less expensive than two individual policies and may be all the couple can allocate to insurance. One of the two insureds may have trouble getting insurance because of poor health, but the insurance company will accept the risk in this situation because it is based on two lives. Also, the purchasers went to a number of agents and carefully bought a policy that required sufficient premium so as not to include much term insurance which might later become more expensive than predicted.

What Went Wrong

Well, here is what really happened. The couple's marriage ended in a divorce. The policy was owned by an irrevocable trust. It took some doing (time and expense) for the attorney to find that the trustee had the right to distribute the policy so that it could be divided into two policies, each for one-half the original face amount and allowing each of the insureds to become the owner of his/her own policy. It was not an inexpensive or easy process because it was not anticipated or provided for in advance.

What Else Could Go Wrong?

Or let's try this. They did not get divorced, but he died before she did and the cost of the policy was a burden to her. The policy did not help her and she began to wonder why she should pay for it. The kids weren't being that great either, so she quit making the gifts to the irrevocable trust that were necessary to pay the premiums on the policy. The mortality (life insurance) costs and expenses were taken from the policy values and the policy terminated, leaving the trust an empty shell. At her death, Uncle Sam took his 50 percent and the estate was destroyed for lack of cash and marketability of other assets. The kids finally realized that they should have taken care of Mom . . . or figured out some way to keep the policy in force.

ANOTHER SCENARIO

Voluntarily Pay Estate Taxes at the First Death

Bob Hales, an attorney from California, tells a story of someone who did not buy second-to-die but elected years ago to pay $90,000 of estate taxes at the first death. This allowed a piece of property to be put in a trust for the limited benefit of the spouse during her lifetime, with the eventual benefit to the children when she died. The trust will not be subject to estate taxes on the value of the property, her interest in the trust was limited, and the $90,000 in taxes was paid when he died using life insurance proceeds from a policy on his life. That piece of property is a sizeable portion of the Napa Valley. The children were not aware of the careful planning their father had done 25 years earlier and came into the lawyer's office recently with their mother who is now 90 years old. They were terribly concerned because they had just attended a seminar on estate taxes and wanted his estimate of the federal estate taxes they thought would be due at their mother's eventual death. The piece of property is now worth $36 million. The seminar leader had told them they would owe Uncle Sam $18 million payable nine months after their mom's death. Bob happily told them that the correct figure was *zero* because of the careful long-term thinking of their father (and the attorney) resulting in payment of a $90,000 tax 25 years earlier. He enjoyed their pleased surprise immensely.

Multiple life policies can be very useful. But excessive use, too little premium and poor planning can turn advantages into disadvantages. Don't consider them defaults in answering a myriad of estate-planning problems.

SUMMARY

Every life insurance policy strategy discussed in this chapter works better with policy-owner control and flexibility of policy face amount, premium input, and investment choice. Diversification is essential in these long-term contracts. The opportunity to invest in various mutual funds, so that the contract can be adapted to both economic environment and policy-owner circumstances throughout the policy's existence, is a paradigm shift in a very basic financial product that few have begun to appreciate. It's usefulness is limited only by your imagination.

In addition, insurance company products enjoy a degree of creditor protection that is unique among assets. Look in the following pages at how your state protects life insurance and annuity assets.

Creditors' Rights in a Nonbankruptcy Context

Editor's note: The following chart has been developed by B. Patrick O'Donnell, Jr., J.D., LL.M., CLU, ChFC, Director of Advanced Sales, Massachusetts Mutual Life Insurance Company. It is reprinted with permission from Massachusetts Mutual.

This is a state-by-state synopsis of the laws regarding the exempt status of personally owned life insurance and annuities in nonbankruptcy situations. The table, which reflects research completed as of August 1, 1992, is based on the following assumptions: 1) no purchase of life insurance policies or annuity contracts or payment of premium thereon, were made with the intent to defraud creditors; 2) life insurance policies were assumed to be owned by the insured, and all rights of policy ownership were retained by the insured (unless otherwise noted); 3) no consideration was given to the creditors of either the beneficiaries or assignees; and 4) assumptions 2 and 3 also were made with regard to the purchase of annuity contracts.

With respect to bankruptcy situations, the general rule seems to be that the exemptions for life insurance and/or annuities would be available. In those situations where that is not the case (or where the exemption is otherwise modified), an asterisk has been placed after the name of the state and the appropriate statutory reference included. In those situations, client's legal counsel needs to consult the specific statutory provisions.

| | | LIFE INSURANCE | | ANNUITIES | |
| | | Death Proceeds (beneficiaries and assignees) | Cash Values | Annuity Values (annuitant) | Annuity Values (beneficiaries and assignees) |
Jurisdiction	Applicable Statutory References				
Alabama	CA Secs. 27-14-29(a) and (b) CA Sec. 27-14-32 CA Sec. 6-10-8	Exempt	Exempt	Exempt up to $250/month if in a pay status	Exempt up to $250/month if in a pay status
Alaska*	AS Secs. 09.38.025(a) AS Secs. 09.38.030(a),(b),(c) and (e)(4) AS Sec. 09.38.050(b) AS Sec. 09.38-115	Considered "earnings income cash, or other liquid assets," subject to an annually indexed limitation	Exempt (however, loan values and accumulated dividends are exempt only up to an aggregate of $10,000)	Same as life insurance death proceeds and cash values	Same as life insurance death proceeds and cash values
Arizona	ARS Secs. 20-1131(A),(B) and (D)	Exempt	Exempt (except modified to maximum of $5,000/$10,000 where policy has been in force for at least two years and dependent named as beneficiary)	No express provisions	No express provisions
Arkansas*	ACA Secs. 23-79-131(a)(1) and (2) ACA Sec. 16-66-209	Exempt	Exempt	Exempt	Exempt
California	Cal. Civ. Proc. Code Secs. 704.100(a),(b) and (c)	Exempt	Exempt (however, loan values are exempt only up to an aggregate of $4,000)	Same as life insurance, except "matured" contracts are exempt only to the extent reasonably necessary for support of judgment debtor, spouse and dependents	Same as life insurance, except "matured" contracts are exempt only to the extent reasonably necessary for support of judgment debtor, spouse and dependents
Colorado*	CRS Sec. 13-54-102(1)(L) CRS Sec. 13-54-106 CRS Sec. 13-54-107	Limited exemption (first $5,000)	Limited exemption (first $5,000)	No express provisions	No express provisions
Connecticut	CGSA Sec. 38a-453	Exempt	Exempt	No express provisions	No express provisions
Delaware*	DCA Title 18, Sec. 2725 DCS Title 18, Sec. 2728 DCA Title 10, Sec. 4914	Exempt	Exempt	Exempt up to $350/month if in a pay status	Exempt up to $350/month if in a pay status
District of Columbia	DCCA Sec. 35-521 DCCA Sec. 15-503(a) and (b)	Exempt	Exempt	Exempt up to $200/month if in a pay status	Exempt up to $200/month if in a pay status
Florida	FSA Sec. 222.13(1) FSA Sec. 222.14	Exempt	Exempt	Exempt	Exempt
Georgia*	GCA Sec. 33-25-11 GCA Sec. 33-28-7 GCA Sec. 33-26-5 GCA Sec. 44-13-100	Exempt	Exempt	Exempt	Exempt
Hawaii	HRS Sec. 431.10-232(a)	Exempt (if payable to spouse, child, parent or other dependent)	Exempt (if payable to spouse, child, parent or other dependent)	Same rules as for life insurance	Same rules as for life insurance
Idaho	IC Sec. 41-1833(1) IC Sec. 41-1836(1) and (2)	Generally exempt	Generally exempt	Exempt up to $350/month if in a pay status	Exempt up to $350/month if in a pay status
Illinois	Ill. Ann. Stat. Ch. 110, Para. 12-1001(f) Ill. Ann. Stat. Ch. 73, Para. 850	Exempt (if payable to spouse, child, parent, other dependent or creditor)	Exempt (if payable to spouse, child, parent, other dependent or creditor)	Same rules as for life insurance	Same rules as for life insurance

*Exempt status may differ in bankruptcy situations. Applicable statutory references included.

Note: This table, which reflects research completed as of August 1, 1992, is provided for general informational purposes only, and not as specific legal or tax advice. Individual clients should consult with their personal advisers about their particular situation.

Jurisdiction	Applicable Statutory References	LIFE INSURANCE		ANNUITIES	
		Death Proceeds (beneficiaries and assignees)	Cash Values	Annuity Values (annuitant)	Annuity Values (beneficiaries and assignees)
Indiana*	IC Sec. 27-1-12-14(c) and (d) IC Sec. 34-2-28-0.5	Exempt (except for dividends paid in cash)	Exempt (except for dividends paid in cash)	No express provisions	No express provisions
Iowa	ICA Sec. 627.6(6)	Exempt (if payable to spouse, child or other dependent)	Exempt (if payable to spouse, child or other dependent), modified further by a $10,000 maximum exemption for policies purchased within two years of any issuance of execution for creditor	No express provisions	No express provisions
Kansas	KSA Sec. 40-414 KSA Sec. 60-2313(a)(8)	Exempt	Exempt	No express provisions	No express provisions
Kentucky	KRS Sec. 304-14-300 KRS Sec. 304-14-330	Exempt	Exempt	Exempt up to $350/month if in a pay status	Exempt up to $350/month if in a pay status
Louisiana*	LSA-RS.22:647 LSA-RS.22:647(A)(1) LSA-RS.22:647(A)(2) LSA-RS.13.3881(B)(1)	Exempt	Exempt (modified by a $35,000 maximum exemption for policies issued within nine months of the process seeking to reach the cash or loan value)	Exempt (except as modified by the same maximum exemption applicable to life insurance cash values for contracts issued within nine months of the process seeking to reach the cash or loan values)	Exempt (except as modified by the same maximum exemption applicable to life insurance cash values for contracts issued within nine months of the process seeking to reach the cash or loan values)
Maine	24-A MRSA Sec. 2428 24-A MRSA Sec. 2431	Exempt	Exempt	Exempt up to $450/month if in a pay status	Exempt up to $450/month if in a pay status
Maryland	48A ACM Sec. 385	Exempt (if payable to spouse, child or dependent relative)	Exempt (if payable to spouse, child or dependent relative)	Same rules as for life insurance	Same rules as for life insurance
Massachusetts	ALM Ch. 175, Sec. 125 ALM Ch. 175, Sec. 132C	Exempt	Exempt	Group annuity contracts exempt (no provisions for individual annuity contracts)	Group annuity contracts exempt (no provisions for individual annuity contracts)
Michigan	MCLA Sec. 24.12207(2)	Exempt	Exempt	Exempt	Exempt
Minnesota	MSA Sec. 61A.12	Exempt	Exempt	No express provisions	No express provisions
Mississippi	MCA Sec. 85-3-11	Exempt up to $50,000 per insured (except all proceeds are exempt if policy ownership other than insured)	Exempt up to $50,000 (except fully available to satisfy a decree for child support and alimony); fully exempt if policy ownership other than insured	No express provisions	No express provisions
Missouri*	VAMS Sec. 377.330 VAMS Sec. 513.430(8) VAMS Sec. 513.427	Exempt	Exempt	No express provisions	No express provisions
Montana*	MCA Sec. 33-15-511 MCA Sec. 33-15-514 MCA Sec. 31-2-106	Exempt	Exempt	Exempt up to $350/month if in a pay status	Exempt up to $350/month if in a pay status
Nebraska	RSN Sec. 44-371	Exempt	Exempt (except limited to $10,000 for individual insured who is also policyowner)	Exempt (except limited to $10,000 per individual annuitant who is also contract owner)	Exempt
Nevada	NRS Sec. 687B.260 NRS Sec. 21.090(i)(k) NRS Sec. 687B.290	Exempt	Exempt (except pro-rata exemption if annual premium exceeds $1,000)	Exempt up to $350/month if in a pay status	Exempt up to $350/month if in a pay status
New Hampshire	NHRSA Sec. 408.2	Exempt	Exempt (except cash values of an endowment policy are not exempt	No express provisions	No express provisions
New Jersey	NJSA Sec. 17B:24-6(a) NJSA Sec. 17B:24-7	Exempt	Exempt	Exempt up to $500/month if in a pay status	Exempt up to $500/month if in a pay status
New Mexico	NMSA Sec. 42-10-3 NMSA Sec. 42-10-5	Exempt	Exempt	Exempt	Exempt
New York*	CLNY, Ins. Law, Sec. 3212 CLNY, Ins. Law, Sec. 3212(d) CLNY, Debtor and Creditor Law, Sec. 282 and 283	Exempt	Exempt	Generally exempt	Exempt
North Carolina	GSNC Sec. 58-58-95 GSNC Sec. 58-58-115	Exempt	Exempt	No express provisions	No express provisions
North Dakota*	NDCC Sec. 26.1-33-36 NDCC Sec. 26.1-33-40 NDCC Sec. 28-22-03.1(3)	Exempt	Limited exemption of $100,000 per policy, with an overall aggregate limit of $200,000 for all policies and annuities. (Note. Must be payable to spouse, children or other dependent, and in force for at least one year.)	Limited exemption of $100,000 per policy, with an overall aggregate limit of $200,000 for all policies and annuities (Note. Must be payable to spouse, children or other dependent, and in force for at least one year.)	Limited exemption of $100,000 per policy, with an overall aggregate limit of $200,000 for all policies and annuities (Note. Must be payable to spouse, children or other dependent, and in force for at least one year.)

*Exempt status may differ in bankruptcy situations. Applicable statutory references included.

Note: This table, which reflects research completed as of August 1, 1992, is provided for general informational purposes only, and not as specific legal or tax advice. Individual clients should consult with their personal advisers about their particular situation

Jurisdiction	Applicable Statutory References	LIFE INSURANCE			ANNUITIES	
		Death Proceeds (beneficiaries and assignees)	Cash Values		Annuity Values (annuitant)	Annuity Values (beneficiaries and assignees)
Ohio	ORC Sec. 3911 10; ORC Sec. 2329.66(A)(6)(b); ORC Sec. 2329.66(A)(10)(a)	Exempt (if payable to spouse, child, dependent relative or creditor)	Exempt (if payable to spouse, child, dependent relative or creditor)		Exempt (if payable to spouse, child, dependent relative or creditor)	Exempt (if payable to spouse, child, dependent relative or creditor)
Oklahoma	36 OSA Sec. 3631; 36 OSA Sec. 3631.1	Exempt	Exempt		Exempt	Exempt
Oregon	ORS Sec. 743.046; ORS Sec. 743.046(3); ORS Sec. 743.049	Exempt	Exempt		Exempt up to $500/month if in a pay status	Exempt up to $500/month if in a pay status
Pennsylvania	42 Pa. CSA Secs. 8124(c)(4) and (6); 42 Pa. CSA Sec. 8124(c)(3)	Exempt (if payable to spouse, child or dependent relative)	Exempt (if payable to spouse, child or dependent relative)		Exempt up to $100/month if in a pay status	Exempt (if payable to spouse, child or dependent relative)
Rhode Island	GLRI Sec. 27-4-11	Exempt	Exempt		No express provisions	No express provisions
South Carolina	CLSC Sec. 38-63-40	Limited exemption of $50,000 (and only if payable to spouse, child or dependent relative)	Limited exemption of $50,000 (and only if payable to spouse, child or dependent relative)		No express provisions	No express provisions
South Dakota	SDCL Sec. 58-12-4; SDCL Sec. 58-12-6,7,8 and 9	Limited exemption of $20,000 (and only if payable to spouse, child or other named beneficiary)	Limited exemption of $20,000 (and only if payable to spouse, child or dependent relative)		Exempt up to $250/month if in a pay status	Exempt up to $250/month if in a pay status
Tennessee	TCA Sec. 56-7-201; TCA Sec. 56-7-202; TCA Sec. 56-7-203	Exempt (if payable to spouse, child or dependent relative)	Exempt (if payable to spouse, child or dependent relative)		Same provisions as for life insurance	Same provisions as for life insurance
Texas	VATS Ins. Code. Art. 21.22. Secs. 1-3, as amended by Acts. 1991. 72nd Leg., Ch. 60-9. Sec. 1. effective Sept. 1. 1991	Exempt	Exempt		No exemption (see Attorney General Opinion DM-125)	No exemption (see Attorney General Opinion DM-125)
Utah	UCA Sec. 78-23-6; UCA Sec. 78-23-7	Limited exemption (only if payable to spouse or dependent, and then only to extent reasonably necessary for support of the beneficiary and his/her dependents)	Limited exemption of $1,500		No express provisions	No express provisions
Vermont	8 VSA Sec. 3709	Exempt	Not exempt if right to change beneficiary is reserved		Exempt up to $350/month if in a pay status	Exempt up to $350/month if in a pay status
Virginia	VC Sec. 38.2-3122; VC Sec. 38.2-3123, as amended by L 1991. Ch. 942	Exempt	Exempt (unless right to change beneficiary is reserved)		No express provisions	No express provisions
Washington	RCW Sec. 48.18.410; RCW Sec. 48.18.430	Exempt	Exempt		Exempt up to $250/month if in a pay status	Exempt up to $250/month if in a pay status
West Virginia	WVC Sec. 48-3-23; WVC Sec. 33-6-27; WVC Sec. 38-10-4(g) and (h)	Exempt	Exempt		No express provisions	No express provisions
Wisconsin	WSA Sec. 815.18(3)(i)(a) and 3(f)	Probably exempt (if payable to dependent but limited to amount deemed necessary for reasonable support)	Probably exempt (not to exceed $4,000)		No express provisions	No express provisions
Wyoming	WS Sec. 26-15-129; WS Sec. 26-15-132	Exempt	Exempt		Exempt up to $350/month if in a pay status	Exempt up to $350/month if in a pay status

*Exempt status may differ in bankruptcy situations. Applicable statutory references included.

Note: This table, which reflects research completed as of August 1, 1992 is provided for general informational purposes only, and not as specific legal or tax advice. Individual clients should consult with their personal advisers about their particular situation.

CHAPTER 12

Universal Variable in Action

A Financial Tool . . . but Which End Do I Grab?

A universal variable life insurance policy is a financial tool that, when used correctly, provides positive financial results that cannot be duplicated by any other financial product. Implicit within this statement is the assumption that the expenses within the product are fair and acceptable. You do have to want the life insurance provided by the product and the cost of the life insurance must be competitive and acceptable. The policy must offer a broad array of competitive mutual funds in the family of funds available so that the policy-owner can profitably manage money within the contract *for a lifetime.* The number of universal variable products that fit that description is rapidly increasing and will continue to increase as the competitive market forces out products that, at one end of the spectrum, are too expensive and at the other end, too cheap and therefore not profitable for the insurance company to support.

To use these products profitably you have to understand them and know how to apply them to your situation and objectives. In this book we will continually do our best to provide this information. However, you will find that very often a salesperson can help you to focus on your objectives and needs and show you how to meet those needs using your policy. Understand that when you pay for this service, be it called a financial-planning fee or a commission, you are paying for help in the selection and delivery of the product and the assistance that an individual can offer in managing the money within the product. There is a cost associated with this service just as there is with any other. But in this case, you may find that the return on your investment as a result of this assistance makes it the most profitable money you have ever spent. This is much the same as in mutual fund purchases. There are more than 4,000 funds from which to choose, so the person who helps you find a suitable family of funds and then shows you how to use them can be very valuable. That educated and informed person cannot work for nothing. You will pay a fee when using no-load funds and commissions when using mutual funds that have sales loads. The point is: get qualified help when you need it, don't be afraid to pay for it, and use it profitably.

Many people have been hurt by the financial press. Writers of books, magazines, and newspaper articles bombard us advising "only buy *no load!*" Since we are not sure how to choose among the no-loads, we pay in lost returns often higher than the costs we are seeking to avoid. Even worse, we don't do anything. Confusion about financial products and the desire to avoid commissions or fees has frozen too many into economic inertia. Doing nothing presents the biggest threat there is to our economic future. The encouragement, motivation, matching product to person and objectives, and coaching in the use of financial products by a paid professional is well worth every dollar investors spend. We can all use a good coach, so be prepared to pay for one as you go about your search for the universal variable product right for you.

Let's look at a case study. Pete does not need life insurance! But his grandfather bought him a $10,000 whole life policy when he was 2, and his dad bought him a $25,000 variable life policy when he reached 18 in 1979. The variable life was one of the very early contracts (the first were issued in 1976). His dad put $266.50 into it for seven years, for a total of $1,865.50. By 1986 it had a value of $2,328.15. This represented a return on that $266.50 annual investment of about 7.3 percent. Not great, but by life insurance standards of the day, it was spectacular.

Anyway, by 1986 these two policies just weren't what Pete wanted, because he knew that an alternative called universal variable had arrived in the life insurance market place. Pete had married Susie and they had become DINKS.

With a mortgage that took both of their incomes to service and with hope in their hearts for kids in the future, Pete and Susie had become economically interdependent. The death of either would leave the survivor in both economic trouble and an emotional state likely to exacerbate the economic problems. They needed to save money as quickly as possible because children would likely increase expenses and possibly reduce income.

THE 1035 TAX-FREE EXCHANGE/TRADING LIFE INSURANCE POLICIES TAX-FREE

The decision was made to trade Pete's two old policies for a single universal variable life policy. But Pete did not wish to pay income taxes on the profit accumulated in the old variable life policy and the 23-year-old whole life policy.

In September of 1986, Pete turned in the application, forms, and medical information that proved he was insurable. He told the insurance company to trade the two old policies on the new one. The insurance company credited $4,380 from the two old policies to a new policy insuring Pete's life for $250,000. A term-insurance rider of $100,000 was added for Susie. Interestingly enough, nine months later their first child, Meggie, was born.

The first-year costs they incurred in September 1986–September 1987 to start the new policy were:

1.	Set-up cost	$250
2.	State premium taxes—Colorado	65
3.	Administrative cost	48
4.	Pete's $250,000 life insurance	285
5.	Susie's $100,000 life insurance	102
	Total year-one costs	$750

The earnings inside the policy that first year were $512, so the earnings did not quite cover costs.

But, Pete and Susie worked hard that first year putting in as much as they could each month. They sent in $135 most months, and one month they were able to put in $435. By the end of the first year their policy value was $5,928, and they were pretty proud of themselves. Most of the money,

$4,417, was in the guaranteed-interest account that first 1986-87 year, earning 8.75 percent. But by February 1987, they were putting their monthly checks into the aggressive stock account within their policy. They paid $161 for their first share of stock in that account.

They chose the aggressive account because they had studied dollar-cost-averaging (see Chapter 9 for a refresher) and concluded that volatility in a mutual fund was their friend, not their enemy. They knew that dollar-cost-averaging is most effective when used in a fund likely to provide the highest highs and lowest lows.

In the second policy year (1987–1988), costs for these two 26-year-olds were:

1.	Colorado state premium tax	$ 65
2.	Administrative expense	48
3.	Pete's $250,000 life insurance	285
4.	Susie's $100,000 life insurance	104
	Total second-year costs	$502

DUAL INCOME, ONE KID

During the second policy year, they were able to send in $135 in nine of the months, $270 one month, and a check for $1,385 another month, for a grand total for the year of $2,870. Our dual income, one kid family was doing a great job, *but* . . . .

The aggressive stock account did what aggressive stock accounts do, it went *down*. During that second year they saw the aggressive fund share value drop from the original $161 to as low as $138 per share! Pete and Susie were learning about volatility, but at this point they had redefined volatility as *it goes down!?*, and they were not very pleased when they looked at their annual report and saw that their investment results for the year were –$114.

ONE INCOME, TWO KIDS!

Checks into their policy did slow down, and they soon learned that another baby would arrive in early 1989.

Pete and Susie were concerned! Loss of Susie's income for at least some period of time, more expenses, and, to top it off, they knew that Susie was becoming ever more dependent on Pete's income—he needed more life insurance. They no longer felt like aggressive investors.

INCREASING YOUR FACE AMOUNT

The decision to double the amount of insurance on Pete's life made them anxious but that feeling was soon replaced by one of relief. They looked at their flexible premium, flexible face amount policy and found that the cost for the extra $250,000 on Pete's life was about $25 per month. Monthly costs in the policy would increase to $50 a month. They would also have a one-time fee of $250 for the change to the policy. What a relief! A one-time cost of $250 to change, and $300 per year for the extra $250,000 of life insurance. The interior costs were going to be a little over $750 in the coming year, instead of the $502 of the year before. They could afford the increase! They began to understand the power of their policy.

HOW DO YOU DECIDE HOW MUCH?

They made the changes. Pete's life insurance was increased from $250,000 to $500,000. The thinking behind the amount of the increase was that each $100,000 of death benefit could provide between $5,000 and $6,000 of investment income. The first $250,000 would give Susie a supplemental income stream of $12,500 per year which, with Pete's group life insurance and the social security benefits for one child, would leave Susie okay, but not great.

But with a second child further hampering Susie's ability to earn, they considered the extra $250,000 of insurance. The $500,000 would generate about $25,000 in supplemental income. The extra insurance was absolutely essential for his family's economic survival if he died.

INVESTMENT MANAGEMENT

After the policy was increased, a material change to keep the policy from becoming a modified endowment contract (MEC), Pete would have to keep his investments each year below $15,000. "No problem!" said Pete. They went back to their dollar-cost-averaging, but the 1988-89 year was tougher for them. They put in seven checks for $135, one for $235, and one for $270, for a total of $1,450. This was about half of what they had invested in the previous year. Approximately $910 of what they paid in 1988-89 was directed to the guaranteed interest account. As the second baby's birth approached, they got more conservative. The volatility (downward trend) of the aggressive stock account was not comfortable for them during this period.

Ellie was born! Susie had to put her employment aside and also wanted to spend more time with their two children. As a result, income was cut. They were concerned. Pete and Susie talked over their concerns with their insurance agent who suggested that they look for an opportunity to move to the *tax-free funding level.*

TAX-FREE FUNDING

This is the funding level within an account that generates enough tax-free interest to pay the expenses of the policy in full. *How much do we need and which account shall we use?*

The account best designed to provide this steady stream of interest payments, with no change in market value is the guaranteed interest account. The good news for Pete and Susie was that the interest was guaranteed at 8.25 percent in 1988-89 year, so if they could get $10,000 into that account, it would earn $825. This would be more than enough to cover the $750 of anticipated costs.

Pete and Susie were going to have to deal with the following considerations as they decided whether to move their money into this guaranteed-interest, guaranteed-principal account.

1. This is a general account of the life insurance company and the guarantees are only as strong as the company. The account is subject to the claims its creditors, so ratings by Standard and Poor's, Moody's, Duff and Phelps, Best's, Fitch, and maybe even Marvin Weiss were important to them. It also meant that whatever information they could have gotten on the company's risk-based capital rating would have been important to them, had it been in exist-

ence in those days. Today, they would feel frustrated in trying to get the same information from their agent. They would probably have trouble understanding or believing that their agent may be under a *gag order* which makes it illegal to talk about risk-based capital. The gag order means that only agents can't talk about it. The press and everyone else is not so restricted. This likelihood means that you will have to pay more to get this theoretically confidential information. The foolishness of our regulators is unbelievable sometimes!

However, if Pete and Susie were able to get at John Ward's brilliant *Ward's Results Life-Health* for the current year (call 513-791-0303), they could get a pretty good idea of the insurance company's risk-based-capital rating.

Pete and Susie decided that as long as their company was considered investment grade by the major rating services, they were not worried about the general account nature of the investment.

2. Once their money went into this guaranteed interest account, there would be some limitations on how quickly and when they could move it out. This is a mechanism wisely set up by most insurance companies to prevent a run on this account, whether caused by a necessary reduction in interest rates or by policy-owners put in a state of panic by the public press.

Pete and Susie could remove 25 percent of the amount in the guaranteed interest account during a 30-day period each year. This they also found acceptable.

MOVING MONEY

On August 4, 1989, they instructed their insurance company to sell their aggressive stock account and move the money into the guaranteed-interest account. The aggressive account unit value on that day was $197.19. They sold 20.97 units and moved $4,136.08. They now had more than $10,000 in the guaranteed-interest account ready to earn enough interest to cover policy costs. Pete and Susie would not have to worry if they could not put more money into their policy in the coming year!

They had two questions:

1. How did their policy do in the third year of its existence? Financial writers love to tell you that it will take 10 years for your policy to be a good investment.

2. How did their dollar-cost-averaging into the aggressive stock account work up to August 4, 1989, when they moved it out?

Third-Year Policy Results (1988–1989)

During the third policy year, September 1988–September 1989, their policy costs were as follows.

State premium taxes	$ 33
Administrative expenses and waiver	49
Pete's life insurance	
$250,000 until February 1989	
$500,000 thereafter	463
Susie's $100,000 life insurance	111
Total policy costs	$656

The policy's gross investment results for the year were plus (+) $1,556. Net of the above expenses, Pete and Susie made $900 tax-free on their total policy investment which, during that year, averaged $9,258. This gave them a *net* return on the capital in their policy of 9.7 percent *plus* the tax-free earnings that paid for the life insurance! Three years, not 10 years! It makes you think that many of those writers have never looked at a real life universal variable policy in action.

AGGRESSIVE STOCK DOLLAR-COST-AVERAGING RESULTS

The following are the actual results of Pete's and Susie's investments in the aggressive stock account.

Date	Gross Investment	Aggressive Stock Unit Value	Aggressive Stock Total # of Shares
2-9-87	$435	161.06	2.67
3-6-87	135	168.26	3.47
4-6-87	135	174.25	4.23
5-4-87	135	174.14	5.00
6-8-87	135	177.05	5.76
7-13-87	135	182.40	6.49
8-3-87	135	184.95	7.20
9-3-87	135	188.92	7.9
10-5-87	135	205.96	8.54

500-point drop on the Dow October 19,1987.

11-10-87	$135	138.23	9.5
1-4-88	270	146.91	11.3
2-5-88	135	142.72	12.22
3-7-88	135	157.16	13.06
4-4-88	135	155.48	13.91
5-2-88	135	155.88	14.75
6-24-88	135	160.44	15.58

7-18-88	1,385	159.52	24.06
8-8-88	135	152.72	24.93
9-6-88	135	149.53	25.81
10-6-88	135	146.62	26.71
11-29-88	135	137.39	27.67
12-5-88	135	142.86	28.59

Total Invest. $4,655   162.82 Avg. Cost Per Share

4-3-89   Sell $1,250   164.06   – 7.62
                                        Bought High Yield at $115.53/unit

8-4-89   Sell $4,136.08 $197.19   –20.97

Total Sales Proceeds $5,386.08   Bought Guaranteed Interest

Less Cost of Shares $4,655.00

Net Non-Taxable
Gain $ 731.08

Cost of Sale = 0
Cost of Purchase = 0
Capital Gains/Income Tax = 0

Looking at this, you might question whether Pete and Susie should have sold or not. But at the time, it was like trying to see what's around the next bend in the road. They sold into the market euphoria that existed after the U.S. won the Gulf war. They sold because they were different investors for a time. With two incomes-no kids, they could be aggressive investors, but with one income-two kids, they could not be aggressive investors. They did the right thing *for them*. Their investment capital had a very near-term important purpose: to pay the cost of their life insurance from the pre-tax earnings in the investment account so that they did not have to worry about those costs until their lives settled down again. It is not relevant that the aggressive stock account went to $462 per share by January of 1994.

UNIVERSAL VARIABLE LIQUIDITY

Policy Loans to the Rescue

By 1989-90, we are into the fourth policy year and things are tight for Pete and Susie. In fact, they put only five $135 checks into the policy, totaling $675 for the year. Susie's happily at home with the two kids, doing some part-time work, but really concentrating on the family.

Income-tax time arrives and they qualify for tax-deductible IRAs, but it is April 9 and they don't have the $4,000 needed. They call their life insurance/investment advisor. What do they do? Here is the advice they get. For each $1,000 they put into one of the IRAs, they will reduce their income-tax burden by $300. They should borrow $4,000 from their policy and put $2,000 into each of their IRAs to reduce income taxes by $1,200. This is exactly what they do on April 9, 1990. The check from the insurance company is dated April 11 and express-mailed to them so they have the money April 12, in time to make the IRA deposits. The loan cost is to be 8 percent annually. The $4,000 is not actually taken from the policy. The policy asset value is merely pledged as collateral to the insurance company for a personal loan, and the collateralized $4,000 is put into the loan guarantee fund in their policy where it earns 7 percent, 1 percent less than the insurance company is to charge.

More good news! The insurance company will not make any charges other than for interest on the loan for the period of time it is in existence. Pete and Susie, upon completing their income taxes, find that their reduced earnings for the previous year and the $4,000 IRA deduction have lowered their taxes enough so they now have the $4,000 to pay off the loan. On April 23 they sent a check to the insurance company for $4,011.65 to pay off the loan and pay the interest for the 13 days involved. Pete and Susie want to get that money back to work in their policy as soon as possible. While they are feeling better about their financial situation, they want all the money back in the guaranteed interest division for this policy year anyway.

Fourth-Year Policy Results (1989–1990)

During the fourth year, their policy costs were as follows.

State premium taxes	$ 15
Administrative expenses and waiver	50
Pete's $500,000 of life insurance	590
Susie's $100,000 of life insurance	117
Total policy costs	$772
Gross policy earnings for the year	$742
Earnings shortfall to cover policy expenses	$ 30

Total account value by year-end	$10,929.33
Investment allocation	100% Guaranteed Interest division; 8% interest for next policy year.

Fifth Policy Year (1990–1991)

Things are looking up! On October 3 Pete and Susie take advantage of the opportunity to move 25 percent out of the guaranteed interest division. They park $2,725 in the money market division while they decide where to invest it within their policy. They are feeling more comfortable with their reduced family income and increased family size.

UNIVERSAL VARIABLE AS A PLACE FOR FAMILY GIFTS

Susie's parents are thrilled to have two grandchildren and decide to make a gift to Pete and Susie for their grandchildren's future educations. They give them $550, not enough to bother fooling around with a Uniform Gift to Minors Act gift and they really don't want the money to belong to the kids at age 18 anyway. They also don't want to have to worry about income taxes on what the money earns each year, so the gift is put into the life insurance policy. On October 12 the $550 check is split:

$275 to the common stock fund which buys 1.8 shares at $146.56 per share.

$275 to the aggressive stock fund which buys 1.5 shares at $178.13 per share.

Pete and Susie are getting back into their consistent saving and investing mode as things settle down to normal frantic. They are able to put in seven checks in the amount of $135, one for $150, and one for $450, for a grand total of $1,545 which, when added to the grandparents' gift, comes to $2095. All of Pete's and Susie's money went into the guaranteed interest division.

Fifth-Year Policy Results (1990-1991)

Policy costs in the fifth year were these.

State premium taxes	$ 47
Administrative expenses and waiver	50
Pete's $500,000 life insurance policy	591
Susie's $100,000 life insurance policy	119
Total costs for the year	$807

On June 20, 1991, they move $1,000 out of the money market fund to a growth asset allocation account; the fund's basic strategy is 70-percent stock (equities) and 30-percent bond (debt). The $1,000 purchases 7.5 shares at a cost of $133.41 per share.

The gross earnings within this policy for this policy year total $1,306, which is sufficient to cover the $807 in policy costs. Their earnings on a very conservative investment for that policy year are $499. This means a 4-percent net cash-on-cash, tax-free return on the policy for the year *plus* the value of the life insurance protection for the year.

Sixth Policy Year (September 1991– September 1992)

Pete and Susie put in five checks for $150 and one check for $300. The $300 went to the guaranteed interest division. Of the five $150 checks, three went to guaranteed interest, two to the aggressive stock account. On December 12, they empty the money market account into the aggressive stock account and pay $1,896.75 ($373.01 per share) for 5.084 shares.

On January 28 they take some more grandparent gift money and some of their own and send in a check for $6,780. They buy 22.6 shares of the global fund at 146.56 per share and 26.1 shares of the conservative asset allocation account at $126.84 that uses a basic investment strategy exactly opposite the one used by the growth asset allocation account (70 percent bond, 30 percent stocks).

Sixth-Year Policy Results (1991–1992)

During the sixth year, their policy costs were as follows.

State premium taxes	$176
Administrative expenses and waiver	60
Pete's $500,000 of life insurance	592
Susie's $100,000 of life insurance	126
Total policy costs	$954
Gross policy earnings for the year	$969
Earnings excess over policy expenses	$ 15
Total account value by year-end	$21,368
Investment allocation:	
Common Stock	$405
Global	$3,157
Aggressive	$2,612
Conservative Asset Allocation	$3,547
Growth Asset Allocation	$1,261

Seventh Policy Year (1992-1993)

On February 16th, Susie obtains a universal variable policy of her own, so they terminate the $100,000 rider insuring Susie's life under Pete's policy.

Seventh-Year Policy Results (1992-1993)

The costs for this policy year were as follows.

| State premium taxes | $ 0 | (no money was invested while they were funding Susie's new policy) |

Administrative expenses and waiver	62	
Pete's $500,000 of life insurance	635	
Susie's $100,000 for five months	55	
Total costs for the year	$752	

The gross investment gain for the year September 1992 to September 1993 was $3,131. Of this amount, $752 was allocated to pay life insurance costs and expenses. This *left* a net gain for Pete and Susie of $2,379 which, when calculated on the amount they had in their policy account at the beginning of the year ($21,368) was a net, non-taxable return of about 11 percent. The asset allocation that generated this return was as follows.

Beginning of Year		Investment Account	End of Year	
Dollars	Percent		Dollars	Percent
$10,386	49%	Guaranteed Interest (6.5%)	$7,508	32%
3,547	16%	Conservative Asset Allocation	6,818	29%
1,261	6%	Growth Asset Allocation	1,483	6%
405	2%	Common Stock	519	2%
3,157	15%	Global	4,211	18%
2,612	12%	Aggressive Stock	3,208	14%
$21,368	100%		$23,747	100%

Their policy prospectus indicates the theoretical split between stocks and bonds in each investment account (growth: 70 percent stock, 30 percent bonds; conservative:

70 percent bonds, 30 percent stock). Adding this to the amount they have in the guaranteed interest account tells us how much of their accounts are in stocks and how much are in bonds. The asset allocation within their policy moved from 38 percent stock, 62 percent bonds at the beginning of the year to 46 percent stock, 54 percent bonds at the end of the year. This occurred for two reasons. First, they moved $2,585 out of the guaranteed interest account into the conservative asset allocation account at the beginning of the year, and second, the overall return on the stocks outperformed the bond investments.

Their strategy for the coming year will depend upon how Pete and Susie feel this year. Are they secure in their employment, income, and family situation, or somewhat insecure because of uncertain employment, etc.? We may suggest to them that they start dollar-cost-averaging the money from their conservative asset allocation account into the common, global, aggressive, and growth asset allocation accounts, moving $100 per month into each. It would take about 18 months to move the bulk of that fund using this strategy. It also would move this young family toward an asset allocation more directed to equities and long-term growth, preparing for the college education years when it is likely that their policy will be called upon to fund some of those expenses.

They may not accept this suggestion. Remember, they have been using the conservative asset allocation account to hold gifts from Susie's parents for the children's education, and they may want to keep the funds where they are or decide to transfer them into Susie's policy so her folks can watch them grow there. Isn't it nice that they have a choice.

The rest of the story: Susie used to sell Xerox machines. Guess what she sells now? Universal variable life!

HOW DOES THE POLICY WORK FOR MATURE FOLKS?

*Ken called again today. Asked how much room
he has in his policy.*

He has *room* for $4,054. That is, he can invest that much more in his policy and still enjoy *all* the tax benefits of the policy. He sent in the $4,054 because, as he said, "My investments in my policy are doing better than my investments elsewhere." Ken is age 62. His expenses, including the cost of $80,000 worth of life insurance, are $92 per month. They *did not* change when he added the $4,054, which he split among five accounts: balanced, common stock, global, aggressive, and growth. Ken now has more than $30,000 in his policy which would be paid out in addition to the $80,000 of life insurance his policy would provide to his beneficiary in the event of his death. The policy is working for Ken, at 62.

BUSINESS OWNER PREPARING FOR RETIREMENT

Jerry is age 57 now. He is a business-owner who must rely on himself for retirement. He is in those years when capital accumulation is important and possible, now that the kids are out on their own. He is using his universal variable life as a private pension plan. That is, he is using it as a place to build capital as fast as he can so it is available when he and Janice finally really do retire. His September 1993 statement reported the following.

Total death benefit	$708,000	
Amount at risk/life insurance	500,000	(Option B)
End-of-Year account value	208,000	
Beginning-of-year account value	176,000	Avg. Acct. Bal. $192,000
Increase in account value	$ 32,000	
He invested	$ 10,000	
Account net investment earnings	$ 22,000	
Net cash-on cash rate of return	$ 22,000	
Average account balance	$192,000	11.5%
		17.4%
		Equivalent Taxable Return

Additional Benefits:
  $500,000 life insurance
  Investments protected from income taxes

Jerry's expenses figured in the preceding numbers were:

State premium tax	$ 200
Administrative expenses	60
Cost of $500,000 in life insurance	3,320
Total Costs	$3,580

The gross earnings in the policy were $25,580. The costs were charged against the guaranteed-interest account that earned $3,650 in interest. The result was that the *net* investment earnings were $22,000.

The asset allocation within the policy:

Guaranteed interest	$58,000	Pays expenses
Balanced division bond	$ 5,000	Bond
Balanced division stock	$ 5,000	Stock
Common stock division	$ 2,000	Stock

Global stock division	$22,000	Stock
Aggressive stock div.	$49,000	Stock
Growth investors division		
30% bond	$20,000	Bond
70% stock	$47,000	Stock
Total	$208,000	100%
Bond	$ 83,000	40%
Stock	$125,000	60%

Jerry will probably continue with this asset allocation for the coming year. It is comfortable, it is doing what he wants it to do, and it is working!

THE BUSINESS OWNER RETIREE

He is 73. I'll bet you think he is retired! Not by a long shot. He's the patriarch of the family business. His policy has a death benefit of $500,000. It has $100,000 of investment capital in it. The cost for life insurance for the year was $9,000, the investment gain in the policy was $10,000.

Result:

The tax-free earnings within the policy were sufficient to cover all policy costs.

Alternatives:

What were this policy-owner's alternatives? He could buy just term insurance—if he could get it for $9,000—which he can't. If he could, he would have to earn $13,637 [$9,000/(1–.34)] in order to have enough to send $9,000 to pay for his life insurance and $4,637 to the IRS. He would have to earn 13.6% on his investment capital of $100,000 to earn enough outside of the policy to pay for his insurance.

Conclusion:

It is easier and less risky to earn the $9,000 within the policy. Yes, variable universal is working well for this business owner—and looking at the big picture—yes, variable universal can work very well for mature individuals.

CHAPTER 13

Understanding Annuities

It's Not Just a Monthly Check

*An annuity is an amount payable yearly
or at other regular intervals for a certain
or uncertain period.*

An annuity is a written contract between an annuity contract-owner, an annuitant, and an insurance company. Frequently, the contract-owner and the annuitant will be the same individual.

Most people think of an annuity as a retirement plan, a series of steady level payments for life, or a way to receive monthly income from a pension plan. A lump sum of money is paid out as continual monthly income with the assurance that the payments will go on for the rest of the annuitant's life. In the *payout mode*, an annuitant can protect against the risk of running out of income during life. The economic risk of living too long, a very serious concern with today's longevity, is protected by the lifetime assurance of income.

Annuities can, in their payment mode, do all of the preceding. However, that is just half the story. Annuities also may be accumulation and investment vehicles.

If you want to use the annuity contract as a payout vehicle, you purchase an *immediate annuity*. You give the insurance company a lump sum of money and the company will commence making periodic payments in accordance with your instructions within a period of time usually ranging from one month after deposit to as long as one year after deposit.

Alternatively, you can use the *deferred annuity* as an income-tax-deferred accumulation vehicle by making deposits, a series of deposits or irregular deposits. You then ask the insurance company to invest those funds on your behalf until further notice, with the objective of earning the highest return possible consistent with your risk-tolerance level.

In the pages that follow, we will deal with annuity contracts in terms of both functions, as payout vehicles and as accumulation vehicles. Exhibit 13.1 is a decision tree that helps in selecting an annuity contract appropriate for the contract owner's objectives and risk-tolerance.

Exhibit 13.1 Annuities

ANNUITIES

A PAYOUT VEHICLE — **IMMEDIATE ANNUITY**

AN ACCUMULATION VEHICLE — **DEFERRED ANNUITY**

Immediate Annuity:
- Variable Annuity
  - Life Annuity
  - Life and Period Certain
  - Life and Refund
  - J&S Life
  - J&S Period Certain
  - J&S Refund
- Fixed Annuity
  - Life Annuity
  - Installment Payout
  - Life and Period Certain
  - Life and Refund
  - J&S Life
  - J&S Period Certain
  - J&S Refund

Deferred Annuity:
- Fixed Annuity
  - Interest Guaranteed
  - Principal Guaranteed
    - 1 Year Initial Guarantee
    - 2 Year Initial Guarantee
    - 3 Year Initial Guarantee
    - 5 Year Initial Guarantee
  - PAYOUT Move to the Immediate Annuity Decision Tree, Take a Lump Sum Distribution or Periodic Withdrawals
- Variable Annuity
  - Interest Guarantee Principal Guarantee
  - Common Stock
  - Agressive Stock
  - Balanced Stock
  - Money Market
  - Bond Account
  - Zero's Account
  - Real Estate Account

IMMEDIATE ANNUITIES: PAYOUT VEHICLES

The purpose of purchasing an immediate annuity is to protect the annuitant against the risk of running out of income during life or, alternatively, to assure a series of payments for a fixed period of time or in a fixed amount. The first decision you have to make when purchasing an immediate annuity is the choice between a *fixed* and *variable* annuity.

Fixed Immediate Annuities

The fixed immediate annuity provides fixed-dollar periodic payments as a result of a deposit. It gives you a safe, secure feeling that, for example, the $1,000-per-month check will be arriving every month for the time period chosen. After deciding on a fixed annuity, you will be asked what guarantees you would like regarding the annuity's continued payment of checks in the event of the annuitant's death.

The immediate annuity guarantees available are as follows.

1. *Installment payment-fixed amount.* You dictate the amount, and the insurance company tells you how long it will be paid, no matter whether you live or die. This is not a life contingent option.

2. *Installment payment-fixed period.* You dictate the period of time for the periodic payments, and the insurance company tells you the amount it can pay based on the interest it will pay and the length of time chosen. The period chosen could be as little as two months or as long as you desire (payments must satisfy the company's minimum payment rules, e.g., no less than $20 per payment). Payments continue

for the fixed period whether you live or die. Like the "installment payment-fixed amount" described above, this is not a life contingent option.

3. *Life annuity (straight life/pure annuity).* Your specified income continues until your death. (Risk: receive one month's payment; die: payments terminate.)

4. *Life and period certain (10 or 20 years).* This is similar to the preceding. The payments continue for your life; however, you may wish to assure that someone other than the insurance company benefits if you die early. The company is instructed to make the payments to your named beneficiary for the remainder of the guarantee period, at least 10 or 20 years, even if you die before that time.

5. *Life and refund certain.* In this case, you again are trying to protect against early termination of payments due to your death occurring prior to getting at least your principal back. The company is instructed to pay you for life, but should your death occur early, to refund your deposit in continuing monthly payments to your named beneficiary until the amount of deposit is returned. If it is a cash refund, the payout will be the discounted present value of the future payments.

6. *Joint and survivor life annuity.* The annuity pays for the whole of the lives of two individuals. It continues to provide level payments until the death of the second-to-die annuitant. Variations of this form of payout include a joint and 75-percent survivor annuity in which the surviving annuitant will receive 75 percent of the original monthly payment, and joint and 50-percent survivor annuity.

7. *Joint and survivor life annuity with period certain.* This is to protect against the early termination of payments if both of the annuitants die early. The insurance company is instructed to continue payments until the death of the last-to-die, with a minimum payout period of at least 10 or 20 years.

8. *Joint and survivor life annuity with refund certain.* This protects against the early termination of payments due to the death of both annuitants. The insurance company is instructed to refund the remaining balance of the deposit by continuing monthly payments to the named beneficiary after the death of both annuitants until the amount deposited is returned, or if it is to be a cash refund, to pay out the discounted present value of the remaining payments.

Fixed-Period/Fixed-Amount Installment Annuities

You may direct the insurance company to make payments of fixed specific dollar amounts at equal intervals until both principal and interest are exhausted or, alternatively, for a fixed period of time. The time chosen would determine the amount of each payment. These annuities are useful in situations where there is an income-tax liability on the payments. You can spread the tax liability over a period of years convenient for the annuitant.

Also, you can purchase such contracts to fund for a specific purpose, such as, an annuity payment commencing when a parent enters a nursing home to assure payments for a specified period.

Whenever funds are needed to provide for a specific need, an annuity can be designed to provide those funds. But there is one caution that we must observe. The Tax Reform Act of 1986 imposed a 10-percent penalty tax on any annuity distributions to an annuitant prior to age 59-1/2 not based on life contingencies. Fixed-period and fixed-amount installments are *not* life contingent annuities.

Life Annuity/Straight Life Annuity/Pure Annuity

The process of selecting from among life annuity alternatives starts with a question to the insurance company: "I want a $1,000 check every month for the rest of my life. I am 65. What will such a contract cost me, and what alternatives are available to me?"

A life annuity costs the least. In other words, this type of annuity will provide the largest possible monthly payment based on a given deposit. It is low in cost because of the high risk of the loss of capital. The risk in a life annuity is that if you die prior to the time the deposit in the annuity has been used up, the balance of the deposit and the interest on the capital are lost, being forfeited to the insurance company or pension plan from which it was being paid. This would occur even if only one monthly check had been paid prior to your death. Most buyers of annuities consider this too great a risk. They want greater safety and assurance that the payout stream will continue to their beneficiaries in the event of their deaths.

Life and Period Certain Annuity

This is one method of assuring the continuation of the payout stream in the event of the primary annuitant's death. Under this election, you would purchase a guarantee of

Exhibit 13.2 Costs for Single Life Annuities Providing $1,000-per-Month for Life (Male–Age 65)

Type	Cost to Purchase	Percentage Increase
A Life Annuity	$143,825	
Life 10-Years Certain	152,655	6.1%
Life Refund Certain	159,754	11.1%
Life 20-Years Certain	175,382	22.0%

Representative 1993 rates.

payments for some minimum time period, such as 10 or 20 years. In Exhibit 13.2, you will note that this guarantee increases the purchase price of the annuity by about 6 percent for a 10-year minimum guarantee and about 22 percent for a 20-year guarantee. The purchaser is buying insurance that costs $8,830 ($152,655 – $143,825 = $8,830) to assure that payments continue for at least 10 years, or $31,830 ($175,655 – $143,825 = $31,830) to assure that payments continue for 20 years.

Life and Refund Certain Annuity

Under this alternative you elect to receive a life income. However, if you don't live long enough to receive all of the principal, it will be refunded to your named beneficiary in continued monthly installments or in a cash settlement (discounted present value of the payments due).

Joint and Survivorship Life Annuity

The joint and survivorship life annuity is designed to function as an assured payout vehicle during the lives of two people. It is to continue the level monthly payments through the life of the last-to-die. It normally is used by married couples for pension income to insure that the income stream will not terminate at the death of the first annuitant.

Under the joint and survivorship annuity option, there also are a number of alternatives. A refund-certain or period-certain guarantee could be selected for 10 or 20 years. You may adjust the continued payments to the surviving annuitant consistent with the survivor's needs. During both the annuitants' lives, the income will be one amount, but after the death of the first, that income could be reduced to 75 percent, 66.6 percent, or 50 percent of the amount of the original payment. Such an election reduces the cost for the income guaranteed. For instance, to assure $1,000 *level* payments for both lives, the cost is $188,421 (see Exhibit 13.3).

Alternatively, providing only $500 per month to the survivor reduces the cost to $159,299, a savings of $29,122. The extra $29,122 could be used to increase the monthly payments to $1,155, leaving $578 to the survivor, if such an arrangement fits the couple's needs.

If you have determined that the greatest need for income is while both annuitants are living, and that the single surviving annuitant will not have as great a need, then this reduction in income to the survivor may be appropriate. The problem is inflation. Enough today is often not enough for tomorrow!

Exhibit 13.4 illustrates the annuity income that could be purchased with a deposit of $100,000 in 1993 for a male age 65 and also the joint and survivorship annuity income that could be purchased for annuitant and spouse age 62. For illustration purposes, we have assumed that they will be in the 28 percent tax bracket. The temptation when looking

**Exhibit 13.3 Costs for Joint Life Annuities
Providing $1,000-per-Month for Life
(Male-Age 65 Female-Age 62)**

Type	Cost to Purchaser	
Joint and Survivor Life	$188,421	100%
Joint and Survivor Refund	190,697	101.21%
Joint and 75% to the Survivor	175,859	93%
Joint and 66.6% to the Survivor	169,008	90%
Joint and 50% to the Survivor	159,299	85%

Representative 1993 rates.

at this table is to convert the annual income figures to a percentage return on the $100,000 of capital invested. That, of course, is invalid, because what is being paid out is a

**Exhibit 13.4 Incomes Purchased by an
Immediate Life Annuity Investment of $100,000**

Male Age 65	Gross Annuity Income	Percentage Tax-Free
Life Income	$8,338	60%
Life Income Refund Certain	7,506	60.6%
Life Income 10-Years Certain	7,855	60.7%
Life Income 20-Years Certain	6,836	60%
Male Age 65, Female Age 62		
Joint and Survivor 100% to the Survivor	$6,363	59.3%
Joint and Survivor Refund Certain	6,287	60%
Joint and Survivor 75% to the Survivor	6,896	60.8%
Joint and Survivor 66.6% to the Survivor	7,094	61.4%
Joint and Survivor 50% to the Survivor	7,524	65%

combination of both interest and principal. It would be misleading to calculate percentage return in that fashion.

However, from a practical standpoint, you may purchase an annuity because you cannot afford to live on just the interest earnings of your $100,000 of capital. You may be reluctant to invest aggressively to earn higher yields for fear of losing your capital during that time. It may be very comforting to seek the shelter of an annuity which promises an income stream that cannot terminate during your lifetime. Your security would be in a constant stream of freely usable income, rather than capital sitting in a bank.

As you review the net after-tax spendable income from the investment of $100,000, you may have one of two reactions. You may think that it assures a pretty good income for the rest of your life, or you may think that you could generate that much income today with $100,000 in some other investment. Your reaction will be based upon the currently available interest rates. In an economic environment in which prevailing short-term interest rates are relatively high, you are not likely to find the annuity principle very appealing. Also, the younger you are, the less appealing it will be. However, in an economic environment in which prevailing interest rates are fairly low, it may look pretty good to you. The reason for this is that when an insurance company guarantees a fixed income for the life of an annuitant, it is looking at a long-term obligation which must be conservatively met with long-term investments. In short, the company must forecast prevailing interest rates available for this block of capital (your investment) for the rest of your life. It will do so in a conservative fashion and likely to use long-term bonds and mortgages as a reserve for the annuity liability, i.e., its obligation to pay you.

OBTAINING ANNUITY QUOTES

Insurance company annuity rates are competitive and constantly changing. The rates shown in the table are based on the prevailing rates effective October 1993. You would be wise to shop carefully for your annuities and to look for not only a competitive rate, but also for a *quality company* that can be expected to perform well *for the rest of your life*. You probably would not even consider an immediate-payout life annuity unless you expected to live a long time, so company selection is very important because future performance will have to be good. There are people out there who did not heed this warning and have had their life income payments interrupted, at best, and lost, at worst, because of insurance company failures. Remember, once a contract is annuitized (payments have commenced), there is no turning back; there are no 1035 exchanges and you *are* dependent on the company you have chosen. When your employer terminates a retirement plan and funds your benefits by buying an immediate-payout annuity, the insurance company risk is being transferred to you. Make sure you have some say in where the employer buys your annuity contract. If you would like to find out what income may be available to you, you may obtain quotes from insurance companies by providing the information shown in Exhibit 13.5 to any company that sells annuities.

Exclusion Ratio (Non-Qualified Annuities)

You may purchase *non-qualified* (obtained using after-tax capital) annuities. A greater portion of your annuity income is usable than if you were living on interest income alone. The fact that a part of your income is return of your personal after-tax capital is recognized in the federal income tax exclusion ratio. The proportion of the annuity income

Exhibit 13.5 Immediate Fixed Annuity Quote Request

Date of Birth _____   Sex _____

If Joint: Date of Birth _____   Sex _____

Marginal Tax Bracket _____   State of Residence_____

Single
Consideration_____ and/or   Monthly Life
Income _____

Non-Qualified (Personal Funds) _____

Qualified Funds (from an IRA or
other qualified retirement plan _____

Insurance company will receive the proceeds by _____ (date).

Please commence payout of the proceeds by _____ (date).
(at least one month later)

Please mail the information to:

Name: _____

Address: _____

_____

Phone Number: _____

that is tax-free (the return of capital) is determined in accordance with Section 72 of the Internal Revenue Code.

The exclusion ratio is determined by dividing the *investment in the contract* by the *expected return* as of the annuity starting date, the day the income stream commences. You might invest $60,000 in an annuity and expect $100,000 as the payout. Therefore, 60 percent of each payment would be a non-taxable return of capital, while the balance would be taxable interest.

$$\text{Exclusion Ratio} = \frac{\text{Investment}}{\text{Expected Return}} = \frac{\$60,000}{\$100,000} = 60\% \text{ Exclusion Ratio}$$

$$60\% \quad \times \quad \$1,000 \quad = \quad \$600$$

Exclusion Ratio × Payment Received = Amount Excluded from Taxation

You know the investment you have put into the contract. However, determining the expected return is complicated by the fact that no one knows how long you are going to live. If we assume you're not going to live long, this would result in a greater portion of your payments being tax-free return of principal. You might be trying to prove to Uncle Sam how sick you are to minimize your income taxes.

To solve this problem, the IRS has provided four life-expectancy tables in Internal Revenue Regulation Section 1.72. These are to be used in determining expected returns. Exclusion ratios vary depending upon the type of annuity purchased. The higher the guaranteed return of capital after the death of the annuitant, the lower the exclusion ratio. It will also vary based upon the age and sex of the annuitant.

The exclusion ratio results in a greater portion of your income stream being usable income, because it is not subject to current income taxes. A comparable stream of fully taxable income would result in increased taxes, thus reducing your spendable income.

Exclusion Ratio-TRA-86 Change

We need to make one final point concerning the taxation of annuity income. One of the advantages of the annuity was the federal income tax exclusion ratio. In our examples in Exhibit 13.4, it was approximately 60 percent of the annuity income. This exclusion ratio used to apply throughout the annuitant's lifetime. Therefore, even if you lived far beyond the time predicted in the life expectancy tables, and had gotten all of your tax-free principal back, you continued to receive approximately 60 percent of your income without taxation throughout your lifetime. The Tax Reform Act of 1986 changed this situation for annuities not yet annuitized on January 1, 1987. Under that law, once the annuitant has received the investment back without taxation, the exclusion ratio ceases to apply. Payments continuing beyond that point are taxed entirely as ordinary income. In our example, this would result in increased income tax for the annuitants at approximately age 85. This means that individuals who have lived on a level monthly income unadjusted for inflation for 20 years, who took the annuity because of their need for spendable income, will be blindsided by Uncle Sam with additional income tax at age 85. Do you suppose our politicians will use those additional tax dollars for the indigent elderly? The politicians' mothers should know what they are doing to them!

VARIABLE IMMEDIATE ANNUITY

With fixed annuities, the insurance company accepts the mortality risk, the expense risk, and the interest risk and you accept the purchasing power risk. With the variable annuity, you trade interest guarantees for variable, increasing (we hope) payments, which leaves the mortality and expense risks with the insurance company.

A variable or equity annuity is one in which the periodic payments received from the contract vary with the investment experience of the underlying investment vehicle. The variable immediate annuity was developed to answer the problem of conventional fixed annuities. The purchasing power of a conventional-payment fixed annuity is eroded by inflation. It was hoped that the variable annuity, with a fluctuating income based on its underlying equity accounts, would adjust itself to current purchasing power and offset the eroding effects of inflation on annuity income. The variable immediate annuity can accomplish this objective, but not without risk to the annuitant. The risk is that the payments can decrease as well as increase. Keep in mind that once you annuitize, there is no turning back. You are not able to change investment accounts (an option available in deferred annuities) if you do not like the performance of the one you are in. There are no 1035 tax-free exchanges once you have annuitized. In short, you are stuck for life. So choose carefully!

The Teacher's Insurance and Annuity Association (TIAA) and the College Retirement Equities Fund (CREF) are *non-profit* organizations providing insurance and annuities to academic personnel. These organizations did a great deal to develop the concept of the variable annuity and were the original source of such contracts. They fought the original regulatory battles starting in 1952. In 1959, the variable annuity contract became subject to dual supervision by the Securities and Exchange Commission and the various state insurance departments.

The investment vehicle in a variable immediate annuity has to be a property that is easy to purchase, easy to sell, and moves with the economy, reflecting the general economic trend on a long-term basis. TIAA's extensive studies covering common stock history from 1880 to 1952 showed that common stock was closest to the ideal investment vehicle. More recent studies confirm this conclusion.

The market for variable *immediate* annuities is small, so understandably there are relatively few sources of supply. The annuity payout principle appeals to conservative older individuals who have a substantial need for income and desire to ensure that the income will not terminate during their lifetimes. It is relatively unusual to find this same risk-adverse individual willing to have funds paid out as a variable annuity, because there is the potential for a decrease in income as well as the hoped-for reward of increased income. The annuity payout principal basically appeals to conservative purchasers unwilling to take the downside risk of the variable immediate annuity. The exploding market for variable annuities is in the accumulation annuities arena, more so than in the immediate annuity.

In an actual case, Aunt Gen deposited $15,288.80 on March 14, 1972, with an insurance company. She was guaranteed a monthly income starting at $100 per month, based on the number of units she purchased. As those units varied in value, so did her monthly income. As a result of the performance of the stock market and the underlying investment account of her annuity, the monthly payments dipped to a low of $63 in 1975. By the time the last payment was made in October 1986, the monthly payment was up to $234. An ironic twist of this particular variable annuity was that by the time the 1980s arrived, and the monthly payments were consistently over $100 per month, most of Aunt Gen's other assets had been used up. Her fear of running out of assets prior to her death was realized. Her annuity income and social security were about all that was available, and as a result she lived in low-income housing. Every time she received an increase in her monthly payment from the variable annuity, the low-income housing authorities raised her rent an equivalent amount. All she would have needed to complete the picture would have been loss of her exclusion ratio and the increased taxation Uncle Sam imposed on post-January 1, 1987 annuitants who managed to live long enough to receive a full return of

Exhibit 13.6 Variable Immediate Annuity with Period Certain
Actual Case: February 28, 1972–October 28, 1986

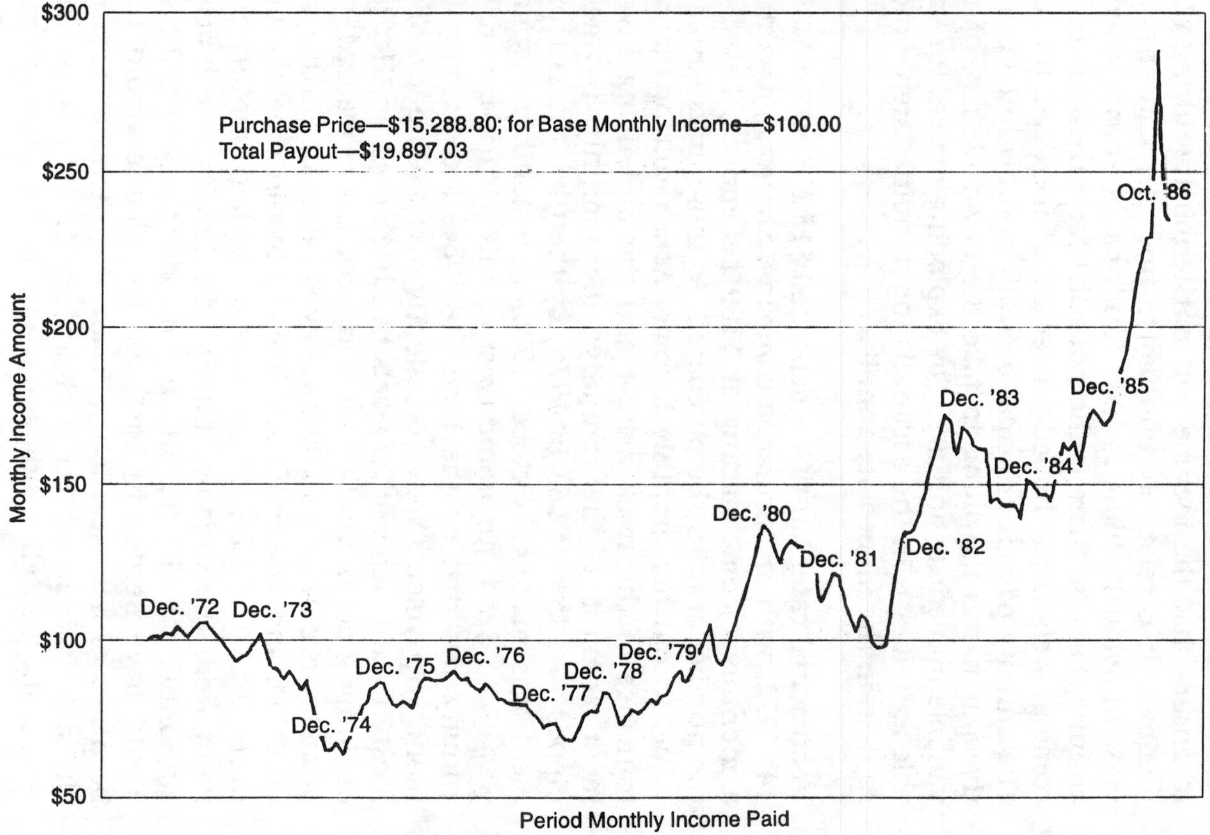

Purchase Price—$15,288.80; for Base Monthly Income—$100.00
Total Payout—$19,897.03
$300
$250
$200
$150
$100
$50
Monthly Income Amount
Period Monthly Income Paid
Dec. '72
Dec. '73
Dec. '74
Dec. '75
Dec. '76
Dec. '77
Dec. '78
Dec. '79
Dec. '80
Dec. '81
Dec. '82
Dec. '83
Dec. '84
Dec. '85
Oct. '86

basis. The actual results from Aunt Gen's immediate variable annuity contract are shown in Exhibit 13.6.

DEFERRED ANNUITIES/ACCUMULATION ANNUITIES/INVESTMENT ANNUITIES

You may be a purchaser of a deferred annuity and not be the least bit concerned about *annuitizing* your annuity, that is, changing it into an immediate annuity. Your primary concern may be to accumulate as much wealth as possible within the contract. Because the inside build-up is not subject to current taxation when owned by an individual, you are provided with greater *net* returns, which is the key to the deferred annuity's appeal. There is no reason to make deposits to a non-deductible IRA when if you do, you're limited to a maximum of $2,000 per year, and required to fill out special income tax forms, make special annual tax calculations at eventual payout, and continue to account for those non-deductible contributions for the rest of your life. Why not use a deferred annuity and avoid these problems. The deferred annuity can provide the following benefits.

1. *Safety*: The originally invested capital is guaranteed by the insurance company offering the annuity. Pick carefully!

2. *Liquidity/Marketability.* You may recover the capital invested subject to insurance company back-end loads, current taxation on interest earnings in the contract, and a 10-percent penalty if you are less than 59 1/2 years old. If it is a variable annuity, it is also subject to principal risk of the accounts to which you have directed your funds.

3. *Tax Benefits.* Deferred taxation on the interest, dividends and gains in market value until withdrawal, at which time ordinary income tax will be due on all earnings. This is identical to the benefits of the non-deductible IRA.

4. *Flexibility.* All of the *immediate* annuity payout options previously discussed are available to you with the accumulation in your deferred annuity.

You have the right to make tax-free exchanges from one annuity contract to another. You may also make a tax-free exchange from a life insurance policy into an annuity, but you may not make a tax-free exchange from an annuity to a life insurance policy.

Deferred annuities come in all varieties. There are single-premium deferred annuities, scheduled-premium deferred annuities (the contract states how much and how often you must pay premiums), and flexible-premium annuities.

The old-fashioned scheduled premium contract which required a stated premium at stated times has fallen out of favor. Its mandatory nature, loads, and penalties for not maintaining payments are unappealing. Single-premium deferred annuities, although marketable and popular, have an unappealing lack of flexibility. There is market appeal for the concept of *single* premium (i.e., no additional payments being required); therefore, marketing departments have been promoting those single-premium annuities that *can accept* additional premiums (non-single premium, single premiums). This may be a new definition of *market-driven*. Ask the market what it wants, and then tell it that whatever you have on the shelf is just that.

In today's market place, annuity contracts with the greatest appeal give the annuitant the option of making payments when convenient and in amounts determined by the annuitant; in other words, flexible-premium deferred annuities.

SINGLE-PREMIUM DEFERRED ANNUITIES

It is within the single-premium, interest only deferred annuity variety that you find much of the competition and publicity regarding annuity contracts. They appeal to the individual, with a lump sum of capital available at a specific time, who is seeking the highest possible interest rate. Buyers often compare the single-premium, interest-only deferred annuity vehicle to certificates of deposit. The insurance companies compete vigorously for this single-premium investment.

When contemplating a single-premium deferred annuity purchase, you will want to check the following features.

1. *The company issuing the contract.* The financial strength and track record of the insurance company is of paramount importance in today's financial world. An annuity contract is only successful when the relationship is long-term, i.e., lifetime.

2. *Current interest rate* if you choose a fixed annuity. Investment accounts, investment management, and competitive current interest and guaranteed principal accounts if you are choosing a variable annuity.

3. *Guarantee period* for the guaranteed interest rate.

4. Minimum guaranteed rate of interest after the initial guarantee period is completed.

5. *Bail-out provisions.* Provisions that allow you to surrender the annuity contract without penalty if the interest rate falls below a contractually stated amount.

6. *Cost of bail-out provision.* That is, do you have the option of accepting higher interest and no bail-out provision or lower initial interest with a bail-out provision?

7. *Interest rate track record* for fixed annuities. Investment accounts track records and interest rate track records for variable annuities.

8. *Free withdrawal privilege.* How much cash can you withdraw from a contract each year without being subject to company-imposed withdrawal charges? Withdrawal from any annuity would be subject to income taxes to the extent of gain and 10-percent penalty if prior to age 59-1/2.

9. *Front-end charges.* Sales charges applied against and thereby reducing your initial deposit.

10. *Surrender charges (back-end loads).* What percentage of the annuity would be left with the insurance company to cover deferred sales charges if you surrendered the annuity, and at what point would such surrender charges no longer exist?

11. *Surrender charges waived.* Under what circumstances are the surrender charges waived, such as death, disability or an annuity payout?

12. *Is there market value adjustment?* If the annuity contract is surrendered, is the surrender value adjusted

as a result of changes in prevailing interest rates? This would be typical of a variable annuity bond account. It is found in some fixed annuities you would be wise to avoid.

13. *On surrender,* may the contract-holder recover the investment in the contract in lieu of the cash surrender value if the investment was greater (i.e., if you paid in more than the contract's current value, can you choose to take your payments back instead)?

14. *At death,* what would be the situation for your named beneficiary? With fixed annuities, it would be unusual for there to be a situation where the amount to be paid out to your beneficiary is less than the amount invested. However, with variable annuities, a significant drop in the stock market could expose an annuitant-owner to significant principal risk. You will find with most variable annuities that the beneficiary will receive the annuity at market value or the owner's gross investments in the contract, whichever is greater. You can expect to find approximately a one-half-percent charge for this guarantee within the prospectus for the variable annuity.

15. *Are there any annual fees?*

16. *What is the commission* and what is its impact on your account?

FLEXIBLE-PREMIUM DEFERRED VARIABLE ANNUITIES

These contracts are recommended because they give you the option of making payments when convenient and in amounts that you determine. Flexible-premium deferred variable annuities offer you many different types of investment accounts. They can have investment accounts that guarantee principal and interest similar to a fixed annuity, while offering you the flexibility of adding to that account in the future if you want to do so. In other words, you could have your flexible-premium variable annuity emulate a single-premium fixed annuity by directing your investment to a guaranteed interest account within the variable annuity and choosing to make only a single payment. In most cases, the variable contract with flexible-premium options offers you greater opportunity to adjust the contract to changing future needs.

Flexible-premium deferred variable annuities also offer various investment funds that range from common stock accounts of the aggressive, blue chip, and balanced varieties to bond funds, zero-coupon, Ginnie Mae, and real estate accounts. You have the option of moving among these funds, switching your contributions and accumulations from one fund to the other, and managing the fund in accordance with your particular objectives.

However, these accounts may contain restrictions on your ability to move funds, such as limitations on the number of moves you can make during a particular time period or charges for making moves from one account to another. Therefore, when you are selecting a contract, you'll want to investigate the variety of funds available, charges for and limitations on movements from fund to fund, the quality of reporting, and the ease, convenience, and promptness of making moves. A telephone call is the easiest way to move among funds. More and more, funds are offering you the convenience and investment advantage of dollar-cost-averaging services whereby you may instruct them to move money for you each month from one account to another.

People who fear the stock market love the ability to put their money into a guaranteed interest account and then just move their interest into the stock accounts each month. This strategy assures that they will have no loss to their principal investment, and can still participate in stock market gains. Since a variable annuity is similar to mutual-fund investing, you will also be interested in the performance of the investment divisions and their management.

The features to be evaluated in variable deferred annuities are these.

1. Professional management.

2. Investment diversification (the availability of various investment alternatives).

3. Flexible payments (including the opportunity to dollar-cost-average with small deposits and minimum expense).

4. Economy of investing and reasonableness of management fees.

5. The variety of payout options available to conform future withdrawals with future needs.

The disadvantages of flexible-premium deferred annuities occur when they are purchased or sold inappropriately or when they are subject to excessive expenses. If you buy an annuity without being aware of the tax consequences, it may cost you at withdrawal, annuitization, or death. If you buy the annuity with the highest interest rate available, without consideration of the other features within the contract or the company behind it, you may set yourself up for a disappointment such as that experienced by the customers of Baldwin United (not related to the author), Executive Life, Mutual Benefit, etc. Many of those annuitants do not know when their capital may be made available to them, let alone if they will receive any interest on that capital.

Accumulation Units

When you buy into a deferred variable annuity, the purchase of the accumulation unit is similar to the purchase of a share in a mutual fund. Your money arrives at the insurance company, and the company calculates the value of the account accumulation unit at the "closing price" the day the money is received or the next business day of the New York Stock Exchange. Your money purchases units of the fund based on that unit value. This procedure is referred to as "forward pricing" to distinguish it from the way stock is purchased based on a quoted price prior to the receipt of payment.

INVESTMENT RESULTS IN VARIABLE ANNUITIES

Variable annuities are similar to fixed annuities. They have the same policy forms, general provisions, and non-forfeiture rights. The settlement options and option tables, actuarial principles, and mortality and expense assumptions are the same. They are subject to similar income tax treatment but differ in underlying investment vehicle. With a variable annuity you accept the investment risk and responsibility, and the insurance company acts as a conduit to pass the investment results on to you.

You purchase accumulation units during the deferred or accumulation annuity stage and receive annuity units at the time you direct the insurance company to annuitize the contract, establishing the payout amount and/or time guarantees.

VARIABLE ANNUITY SELECTION

Flexible-premium *variable* annuities are the only type of annuity recommended by *The New Life Insurance Investment Advisor*. Single-pocket, interest-only annuities are things of the past. Our world and our needs change too often to select one investment and think that we will be happy with it for the rest of our lives. We must have flexibility, and we must retain control over our investments. We must have multiple-pocket contracts (multiple investments including general account investment options and separate account investments), so that we can make our insurance investments adapt to our needs now and in the future.

When evaluating a variable annuity, keep in mind that your objective is long-term investment growth for your retirement. You have chosen the annuity in order to grow capital faster, since income taxation on interest, dividends, and most importantly capital gains taxes is deferred until you start using your money. Avoiding taxation on profits, as you sell out of very profitable accounts and move to less volatile accounts to safeguard your gains, is very important for two reasons. First, hopefully they will provide a good percentage of your return and exceed the amount you will earn from interest and dividends. Secondly, if you have ever owned a stock or mutual fund that has increased substantially in value, what would keep you from selling it? Either you think it is going to go higher, or you don't want to sell and give about one-third of your profits to Uncle Sam. If you had hesitated and not sold an investment like this in September of 1987 just before the 500-point drop in the Dow Jones average (October 19, 1987), you would know how unwise it can be to let taxation drive your investment decisions. Investments inside of variable annuities are not subject to taxation, so remove that from consideration in your annuity investment decisions. Ability to sell various sub-accounts and buy into others without taxation or transaction costs is one of the most profitable of annuity features. As a result, you want sub-accounts or mutual funds within your variable annuity that can accommodate your investment needs over a lifetime and that are profitably managed.

SUB-ACCOUNT/MUTUAL FUND SELECTION

Morningstar publishes its *Variable Annuity/Life Sourcebook* annually and will give you information about the performance, features and expenses of variable annuities (800-876-5005). You could also find an advisor with the Morningstar data on disk who could help you search for a variable annuity with acceptable costs, fund diversity, and good performance.

INSURANCE EXPENSE/MORTALITY AND EXPENSE CHARGES (M&E)

Insurance expenses, often referred to as M&E charges for mortality and expense, are charged against the investment sub-accounts within your variable annuity. These are charges made by the insurance company for the guarantees it provides within the annuity contract, such as a maximum on expenses, guaranteed annuity rates, and a minimum guaranteed interest rate in the general account investment alternative. It also guarantees that in the event of death, the annuitant's beneficiary will receive the greater of the deposits in the contract or the account value, a protection against adverse investment results.

Low	Average	Maximum
1.00%	1.25%	1.75%

FUND EXPENSE

This may also be referred to as a management fee or operating expense charge. It is the expense charged against your sub-accounts (mutual funds) for paying the fund managers and the operating expenses of the fund. It may not include the brokerage costs.

Low	Average	High
1.43%	2.00%	4.9%

You can see from these charges that bond funds within a high expense variable annuity will not be able to do much for *you*, since their long-term rate of return is about equal to the expenses. It is important to be aware of these expenses as you invest in these products. You are looking for an acceptable net-after-expense rate of return. If you have a general account investment within your variable annuity, the interest quoted normally is *net* rather than gross interest from which you would have to deduct these charges so it may be a better alternative than a bond account, particularly in a potentially increasing interest rate environment.

SURRENDER CHARGES

A surrender charge is paid from your annuity if you cash it in (surrender it) in the early years of the contract. It is usually highest within the first years your contract is in force and will decrease and be eliminated over the years.

Low	**Average**	**High**
5 yrs.	7 yrs.	15 yrs.

If you elect to make an early withdrawal of just part of the funds within your annuity contract, you may have a free corridor amount you can withdraw without any charge.

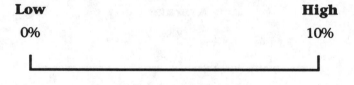

Low	**High**
0%	10%

Free Corridor Amount

Amounts in excess of the free corridor amount would be subject to proportional surrender charges. Since most of these are flexible-premium contracts, you may have *rolling surrender charges* meaning that each investment within the contract must stay within it for a certain period of time before the surrender charge is lifted.

Examine these charges carefully to make sure that you can leave your money in the contract long enough so as not to have to pay the surrender charge. If you do so, it will be profitable to the insurance company. If you do not, the company will try to recoup the expenses of putting the contract in force through surrender charges. Remember, it is in your best interest to buy products that are profitable to the company. You do not want to be exposed to a disappearing company even though your separate account investments (mutual funds) within these contracts are not subject to the creditors of the insurance company.

Since variable annuities are a securities product, it is usually easier to identify all expenses within them as opposed to within a fixed annuity that is not subject to the security disclosure regulations. The Morningstar reports on the products you are considering summarizes all of this information; however, you should also carefully check a current prospectus before buying. You will find the prospectus information surprisingly simple to read. It is fairly easy to find all of the expenses and surrender charges carefully itemized and compare them to the ranges just shown.

ANNUITY TAXATION

Non-Qualified or Qualified Annuities

Up to this point, we have been discussing non-qualified annuities, after-tax investments in which you establish a cost basis in the contract which you will receive back without taxation upon distribution. This is a major difference between the non-qualified and the qualified annuity. In the qualified plan, you have no cost basis because you have made no taxable contributions into the contract. Therefore, when payout-day comes, the tax liability will be on the entire amount coming out.

A principle advantage of the qualified plan is that any investment you make, or that is made by your employer on your behalf, can be exempt from current income taxation.

The investment itself will escape current taxation and, in addition, you will have all the benefits of tax-deferred compounding. For example, to make a $1,000 investment into a *non-qualified* annuity, you would have to earn $1,388.89 (assuming the 28-percent tax bracket). You would pay your 28-percent taxes on those earnings ($1,388.89 × 28% = $388.89) and send the remaining $1,000 into your annuity contract. If you are fortunate and able to put money into a qualified annuity, you don't have to pay taxes on your earnings to net $1,000. You just take $1,000 off the top of your income without taxation, save the $388.89 that would otherwise have been lost to taxation, and also reduce your current income taxes by $280. Your net cost to put away $1,000 is $720, about one-half of what it costs you to save after tax. Your IRA, SEP, TSA, 401(k), PDEC, profit-sharing, and pension plans are all practical opportunities for qualified annuities. If you qualify for any of these, take maximum *advantage of them*. You will find that in addition to the tax benefit of the qualified plan, there are often other advantages. There may be higher interest rates, and in many instances you may find employers making contributions on your behalf without taxation to you.

For example, IBM has had a qualified plan called the Employee Tax Deferred Savings Plan. An employee can choose to contribute up to 5 percent of pay on a pre-tax basis. IBM will match with 30 cents for every $1 contributed. What does that mean to an employee whose combined state and federal tax bracket amounts to 30 percent?

Employee's Gross Investment		Employee's Tax Reduction Due to Contribution		Employee Cost of Investment	IBM's Contribution (.30/$1.00)	Total Working on Employee's Behalf
$1,000	–	$300	=	$700	$300	$1,300

A $1,000 investment (costing only $700) has resulted in $1,300 being added to the employee's investment account—a gain of $600 over the employee's $700 cost of investment and an 86.7 percent gain! How much would this employee have had to make to add $1,300 to his/her own account with after-tax dollars? Take the amount to be deposited ($1,300) and divide by 1 minus (–) the tax bracket (1 – .30 or .70). The earnings required to make this investment on an after-tax basis would be $1,857.14. To check this, merely multiply by the 30-percent tax bracket figure ($1,857.14 × 30%). You find that the tax would be $557.14, leaving $1,300 to invest. That is 2.57 times what it cost through the IBM plan.

Qualified plans offer such an advantage that you should participate whenever practical to the maximum extent possible.

Annuity contracts, qualified or non-qualified, offer outstanding investment and family wealth-building opportunities. Tax-deferred compounding is a powerful tool. Tax-deferred compounding throughout two lives, both husband and wife, is even more powerful. There is no computation, no reporting, and no current dividends, interest, or gains to keep track of or report. Opportunities to change your investment orientation without current taxation are available, as is the opportunity to control your future taxation by controlling payouts from your contracts.

Non-qualified annuities are those that you invest in individually, without the tax advantages of one of Uncle Sam's formal retirement plans (such as those provided through your employer or qualified IRAs). The premium payments into a non-qualified annuity are non-deductible. If the premium-payer and the contract-owner are one and the same,

the assets of the annuity are part of the estate of the contract-owner for estate-tax purposes.

CHANGES IN OWNERSHIP

TRA-86 declares that a change in ownership of an annuity
is a taxable event that will be treated, for tax purposes, as if
the owner/annuitant had died. In short, it means that unless the recipient beneficiary is the owner/annuitant's
spouse, the tax deferral cannot continue. To avoid this
problem, do not make gifts of annuities; rather make cash
gifts into annuities already owned by the individual to
whom you wish to make the gift. To qualify for the
$10,000 gift exclusion, the annuitant should have a present
interest in the use and enjoyment of your gift.

Anyone may make a gift into an annuity contract that
someone else owns. If the recipient of this gift happens to
be a spouse, the gift will be sheltered from gift taxation by
the unlimited marital deduction. Non-spousal gifts will
have to be considered more carefully.

At the present time, each of us can give $10,000 per year to
any individual and, if it is a *bona fide* gift and a gift of a
present interest, it will be exempt from gift taxation. If you
join together with your spouse in making the gift to a third
person, then $20,000 may be gifted without the imposition
of gift taxes. This is commonly referred to as a *split gift*.
However, if you plan to use the shelter of the split gift, you
will have to file a current gift tax form with the IRS.

To qualify for the $10,000-per-year, per-individual gift tax
exemption, the payment of the premium into the annuity
contract must create a gift of a present interest for the con-

tract-owner (ability to control the benefits of the contract currently). If the gift of the premium into the annuity contract is deemed to be a gift of a *future interest* (enjoyment of contract benefits is deferred) and/or is in excess of $10,000, it will be subject to gift taxes. A gift tax return should be filed and, if the gift-giver has used up the lifetime *unified credit* of $600,000 available under the Unified Transfer Tax System, then gift taxes would be due as determined under the Unified Transfer Tax Rate Schedule. Once an individual has used up the $600,000 exemption, additional gifts are taxed at a rate starting at 37 percent and increasing to the top tax rate of 55 percent in 1993.

If a gift is being given for the payment of tuition or medical expenses, it can qualify for an unlimited exclusion by complying with the regulations controlling such gifts. You might wish to utilize this special exclusion. It would enable you to give a non-taxable gift and would not be drawn back into your estate for federal estate-tax purposes. An annuity contract can be useful in providing for a non-spouse's medical expenses, such as an aging parent's nursing home expenses.

To IRA or Not to IRA

Contributions to *qualified* annuities are tax deductible to the extent that the annuitant qualifies to participate in such plans. There are times when you may continue to make contributions to a qualified annuity even though you do not qualify for deductible contributions. Your income may be too high for a deductible IRA contribution, and/or either you or your spouse are already participating in an employer-sponsored plan. Non-qualified IRA contributions are limited to $2,000 per year ($2,250 with a non-working spouse). Non-deductible IRA contributions create a tax-reporting and record-keeping requirement that goes on for the rest of your life. You must be able to establish the portion of the funds put into the IRA that qualify for a tax deduction as well as those that do not. You have to be able to do this when you are ready to take the funds out at retirement. An exclusion ratio will be established that will reflect the non-deductible contributions made to the contract, so that these funds may be excluded from taxation at distribution. To avoid the $2,000 limitation, the reporting requirement, and the record-keeping problems non-deductible IRAs could create, you could use an individually purchased, non-qualified deferred annuity contract. The taxation of the contract upon distribution would then stand on its own. It would not be subject to the $2,000-per-year limitation, the reporting requirement, or IRS record-keeping requirements.

The people in the press constantly advise you to continue non-deductible contributions to IRAs. The argument is that you still receive the value of the tax-deferred earnings which is a valuable wealth accumulation opportunity not to be passed up. All of this is true, but it does not address the fact that you can enjoy tax-deferred or even tax-free earnings from a number of other investments. These other investments will not impose current limitations and reporting requirements and will probably offer fewer future complications in your life than non-qualified IRA contributions do. Exhibit 13.7 is provided to help you compare non-qualified IRA contributions to annuities, life insurance, and other investments.

ANNUITY INSIDE BUILD-UP

The interest and/or investment return earned within an individually-owned annuity contract accumulates without current taxation.

Exhibit 13.7 Alternatives to a Non-Qualified IRA

	Regular IRA	Non-Qualified IRA	Non-Qualified Annuities	Variable Universal Life Insurance	Independent Investment
Tax Deductible Contributions	Yes	No	No	No	No
Tax Sheltered Investment Results	Yes	Yes	Yes	Yes	No
Dollar Limit on Contributions	$2,000	$2,000	No Limit	No Limit	No Limit
Access to Cash	Limited	Limited	Limited	No Limit	No Limit
Loans	No	No	No	Yes	Yes
Withdrawals					
(A) Pre-age 59-1/2	Yes	Yes	Yes	No	No
IRS Penalties	10%	10%	10%	No	No
(B) IRS Taxation on Gains	Yes	Yes	Yes	Owner Controlled	Yes
(C) Cause SS to be Taxed	Yes	Yes	Yes	No	Yes
Mortality Charge From Investment Results	No	No	No	Yes	No
Tax-Free Inflated Death Benefit	No	No	No	Yes	No
IRS Accounting Difficulties Anticipated	No	Yes	No	No	No
Mandatory Taxable Withdrawals Past 70 1/2	Yes	Yes	No	No	No

Conclusions: Rules of Thumb (ROT) concluded from the above:

1 - Regular IRA, if available, should be utilized. The tax deductibility of the contribution is such an advantage that it overwhelms the disadvantages of limited access to the assets.

2 - There is but one advantage in the non-qualified IRA column, tax sheltered investment results, versus eleven in the life insurance column.

This is, of course, one of the primary benefits of the *accumulation* annuity contract. The Tax Reform Act of 1986 terminated the tax deferral on inside build-up of corporate-owned annuity contracts commencing with contracts purchased, or added to, after February 28, 1986. Annuities contributed to by February 28, 1986, have been grandfathered for contributions made up until that time; in other words, tax-deferred earnings will continue.

This tax deferral on the inside build-up of annuity contracts combined with the extensive menu of investment alternatives available within variable contracts is the key to their popularity. Prior to TRA-86, when long-term capital gains were tax-favored (60 percent of the gain was excluded from taxation), many questioned the advisability of earning long-term capital gains within an annuity contract. Now, with the change in 1993, income tax law limiting taxation on capital gains to 28 percent, while taxing high-income taxpayers at up to 40 percent, will again be an individual consideration. Capital gains within annuities are subject to ordinary income tax upon distribution, rather than the lower capital gains tax. When considering whether to own your mutual fund or common stocks inside or outside of an annuity contract, also remember that losses incurred within your annuity contract cannot be written off. Outside of an annuity contract, you have the opportunity to deduct up to $3,000 of your losses each year against ordinary income. This is not available to you if these losses occur within an annuity contract or a life insurance policy.

INVESTMENT MANAGEMENT INSIDE OF VARIABLE ANNUITIES

With 20/20 hindsight, it would have been wonderful to have invested a single large premium into common stocks or other equity investments within an annuity or a life insurance policy in July of 1982. The results would have been almost as exciting if you had invested, with a single-premium deposit, in long-term interest-yielding securities in December of 1980 at the top of the interest rate curve. Looking back at it from the present, there would not seem to be much opportunity for loss (interest rates continuing to go down and the stock market continuing to go up), and therefore the single deposit into a life insurance or an annuity contract would not expose you to excessive risk of loss. It's amazing how clear it all seems looking back and how foggy it always is looking forward.

In an early 1994 economic scenario, the question is, *What do I do now?* From here, with long-term bonds yielding about 6 percent, it appears that interest rates may decline another 1 percent. The stock market, from a level of almost 3,900 on the Dow, appears to offer an opportunity for near-term losses as well as gains. It is interesting to note that six years ago, the Dow was at 2,700 and we said the same thing. The clarity of our hindsight and the fogginess of our foresight will always plague us. Dollar-cost-averaging (the consistent investment of equal periodic payments into a diversified equity-based investment), rather than large single-sum investing, is a relatively conservative and often successful strategy. Alternatively, if you obtain a contract that offers a guaranteed-interest, guaranteed-principle account from which you can move monies at your discretion into equity accounts, you can put your single-sum deposits in these accounts and then move portions into the equity accounts using the dollar-cost-averaging arrangement.

Dollar-cost-averaging can best be described by illustration. The one following indicates what happened when one extremely fearful investor was persuaded to put $100 per month into the stock account of a variable contract for five months, even though he was convinced that the entry of his $100 investment was sure to trigger substantial market declines. As you will note in the illustration, he was right. The market had two 50-percent declines before it started to recover during the first two months of his participation, and as soon as it came back to where it was, he got out. Had he made a substantial single-premium deposit, it would have been merely a very agonizing ride with no reward; however, with dollar-cost-averaging, he was repaid with a 100-percent return on his investment.

The discipline of dollar-cost-averaging provides a successful long-term investment strategy when applied to equity-based annuity and life insurance contracts, as well as mutual funds and other investments. It is a lower-risk strategy than lump-sum investing. If the scenario above had described a market going straight up, it certainly would have been more profitable to go into equities with the whole investment at the outset. But who knows?

Dollar-Cost-Averaging

Month	1	2	3	4	5		Totals
Investment:	$100	$100	$100	$100	$100	=	$500
Share Value on Purchase Date:	100	50	25	50	100		
Shares Purchased:	1	2	4	2	1	=	10 shares

Sell all shares at the end of the fifth month:

10 shares × $100 market price	=	$1,000
Less investment		− 500
Gain on investment		$ 500

As time goes on and your investments build within your annuity or life insurance contract, you may find that you want to cash in some of the gains that have built up over the years in the stock funds. You may move the accumulated funds out of the stock accounts into some more conservative account. If you made this decision with a mutual fund or a personally-managed portfolio of common stocks, you would no doubt agitate over the fact that the sale would trigger current taxation. Two things would be on your mind. First, will the stock market keep going higher? If so, you will lose the opportunity to enjoy further gains. Second, if you sell out now, Uncle Sam's going to take his income-tax bite. For 1993 that could be 30 percent of your profits—not an insignificant amount. That is 30 percent less to reinvest to provide for your personal security. If the assets you are considering moving are within the annuity or the life insurance policy, you have only one of these worries to contend with: if you move out now, you will miss the additional potential profits if the market continues to move up. Taxation, however, will not be a consideration. You will not be required to turn over 30 percent of your profits to Uncle Sam. They can stay in your account and continue to work for you. Not having to consider taxation in evaluating your investment alternatives is a substantial advantage.

TAX REFORM ACT 1986: IMPACT ON ANNUITIES

The general rule has been that the annuity earnings accumulate within the annuity on a tax-deferred basis.

TRA-86 modified the general rule, so that only an annuity that is owned by a natural person will enjoy this tax-deferred income. Code Sections 72(u) and 71(q) provide that an annuity contract issued or added to after February 28th, 1986, owned by a corporation, partnership or other non-natural person, will not enjoy the tax deferral on the inside build-up. Taxes will have to be paid each year on contract earnings. Contracts contributed to by February 28, 1986, have been grandfathered and will not be taxed on prior or continued earnings on such contributions.

To determine the way funds will be taxed when distributed from tax-deferred annuities, we have to look to the date that the funds were put into the annuity. If the funds were received by August 14, 1982, withdrawals will be received by the annuitant as principle first and income second (first in, first out—FIFO). If a contract received deposits after the August 14, 1982, withdrawals are taxed as income first and principal last, to the extent of earnings in the contract (last in, first out—LIFO). The annuitant is exposed to ordinary income tax immediately on withdrawals from such contracts. The ordinary income-tax liability is created when a partial withdrawal or lump-sum distribution is made. If the annuity contract is pledged or assigned as collateral for a loan, ordinary income taxes are due on the amount collateralized up to the amount of the accumulated earnings in the pledged contract, and the 10-percent penalty applies if prior to the annuitant's age 59-1/2.

TRA '86 also increased the penalty tax from 5 percent to 10 percent on withdrawals prior to age 59-1/2 from both non-qualified and qualified deferred annuities. The penalty tax is waived if the owner of the annuity is age 59 1/2 or older, dies, or becomes disabled; or if the annuity contract is being used relative to the periodic payments required under a personal injury suit. The penalty also will be waived if benefits are annuitized, paid out in a series of substantially equal payments over the life of the annuitant or over the joint life of the annuitant and the primary beneficiary. This 10-percent penalty tax is also applicable to withdrawals from pre-August 14, 1982 annuities. These contracts were grandfathered from the standpoint that you may still consider withdrawals to be of principal first and thus not subject to tax up to your pre-August 14, 1982 cost basis. However, you will now have to pay the 10-percent penalty tax to take *taxable funds* out prior to age 59-1/2. Once your pre-August 14, 1982 basis has been recovered without taxation, your next withdrawals will be entirely taxable annuity earnings and thus also subject to the 10-percent pre-59-1/2 penalty.

ANNUITY TAXATION AT THE DEATH OF THE ANNUITANT

The taxation of annuity proceeds in the event of the death of the annuitant will depend upon two things: (1) whether income has commenced, or has not yet commenced, at the death of the annuitant, and (2) whether the beneficiary receiving the proceeds of the annuity contract is the annuitant's spouse.

First, let us assume that payments had not yet begun at the annuitant's death, leaving the proceeds of the annuity to the surviving spouse. The spouse has the option of continuing the annuity and enjoying the tax-deferred earnings or taking a distribution and paying the taxes. However, if the annuitant *had* started to receive benefits and died leaving the annuity proceeds to the surviving spouse, the benefits would have to be distributed at least as rapidly as through the method in effect at the time of the annuitant's death. Taxation will continue to apply to those proceeds.

If a non-spousal beneficiary receives the proceeds in the event of the annuitant's death prior to the distribution of any income, the non-spousal beneficiary may elect a lump-sum distribution without penalty but with full taxation on

323

the accrued interest or gain within the contract. Alternatively, the annuitant may elect a series of payments to be made over a period of time not to exceed the beneficiary's life expectancy, beginning within one year of the annuitant's death. The non-spousal beneficiary has no option to continue the contract, and, although the payment is not subject to a 10-percent penalty tax since it is the result of the annuitant's death, it will be subject to ordinary income tax to the extent of the decedent's earnings in the contract. If the annuity income had started prior to the annuitant's death, then the proceeds would have to continue to come out of the annuity at least as rapidly as the method in effect before the annuitant's death, with normal taxation continuing.

The taxation of these benefits from non-qualified annuities will be based upon the exclusion ratio; that is, the investment in the vehicle will be divided by the expected return to be enjoyed by the beneficiary to determine the exclusion ratio. Each payment to be received by the beneficiary is multiplied by the exclusion ratio to determine the amount of the payment that would be excluded from current taxation as a return of principal, up to a point where basis has been fully recovered. After that, all payments are fully taxable as ordinary income.

ESTATE TAXATION OF ANNUITIES

Usually, you begin to be concerned about estate taxes when your estate reaches the level which would cause them to be paid. One of the first changes of the Reagan administration was the elimination of taxation on assets passing between husband and wife, either during life or at death. You can be assured that, under current law, no matter how much you leave to your spouse, it will not incur any estate or gift tax. The estate tax is levied against that which you own at death and leave to those other than your spouse. However, the first $600,000 of assets passed by gift or at death to non-spousal beneficiaries incurs no tax, since the tax is off-set by a credit against the tax for which we are all eligible. Transfers above $600,000 are taxed at a 37-percent rate up to $750,000 and a 39-percent rate from that level to $1,000,000. Over the $1,000,000 mark, the rate begins at 41 percent and rises to the maximum of 55 percent.

In brief, the Unified Transfer Tax System establishes a means of taxing everything that you or I own and pass to others with certain exceptioons:

1. Except if the recipient is your spouse (spousal gifts and marital deduction).

2. Except if it is a present interest gift of less than $10,000 in a year per individual recipient (joint with spouse gifts $20,000).

3. Except if the total of all the gifts, not counting the $10,000-per-year gifts, totaled less than $600,000 in your whole lifetime including the total of all you passed by inheritance at your death.

Some estate-planning strategies suggest that an estate owner arrange his/her estate with the spouse so as to pay some estate taxes at the 37-percent level, so that at the spouse's death the taxes will not have to be paid at the 55-percent level. The relatively small difference of 18 percent between the lowest bracket and the highest bracket makes it difficult for most estate-owners to understand the logic of pre-payment. You might feel that if you could retain the 37 percent, you probably could earn the extra 18 percent and

1994 Federal Estate and Gift Tax Rates

If the Tax Base Is—		The Tentative Tax Is—		
Over	But not over	Flat amount	+%	Of excess over
$ 0	$ 10,000	$ 0	18%	$ 0
10,000	20,000	1,800	20%	10,000
20,000	40,000	3,800	22%	20,000
40,000	60,000	8,200	24%	40,000
60,000	80,000	13,000	26%	60,000
80,000	100,000	18,200	28%	80,000
100,000	150,000	23,800	30%	100,000
150,000	250,000	38,800	32%	150,000
250,000	500,000	70,800	34%	250,000
500,000	750,000	155,800	37%	500,000
750,000	1,000,000	248,300	39%	750,000
1,000,000	1,250,000	345,800	41%	1,000,000
1,250,000	1,500,000	448,300	43%	1,250,000
1,500,000	2,000,000	555,800	45%	1,500,000
2,000,000	2,500,000	780,800	49%	2,000,000
2,500,000	3,000,000	1,025,800	53%	2,500,000
3,000,000	. . . .	1,290,800	55%	3,000,000

These rates apply to gifts made and estates of persons dying in 1994.

The tax base is the sum of the taxable estate and any adjusted taxable gifts made during life.

The unified estate and gift tax credit is set at $192,800. This credit exempts the estate from tax if the tax base is $600,000 or less.

more and thus justify paying the higher level of estate taxes later. The way to reduce your estate and thus your estate taxes is to make gifts, preferably that qualify as gifts of a present interest and are thus protected from taxation by the

$10,000 gift-tax exclusion, or split-gifts with your spouse, which warrant a $20,000 exclusion.

Also, if you are able to give gifts of rapidly appreciating property, you can keep the growth out of your estate.

Just as with any property, you will find the value of the annuity included in the owner's estate at death. Whether it will cause estate taxes or not depends upon the contract-owner's total estate. If the estate is less than $600,000, all estate taxes will be offset by the unified credit. If the beneficiary of the contract happens to be the contract-owner's spouse, it is protected from estate taxes by the marital deduction. However, if the beneficiary of the contract is other than the annuitant's spouse, not only will the contract be included in the contract-owner's estate for estate-tax purposes, but the beneficiary will incur an immediate income-tax liability as he or she is forced to begin taking withdrawals from the contract within one year of the annuitant's death. Since a single-sum payout could create a substantial ordinary-income-tax burden, beneficiaries may elect a payout arrangement that stretches out the income-tax liability. Annuities in this case have a disadvantage in comparison to other assets owned by the deceased. Other assets take on a new basis as of the death of the owner that wipes out gain and eliminates income-tax liabilities on accumulated gains. This is referred to as the step up in basis. Step up in basis at death does not apply to annuity contracts.

Annuity Contract: Pre-59-1/2 Liquidity

You might as well consider pre-age 59-1/2 annuity accumulation and liquidity as a contradiction in terms. There are three reductions in value to which your annuity can be exposed should you decide to take money out of the post-

TEFRA deferred annuity (issued after August 13, 1982). First, there can be charges from the insurance company that is-sued the contract. Many annuity contracts are back-end loaded. They make little or no up-front charges when you deposit money into the contract, but they do make charges for premature withdrawals referred to as back-end loads. These charges usually disappear after five to 10 years. Some companies have what are referred to as rolling back-end loads, which means that when new money is put into the contract, the time period for the back-end load for those new funds starts all over again on the day of the deposit.

In addition to the charges made by the insurance company, there are two potential charges from Uncle Sam. The first is ordinary income tax on the amount of money withdrawn from the annuity contract to the extent that there are earn-ings within the contract. It is not until all of the interest earnings on your annuity contract have been removed and subject to taxation that your principal will come out with-out further taxation for post-August 13, 1982 contracts.

In addition to the income tax, there will be the excise tax. There is a 10-percent tax penalty for making withdrawals from your annuity contract prior to age 59-1/2.

Withdrawals from annuities purchased before August 14, 1982, are considered to be all principal first and interest earnings after all principal has been withdrawn. Therefore, withdrawals from such annuities up to the contract-owner's basis escape current income taxation. They also escape the 10 percent penalty tax since the penalty is 10 percent of the amount withdrawn "that is included in income" and retrieving your principal means nothing is included in in-come. Withdrawals in excess of principal will incur the penalty. After 59-1/2 years of age, you can eliminate this penalty tax from consideration.

QUALIFIED PLAN ANNUITY DISTRIBUTIONS

By April 1, following the year you attain age 70-1/2, you must make at least minimum annual distributions from your qualified plan, that is, retirement plans such as your Individual Retirement Accounts (IRA), SEP plans, profit-sharing, 401(k)s, and pension plans.

Most people choose to take their first minimum distribution in the year they attain age 70-1/2, rather than waiting until the first quarter of the following year. If you wait until the following year, you would have to take two minimum distributions, one for the year in which you were 70-1/2 and one for the year in which you were 71-1/2. This could stack too much income into that one year.

When calculating the amount of your minimum annual distribution (Exhibit 13.8), you may choose to do it on a *joint life basis* with your beneficiary or just based upon your own *single life* (Exhibit 13.9). Choosing to do it on a joint basis will reduce the amount you have to take out because, as you will note in the tables, two 70-year-olds have a longer life expectancy (20.6 years) than one 70-year-old (16 years). So if slow withdrawal is your objective, so that your money can continue to earn without current taxation, then using the joint life tables will work better for you up to a spread in ages of 10 years (Uncle Sam's limit).

There are also two different methods you can use to calculate each year's withdrawal: the *annual reduction* method or the *annual recalculation* method.

Annual Reduction Method

Under this method, you reduce your life expectancy by one year each year. For example, if you started out using 20.6

Exhibit 13.8 Ordinary Joint Life and Last Survivor Annuities
Two Lives Expected Return Multiples

(Reg. 1.72-Table 6, Gender Neutral)

	70	71	72	73	74	75	76	77	78	79	80	81	82	83	84	85	86
60	26.2	26.0	25.8	25.6	25.5	25.3	25.2	25.1	25.0	24.9	24.8	24.7	24.6	24.6	24.5	24.5	24.5
61	25.6	25.3	25.1	24.9	24.7	24.6	24.4	24.3	24.2	24.1	24.0	23.9	23.8	23.8	23.7	23.7	23.6
62	24.9	24.7	24.4	24.2	24.0	23.8	23.7	23.6	23.4	23.3	23.2	23.1	23.0	23.0	22.9	22.8	22.8
63	24.3	24.0	23.8	23.5	23.3	23.1	23.0	22.8	22.7	22.6	22.4	22.3	22.3	22.2	22.1	22.0	22.0
64	23.7	23.4	23.1	22.9	22.7	22.4	22.3	22.1	21.9	21.8	21.7	21.6	21.5	21.4	21.3	21.3	21.2
65	23.1	22.8	22.5	22.2	22.0	21.8	21.6	21.4	21.2	21.1	21.0	20.8	20.7	20.6	20.5	20.5	20.4
66	22.5	22.2	21.9	21.6	21.4	21.1	20.9	20.7	20.5	20.4	20.2	20.1	20.0	19.9	19.8	19.7	19.6
67	22.0	21.7	21.3	21.0	20.8	20.5	20.3	20.1	19.9	19.7	19.5	19.4	19.3	19.2	19.1	19.0	18.9
68	21.5	21.2	20.8	20.5	20.2	19.9	19.7	19.4	19.2	19.0	18.9	18.7	18.6	18.5	18.4	18.3	18.2
69	21.1	20.7	20.3	20.0	19.6	19.3	19.1	18.8	18.6	18.4	18.2	18.1	17.9	17.8	17.7	17.6	17.5
70	20.6	20.2	19.8	19.4	19.1	18.8	18.5	18.3	18.0	17.8	17.6	17.4	17.3	17.1	17.0	16.9	16.8
71	20.2	19.8	19.4	19.0	18.6	18.3	18.0	17.7	17.5	17.2	17.0	16.8	16.6	16.5	16.3	16.2	16.1
72	19.8	19.4	18.9	18.5	18.2	17.8	17.5	17.2	16.9	16.7	16.4	16.2	16.0	15.9	15.7	15.6	15.5
73	19.4	19.0	18.5	18.1	17.7	17.3	17.0	16.7	16.4	16.1	15.9	15.7	15.5	15.3	15.1	15.0	14.8
74	19.1	18.6	18.2	17.7	17.3	16.9	16.5	16.2	15.9	15.6	15.4	15.1	14.9	14.7	14.5	14.4	14.2
75	18.8	18.3	17.8	17.3	16.9	16.5	16.1	15.8	15.4	15.1	14.9	14.6	14.4	14.2	14.0	13.8	13.7
76	18.5	18.0	17.5	17.0	16.5	16.1	15.7	15.4	15.0	14.7	14.4	14.1	13.9	13.7	13.5	13.3	13.1
77	18.3	17.7	17.2	16.7	16.2	15.8	15.4	15.0	14.6	14.3	14.0	13.7	13.4	13.2	13.0	12.8	12.6
78	18.0	17.5	16.9	16.4	15.9	15.4	15.0	14.6	14.2	13.9	13.5	13.2	13.0	12.7	12.5	12.3	12.1
79	17.8	17.2	16.7	16.1	15.6	15.1	14.7	14.3	13.9	13.5	13.2	12.8	12.5	12.3	12.0	11.8	11.6
80	17.6	17.0	16.4	15.9	15.4	14.9	14.4	14.0	13.5	13.2	12.8	12.5	12.2	11.9	11.6	11.4	11.2
81	17.4	16.8	16.2	15.7	15.1	14.6	14.1	13.7	13.2	12.8	12.5	12.1	11.8	11.5	11.2	11.0	10.8
82	17.3	16.6	16.0	15.5	14.9	14.4	13.9	13.4	13.0	12.5	12.2	11.8	11.5	11.1	10.9	10.6	10.4
83	17.1	16.5	15.9	15.3	14.7	14.2	13.7	13.2	12.7	12.3	11.9	11.5	11.1	10.8	10.5	10.2	10.0
84	17.0	16.3	15.7	15.1	14.5	14.0	13.5	13.0	12.5	12.0	11.6	11.2	10.9	10.5	10.2	9.9	9.7
85	16.9	16.2	15.6	15.0	14.4	13.8	13.3	12.8	12.3	11.8	11.4	11.0	10.6	10.2	9.9	9.6	9.3
86	16.8	16.1	15.5	14.8	14.2	13.7	13.1	12.6	12.1	11.6	11.2	10.8	10.4	10.0	9.7	9.3	9.1

Exhibit 13.9 Ordinary Life Annuities
One Life-Expected Return Multiples

Age	Multiple	Age	Multiple	Age	Multiple
5	76.6	42	40.6	79	10.0
6	75.6	43	39.6	80	9.5
7	74.7	44	38.7	81	8.9
8	73.7	45	37.7	82	8.4
9	72.7	46	36.8	83	7.9
10	71.7	47	35.9	84	7.4
11	70.7	48	34.9	85	6.9
12	69.7	49	34.0	86	6.5
13	68.8	50	33.1	87	6.1
14	67.8	51	32.2	88	5.7
15	66.8	52	31.3	89	5.3
16	65.8	53	30.4	90	5.0
17	64.8	54	29.5	91	4.7
18	63.9	55	28.6	92	4.4
19	62.9	56	27.7	93	4.1
20	61.9	57	26.8	94	3.9
21	60.9	58	25.9	95	3.7
22	59.9	59	25.0	96	3.4
23	59.0	60	24.2	97	3.2
24	58.0	61	23.3	98	3.0
25	57.0	62	22.5	99	2.8
26	56.0	63	21.6	100	2.7
27	55.1	64	20.8	101	2.5
28	54.1	65	20.0	102	2.3
29	53.1	66	19.2	103	2.1
30	52.2	67	18.4	104	1.9
31	51.2	68	17.6	105	1.8
32	50.2	69	16.8	106	1.6
33	49.3	70	16.0	107	1.4
34	48.3	71	14.3	108	1.3
35	47.3	72	14.6	109	1.1
36	46.4	73	13.9	110	1.0
37	45.4	74	13.2	111	.9
38	44.4	75	12.5	112	.8
39	43.5	76	11.9	113	.7
40	42.5	77	11.2	114	.6
41	41.5	78	10.6	115	.5

years, the next year you would merely subtract one year and use that number as your divisor. You divide your retirement plan balances by your life expectancy. Specifically, your calculation in the year you attained age 70-1/2 would be as follows. Add up *all* of your qualified plan balances on December 31 of the year-end prior to your 70.5 year. It certainly will simplify your life if you have consolidated all of those small IRA accounts and your qualified plan incomes in one place by this point in your life.

Divide the total of all retirement account balances by your life expectancy or joint-life expectancy factor, whichever you have selected. If it happens to be 20.6, dividing by that number will tell you your minimum distribution requirement for that calendar year. It would be wise to take the distribution out during that calendar year, even in the first year, if you wish to avoid a double withdrawal in the following year.

If you have chosen the annual reduction method you will take the balance on the *next* December 31 and divide it by 19.6 to determine the minimum distribution requirement for the second year. Do likewise in each succeeding year (e.g., 18.6, 17.6, etc.)

Annual Recalculation Method

With the recalculation method, you use the IRS table factor for your ages each year, rather than just subtracting one year from the previous year's life expectancy. Thus, instead of going from 20.6 to 19.6 as you do in the reduction method, you would go from 20.6 to 19.8 as indicated by the table for the life expectancy of two 71-year-olds. As you can see, this method reduces the amount you have to take out and thus allows you to leave more in your plans to enjoy tax-deferred compounding.

However, there can be an income-tax disadvantage in this recalculation method. A surviving spouse will have to recalculate based only on his or her own life expectancy. It also affects how your non-spousal beneficiaries are taxed. Uncle Sam in his infinite wisdom says that under the recalculation method, your life expectancy *is now zero* in the year *after* your death! Thus, your non-spousal beneficiaries must take total distribution and pay all income taxes due in that year. No more tax deferral for them! However, if you had chosen the annual reduction method, they could continue the payment schedule you had set up, or take it faster, but no slower.

CONCLUSION

Keep in mind that annuities are for *you* and your retirement income. They are designed to be used up within your own and your spouse's lifetime. Annuities pass to non-spousal beneficiaries and incur income taxes, whereas many other assets receive a step up in cost basis at the death of the owner and are thus forgiven income-tax liabilities that the living owner would have incurred. The net benefit to beneficiaries of annuities can be reduced by income taxes, estate taxes, and even excise taxes at death. Thus annuities are best used during the lives of the annuitants.

CHAPTER 14

Where to Go for Products and Assistance

I'm So Confused!

Prior to the mid-1970s, few financial professionals or consumers worried about the financial integrity of insurance companies. Street talk regarding a company, its products, service, and stability served as a good enough indicator for most people.

We have learned that such confidence was unjustified. Many of you will remember the Equity Funding fiasco in which the insurance company staff people actually manufactured phoney policies for non-existent insureds. The fraud was finally exposed by an alert reporter. Then came the Baldwin-United failure in which the consumer was promised *too good to be true* interest rates and salespeople received *too good to be true* commissions. Many have been shocked by the fact that insurance companies can fail, that they fail to provide service, that their products fail, and that they abandon products. On April 11, 1991, Executive Life of California was placed in conservatorship by the state insurance commissioner, and the world learned a new lesson. Even when dealing with fairly large insurance companies, company selection is important to your economic health. When you consider that there are more than 2,200 life insurance companies to choose from, and 125 of them do 85 percent of the business, you can understand why a substantial reduction in the number of companies is inevitable.

How do you protect yourself against potential insurance company failures? You deal with only the biggest and the best, those that have been in business for many years. Avoid those with portfolios that are obviously taking exceptional risk to earn higher yields and/or avoid the general accounts of insurance companies entirely by using their separate accounts. Make sure the company you deal with has multiple-pocket policies (separate accounts) available and use them. Fortunately, there are a number of public sources of information to offer assistance in this area.

STATE REGULATION

Insurance companies are regulated primarily by the individual states. Assuming the insurance company that you have chosen is licensed to do business within your resident state, you have that level of protection. You may assume that your state insurance department has examined the company and its products and found them in compliance with state regulations. Unfortunately, this first level of protection isn't always totally reliable. In spite of state regulations, insurance companies have failed and caused economic harm to their customers. As William H. Smythe said while executive director of the National Association of Insurance Commissioners (NAIC) securities valuation office in New York, "We regulators don't have the authority to tell guys how to run their businesses. We almost have to wait for a disaster to happen, when it comes down to it."

The state does, however, collect information about companies doing business within the state that can be of value. Items such as the company's annual convention statements and Schedule M should be available upon request. They will give you the information the company is providing to the regulators regarding its financial condition and the assumptions used in its illustrations. If you have a concern about a company, call your state insurance commissioner's office and ask questions. Your call may trigger action that saves you and possibly others from economic harm.

The states vary in the quality and quantity of their regulation. New York State is noted for being the toughest within the industry. Many people say that New York is too conservative and difficult, but a restrictive approach can be an advantage to you as you try to pick a company that will be a survivor in these volatile times. Ask if it is licensed to do business in New York. If it is and has agreed to follow New York rules wherever it does business, you have another level of assurance from New York regulators. A relatively small minority of the 2,265 life insurance companies you have to choose from are licensed in New York.

Risk-Based Capital Ratio

The NAIC has created model legislation for the states to adopt. This legislation would create *risk based capital* regulations to help regulators identify how much capital (surplus) is *enough* for various companies, depending upon the *riskiness* of their assets and business. Risk-based capital is liable to become a more important consideration in evaluating insurance companies and is discussed in Chapter 1 and other places within this book. In the author's opinion, the strict regulation of all insurance company general accounts will be detrimental to the insurance buying public, the long-term economic health of good insurance companies, and the thousands of businesses who look to the life insurance industry for capital to expand their businesses.

A.M. Best Company

Another source of public information is the A.M. Best Company of Oldwick, New Jersey, the oldest insurance industry-rating service. A.M. Best provides information regarding a company's financial condition, a synopsis of its history, and data on its management, operating commitments, and the states in which it may write business. A.M. Best also provides its own company ratings, designed to evaluate strengths and weaknesses in four areas: underwriting, expense control, reserve adequacy, and investments. In most cases, you would be wise to place your trust in companies with A ratings by Best. A.M. Best Company may be contacted directly at Ambest Road, Oldwick, NJ, 08858.

You will find the Best's reports in your local library. Use only the most current book. Many insurance companies and agents also can provide summaries of Best reports regarding the companies they are recommending.

Standard and Poor's

Standard and Poor's has a service that rates a very modest number of companies on their *claims paying ability*. Major employers trying to find a source for Guaranteed Interest Contracts (GICS) for their retirement plans use this service to evaluate the financial strength of competing insurance companies. An insurance company pays about $20,000 to obtain a rating from Standard and Poor's Corporation. If the company is dissatisfied with the rating S&P has given it, it has the option of instructing S&P not to publish it. The S&P modifies its ratings with the addition of a plus (+) or minus (–) sign. A company could have an A+ rating from S&P and be in on the third ratings level. You easily could be misled if you assumed that this A+ rating was equivalent to a Best's top rating. If you use these ratings in your decision-making, know what they mean and how they vary.

Standard and Poor's also provides ratings on a broader number of companies for which it does not charge.

Moody's

Moody's concentrates more heavily on the quality of the company's investment portfolio. It is located at 99 Church Street, New York, New York 10007. Moody's ratings, like S&P's, are not generally available unless the insurance company chooses to make them available to you.

Duff and Phelps

Duff and Phelps (55 East Monroe Street, Chicago, IL 60603) provides an overall approach in its credit ratings and has a reputation for quality and integrity. The Duff and Phelps ratings apply to corporate debt, preferred stock, real estate, asset-backed financing, and the insurance company's claims-paying ability. When rating a company, Duff and Phelps' evaluation includes a management interview, quantitative analysis, and a view of the company's future. The ratings are updated quarterly in an effort to make the material more timely. Duff and Phelps ratings are available from insurance companies that have contracted for their services and are included in the annual Morningstar *Life and Annuity Sourcebook*.

Company Annual Reports

A review of the company's financial statements and annual report also is in order. These annual reports are readily available from all insurance companies, and you definitely should ask for them. At least read the president's letter. It should help you to determine what is going well for the company and what is going poorly. Obviously, you want products and services that are doing well because they have a greater claim on the resources and attention of the company. Poorly performing products and services are likely to receive less enthusiastic attention and may even be eliminated. Scan the remainder of the report for information pertinent to the sector of the company in which you are interested. Don't skip the footnotes, which often contain the most important warnings.

Caution

The bottom line is that you can't know everything. The information you obtain will inevitably be dated. If an insurance company is trying to fool you and the regulators, you are likely to find that out too late. For this reason, we continue to advise you to work with the biggest and the best. Companies whose primary business is insurance. Others will find it very easy to rid themselves of underperforming insurance subsidiaries. We also recommend that you use companies that offer multiple-pocket variable contracts.

State Guarantee Funds

There are state guarantee funds for insurance and, if your state has an adequate guarantee, you may benefit. When Baldwin-United failed (primary business: piano-making) in 1983, the life insurance industry and regulators worked diligently for five years to contain the damage. Those who owned Baldwin-United contracts endured five years of uncertainty about their investments. They finally did receive a settlement that generally covered the principal they had invested, but not the exorbitant interest rates they had been promised. You certainly couldn't say that they did not suffer a loss!

In 1989, 48 life and health companies failed. They were followed by 33 in 1990, 40 in 1991, and 19 in 1992. Companies that promise unachievable interest rates take business away from honest ones, and then leave a mess when they fail, e.g., Executive Life. Informed taxpayers are objecting to bail-out practices at their expense in the banking and savings and loan industries. Eventually, we will see the same reaction in the insurance industry. Responsible insurance companies cannot and eventually will not absorb insurance company failures at the expense of their own contract-owners and stockholders. You, the consumer, must consider carefully the credit worthiness of the general accounts of the insurance companies to which you are entrusting your funds. In short: don't bet on state guarantee funds, mergers, acquisitions, and reorganizations in the insurance industry to bail you out of a failing company.

Joseph M. Belth

Joseph M. Belth, Ph.D., whom we have previously introduced, has been referred to as the Ralph Nader of the insurance industry. He exhibits a bulldog-like tenacity in his pursuit of financial information on insurance companies to keep consumers and financial professionals informed. He is not the least bit hesitant to point out the companies that he believes are involved in questionable practices. His monthly publication can be obtained by writing to: *The Insurance Forum*, P.O. Box 245, Ellettsville, IN 47429.

Belth is a controversial source of information. He has the courage to express his opinions in no uncertain terms, and, consequently, many take issue with him. However, he does give the background data that leads him to his conclusions. This helps you to understand the issues and risks involved so that you can make more informed purchase decisions.

Product Impact on Company Selection

Another important factor in company selection is the product line offered by the company you are considering. There are some multi-line companies that will provide for both the property and casualty needs of individuals and companies, as well as the life, annuity, and health insurance needs. However, it is unusual for one insurance professional to have expertise in all of these fields although there are, of course, exceptions. There are many partnerships of property/casualty and life agents who combine their expertise to serve their clients. Most insurance companies are oriented toward property/casualty or toward life, annuity, and health. One rule of thumb to remember is that the company you choose should have a sufficiently diverse product line so that if one of its products is legislated out of existence, the company does not fail with it, leaving you *orphaned*. Diversification of product provides a degree of safety and flexibility for insurance companies, just as it does for individuals.

You want to avoid the risk that the insurance product you select may fail to perform as promised. This can happen not only as a result of insurance company insolvency, but also if the product becomes unprofitable and the company decides to divest itself of the unprofitable unit.

Company Selection Involves Intermediary Selection

Intermediaries can greatly influence product selection and satisfaction. You should learn to distinguish the *client-oriented* salesperson from the *product* salesperson. The product salesperson develops an expertise and an efficient marketing plan for a specific *hot product*. Product specialists can be used to your advantage because of their comprehensive knowledge. However, it could be to your disadvantage if the product is sold to you as a solution to a problem you don't have. For example, single premium life is a good product, but it is not appropriate for every client. In 1986-87 it was sold indiscriminately by hot-product salespeople who marketed it more for their personal wealth enhancement than for that of their clients.

On the other hand, highly technical products such as pension plans, profit-sharing plans, 401(k)s and other qualified plans may be more efficiently handled and serviced by product specialists. Frequently, a client-oriented generalist works jointly with a product specialist to ensure you get adequate service and technical assistance.

You need to understand the type of salesperson with whom you are working so that you can determine his/her role in your risk-management process. The choice is yours. Hiring a qualified, empathetic salesperson is not an admission of naivete. Can you go through the selection process alone? If so, could you do it better than if you had the proper help? Exactly what would that help cost you?

Know what you are *paying* the salesperson. How much of the money transferred to the insurance company is allocated for that pay? In these days of products that have contingent deferred sales loads, you often will find that the salesperson receives more commission dollars than are subtracted from your funds. This is because the insurance company advances the pay and plans on recouping this expense from profits on your product over the years you keep your business there. If you keep the business there long enough, for example 15 years, it is all recouped and you are charged no contingent deferred sales charge after that point. However, if you take your business away too soon and the company is unable to recoup these expenses, it will charge you a contingent deferred sales charge or "back-end" load. It is really a rather fair and economical way to pay for the services of good salespeople. If you choose to pay them simply because they are persistent rather than helpful, it is a waste and nobody's fault but your own. In short: know who you are buying from, what you are paying, and why.

Front-end loaded products are still prevalent in the industry today. Expenses in the various products vary greatly. Yet consumers and financial advisors still look at 10- and 20-year projections that distract from what is really important:

the expenses taken from funds which limit the amount of money that can go to work *for you* in the product. Minimize front-end loads to the greatest extent possible, and by all means know how much of your money is going to be working for you in the product in the early years. If the company treats you fairly then, it is more likely to treat you just as fairly in the later years. You can check performance by comparing results annually.

Financial journalists like to debate the need for intermediaries. They contend, "Read our magazine or column and you will not have to pay salespeople." Some suggest that you are best served by dealing directly with a company like USAA that markets by direct mail and referral because you avoid the salesperson's commission. Alternatively, you have the choice of dealing with the no-load or low-load companies that market directly to the public, or in some cases to financial planners who then add an independent charge for acting as your intermediary. Don't be deceived—you pay marketing expenses whether they involve commissions to salespeople, overhead costs of direct mail and advertising, or direct fees to those who find you a product.

If you are going to hire a salesperson or other intermediary, that person should have the education, integrity and expertise to be your staff employee, preferably with special background in your area of need. Interview potential salespeople, looking for those qualities. There are approximately 400,000 insurance agents eager to serve you, so you needn't give the business to either the first who knocks on your door or the one who keeps knocking. Keep in mind that fewer than one-third of those 400,000 are even properly licensed to sell you all the products mentioned in this book. If someone makes negative statements about a particular product, make sure it is because of the product, and not just because the salesperson is not licensed to sell it. In most cases, you will find that the fee-only salespeople of life insurance (yes, the fee is no different than a commission, so they are salespeople), may not be informed about variable universal life. Make sure they are educated in this product or you are likely to end up in a single-pocket policy because that is all they are qualified to deal with.

Paying for the Product and Service

Understand that you will pay for the sales process. Even if a product is supposedly *no-load* there is a cost of bringing that product to your attention, and you pay that cost. No-loads and low-loads typically have substantial marketing costs and can be expected to make more use of advertising than companies that employ a sales force. Companies that market to independent agents do so with good products and services, along with high commission promises and loss-leader interest rates that they do not intend to maintain. What is your independent agent recommending—superior products or higher commission products?

Common wisdom used to suggest that you would be better served by dealing with a *broker* or *independent agent* than with a *captive* agent. The former would have access to all products from all companies while the latter would have access only to those products provided by the employing company. This theory never did work very well because all insurance salespeople, captive or independent, are limited in their capacity to know everything about every product available. Now, more than ever, they must question the promises made by the product-providers and limit their product search to companies they trust.

The distinction between the independent and captive insurance agent is irrelevant when you consider registered products, i.e., those that are related to the securities markets and sold with a prospectus. These stock and bond-based products are provided to a salesperson through a *broker-dealer* or parent organization that screens the products before they are sold. Most broker-dealers insist that their salespeople sell only the securities-based products that they have pre-approved, which means that the salesperson's broker-dealer affiliation limits the products the salesperson can offer.

We have recommended that you make your first cut based on the financial strength and integrity of the insurance company and your second cut based upon *making sure that the companies you have selected offer the products you want* currently, together with a diversified portfolio of products available for your use.

INTERVIEW INTERMEDIARIES

The third cut is the agent or intermediary. Interview a number of them. Find out what products they are licensed to sell. Ask them questions about their background, their approach to the business, their present educational credentials, and those they expect to attain in the future. If the agents you are interviewing are relatively new in the business, find out what back-up services are available to them. Ask who they go to for help in a difficult case, and if you think you'll be needing them, ask to meet those individuals also. Never before has an insurance expert's advice been more important to you.

You will find that financial planners like to have quality insurance professionals available to them. Certified Financial Planners (CFP) and Chartered Financial Consultants (ChFC) will look for insurance professionals with educational credentials comparable to their own in the insurance field. They will look for a Chartered Life Underwriter (CLU) who has received the designation from the American College in Bryn Mawr, Pennsylvania.

CLUs must have completed 10 semester courses and 10 examinations over approximately a five-year period to attain this designation. Certified Financial Planners and Chartered Financial Consultants also have had education in the personal risk-management area. If the agent that you are interviewing has taken any of these advanced courses, it indicates two things that are advantageous to you. First, the individual is committed and capable of taking and passing such exams; and second, he/she is committed to learning more in order to serve you better. The agent has, in effect, worked to become qualified to serve as your insurance consultant.

When you find a person who meets your requirements, with whom you can communicate, and who you know can obtain the insurance products that you want, the person will *earn* what you pay for services. The individual will either have integrity and a professional approach in serving your best interests, or not. It will be up to you to sense the presence or absence of such integrity. That is why the interview is so important.

When dealing with professional insurance intermediaries, your most effective questions are, *What would you do to solve this problem if you were in my shoes? Why? How have you handled this need for yourself?* and *Show me!* This puts a good deal of pressure on the professional, and it is likely that response will help you to judge if the two all-important qualities—personal integrity and empathy—are present. If they are not, do not do business with that intermediary.

The bottom line is that most of us need help in selecting and managing insurance products. We will pay for this help one way or the other. Seek the best qualified help you can find because poorly designed insurance is detrimental to your economic health, whereas properly owned, designed, funded, and managed insurance products are productive and valuable in enhancing your family's financial security.

Once you have found the company, product line, and professional intermediary, you are in an excellent position to compare costs and benefits. Our objective at the outset of this book was to give you the tools to manage the products you purchase from insurance companies profitably and efficiently. By now, we hope you are able to do just that. With the tools we have provided herein, you are the new sophisticated consumer. You know the questions to ask and the benefits to demand. You know that when you are offered choices within the various insurance company products, your basic rules of thumb will be to:

1. Know the costs built into the product, especially in the early years.

2. Establish long-term relationships with quality insurance companies and quality intermediaries.

3. Choose multiple-pocket contracts.

4. Choose control over no-control.

5. Choose flexibility over inflexibility.

6. Choose quality and alternatives over current or future interest rate promises.

7. Choose a survivor among insurance companies and intermediaries.

8. Accept the fact that assets within insurance contracts require your management, as does every other asset on your balance sheet. Vigilance pays.

Life insurance and annuity contracts that are carefully purchased and well-managed are wealth-building and wealth-preserving vehicles. The basic truth is that you can do almost everything you can do with CDs, stocks, bonds, and mutual funds within life insurance and annuity products today and at the same time protect the return on those investments from being diminished by current income taxes.

CONCLUSION

As this book goes to press, the most important risk facing the life insurance industry and *you*, if you are an owner of a whole life or universal life policy, is the possibility of continuing low interest rates. The effect of low interest rates on the general accounts of insurance companies is being exacerbated by the regulators and raters of insurance companies. The National Association of Insurance Commissioners, through the *risk-based capital* model legislation being encouraged in every state at this time, is telling insurance companies that they must reduce risk (and thus return) in their investments. This over-reaction by the regulators and raters, pushing toward lower-return investments, is happening at a time when it is conceivable that the yield on long-term bonds could decrease to 5 percent and that the lower-risk investments being forced upon insurance company general accounts could go to 4 percent, the minimum guaranteed interest rate in many of your whole life and universal life policies. If you are shaking your head and don't believe this can happen, keep in mind that we would be merely returning to historical norms because the average annual yield on long-term bonds over the past 199 years is 5.2 percent. If this condition prevails for an extended period of time, you can forget about your dividends or excess interest—there will not be *any!* You will then understand the constraints of a single-pocket (only one investment) contract. You do not have choice and you do not have control, and in today's world that is a risky investment. You will then appreciate the importance of owning multiple-pocket contracts (multiple investments). Flexibility, control, and the opportunity to diversify produces policies with less risk as opposed to policies in which you put your money and the insurance company decides on the investment.

You'll hear the hand-wringers say, "What will happen to variable universal policy-owners when the market falls? What about guarantees, etc.?" Well, who said that all the money in your universal variable policy will be in the stock market? Won't you indeed diversify? Use a little guaranteed interest or conservative government bond fund and dollar-cost-average into your volatile stock accounts. The most important factors affecting performance will be the amount of your investment and asset allocation. *Invest enough!* Overfund your policies or do not buy them. Try to get them up to the maximum they will hold and still allow you to borrow or withdraw from your policy without fear of income taxes or pre-59-1/2 age penalties below modified endowment contract (MEC) status. That is when they work best for you and provide the best investment results along with life insurance purchased with income-tax-free earnings. As our grandchildren would say, "Fill it up to the top!"

Bibliography

AIPCA. *Guide to Risk Management and Insurance*. American Institute of Certified Public Accountants, 1992.

American Bar Association. *The Life Insurance Products, Illustrations, and Due Diligence*. Chicago, IL: American Bar Association, 1989.

_____. *Life Insurance Counselor Series American Bar Association's Federal Income Taxation of Life Insurance*. Chicago, IL: American Bar Association, 1989.

_____. *Insurance Counselor Series American Bar Association's Split-Dollar Life Insurance*. American Bar Association, 1991.

Amling, Frederick and William G. Droms. *Investment Fundamentals*. New York, NY: Dryden Press, 1994.

Armstrong, Alexandra, CFP and Mary R. Donahue, Ph.D. *On Your Own*. Chicago, IL: Dearborn Financial Publishing Inc., 1993.

Baldwin, Ben G. and William G. Droms. *The Life Insurance Investment Advisor*. Chicago, IL: Probus Publishing Company, 1988, 1990.

_____. *The Complete Book of Insurance*. Chicago, IL: Probus Publishing Company, 1989, 1991.

_____. *Risk Management and Insurance in Personal Financial Planning*. AICPA, 1992.

Becker, Benjamin M. *Simplified Estate Planning*. Chicago, IL: Twentieth Century Press Inc., 1965.

Bibliography

Belth, Joseph M., Editor. *The Insurance Forum Monthly Newsletter.*

Breitbard, Stanley H. and Donna Sammons Carpenter. *The Price Waterhouse Book of Personal Financial Planning.* New York, NY: Henry Holt and Company, 1987, 1988.

Browlie, William D. with Jeffrey L. Seglin. *The Life Insurance Buyers Guide.* New York, NY: McGraw-Hill Publishing Company, 1989.

Craig, Ernest E. *The Craig Commentary.* New York, NY: Farnsworth Publishing Company, 1979.

Crowe, Robert M. and Charles E. Hughes, Editors. *Fundamentals of Financial Planning.* Bryn Mawr, PA: The American College, 1993.

Daily, Glen S. *Low Load Insurance Products.* Chicago, IL: International Publishing Corporation, 1991.

Dacy, Norman F. *What's Wrong With Your Life Insurance.* New York, NY: Macmillan Publishing Company, 1963, 1989.

Dolan, Ken and Daria Dolan. *Smart Money.* New York, NY: Random House, 1988.

Dorf, Richard C. *The Mutual Fund Investment Advisor.* Chicago, IL: Probus Publishing Company, 1986.

Dorfman, Mark S. and Saul W. Adelman. *The Dow Jones Guide to Life Insurance.* Homewood, IL: Dow Jones-Irwin, 1988.

Droms, William G., B.A., C.F.A. and Frederick Amling, Ph.D. *The Dow Jones-Irwin Guide to Personal Financial Planning.* Homewood, IL: Dow Jones-Irwin, 1982, 1986.

Droms, William G. and Ben G. Baldwin. "Evaluating the Investment Merits of Life Insurance." *Journal of Accountancy* (May, 1989), pp. 63–72.

Duff, Richard W., J.D., CLU. *Preserving Family Wealth Using Tax Magic.* Denver, CO: RDW Enterprises, 1993.

Dunton, Loren. *Financial Planning Can Make You Rich.* Englewood Cliffs, NJ: Prentice Hall, 1987.

_____. *The Financial Planner: A New Professional.* Chicago, IL: Longman Group USA Inc., 1986.

Bibliography

_____, *Your Book of Financial Planning.* Reston, VA: Reston Publishing Company Inc., 1983.

_____, *About Your Future.* San Francisco, CA: Allen M. Associates, 1988.

Genetski, Robert J. *Taking the Voodoo Out of Economics.* Lake Bluff, IL: Regency Gateway Inc., 1986.

Gibson, James H. *Winning the Investment Game.* New York, NY: McGraw-Hill Book Company, 1987.

Gourgues, Harold W., Jr. *Financial Planning Handbook.* New York, NY: New York Institute of Finance, 1983.

Huebner, Solomon S. and Kenneth Black, Jr. *Life Insurance.* Englewood Cliffs, NJ: Prentice-Hall, Inc., 1915, 1923, 1935, 1950, 1958, 1964, 1969, 1972, 1976, 1982.

Ibbotson Associates. *Stocks, Bonds, Bills, and Inflation 1993 Yearbook.* Chicago, IL: Ibbotson Associates, 1993.

Janeway, Elliott. *You and Your Money.* New York, NY: David McKay Company, Inc., 1972.

Journal of Financial Planning. Institute of Certified Financial Planners. Quarterly Issues, 1993, 1994.

Kay, Barry. *Save a Fortune on Your Life Insurance.* New York, NY: Simon & Schuster Inc., 1991.

Leimberg, Steven R. *The Tools and Techniques of Estate Planning 1992.* National Underwriter.

_____. *The Tools and Techniques of Estate Planning 1993.* National Underwriter.

Life Association News. The National Association of Life Underwriters, Monthly, 1993, 1994.

Loeb, Gerald M. *The Battle for Investment Survival.* New York, NY: Simon & Schuster, 1935-1965.

Lynch, Peter with John Rothchild. *Beating the Street.* New York, NY: Simon & Schuster, 1993.

Mackim, Robert E. *Insurance Legislative Fact Book and Almanac.* The National Conference of Insurance Legislatures, 1988.

Bibliography

McFadden, John J., Editor. *The Financial Service Professional's Guide to the State of the Art Third Edition.* Bryn Mawr, PA: The American College, 1994.

Mehr, Robert I. *Fundamentals of Insurance.* Chicago, IL: Richard D. Irwin, Inc. 1983.

Munch, James C., Jr. *Financial and Estate Planning with Life Insurance Products.* Little Brown and Company, 1990, 1991, 1992, 1993.

Murray, Nick. *Serious Money.* New Jersey: Robert A. Stanger and Company, 1991.

National Underwriter Life and Health/Financial Services Edition (newspaper/weekly).

Porter, Sylvia. *Sylvia Porter's Money Book.* Garden City, NY: Doubleday & Company, Inc., 1975.

O'Donnell, Jeff. *Insurance Smart.* New York, NY: John Wiley and Sons Inc., 1991.

O'Neill, Terry R. *The Life Insurance Kit.* Chicago, IL: Dearborn Financial Publishing Inc., 1993.

Reichard, Robert S. *The Figure Finaglers.* New York: McGraw-Hill Book Company, 1974.

Savage, Terry. *Terry Savage Talks Money.* Chicago, IL: Dearborn Financial Publishing Inc., 1990.

Schwed, Fred, Jr. *Where Are the Customers' Yachts?* Burlington, VT: Simon & Schuster, Frazier Publishing Company, 1985.

Trusts & Estates Magazine. Argus Inc., Monthly Issues, 1993, 1994.

VanCaspel, Venita, CFP. *The Power of Money Dynamics.* Reston, VA: Reston Publishing Company, Inc. 1983.

Vaughn, Emmet J. *Fundamentals of Risk and Insurance.* New York, NY: John Wiley and Son, 1986.

Ward, John L. *Ward's Results.* The National Underwriter Company, 1991, 1992, 1993.

Watts, John M. *The Financial Services Shock-Wave.* Englewood Cliffs, NJ: Prentice-Hall Inc., 1987.

INDEX

INDEX

INDEX

INDEX

INDEX

INDEX

see Cash
Survivor, 350
annuity, 285
Survivor life
annuity, 285
insurance, 248
Survivorship
annuity option, 289
life annuity, 288-291
Swiss army knife, 157
approach, 201-202

T

1035 tax-free exchange, *see* Internal Revenue Code
TAMRA, *see* Pre-TAMRA, Technical
Target premium, 65, 101-103
Tax(es)
see After-tax, Alternative, Capital, Corporate, Estate, Federal, Gift-tax, Income, Premium, State, Tax-free, Untaxed
basis, 139
benefits, 300
bracket, 191
deferral, 322
earnings, *see* Pre-tax
liability, 17, 49
return, 157
Tax Reform Act of 1984, 4
Tax Reform Act of 1986 (TRA-86), 52, 214, 215, 287, 314, 318, 321
see Annuities, Exclusion
Section 7702, *see* Internal
Taxable
earnings, 209
funds, 323
income, 204
interest, 219
Taxation, 19, 21-22, 135, 138, 140, 297, 312, 321, 324, 326, 329
see Annuity, Estate, Income
Tax-deferred
annuities, 322
see Non-qualified
compounding, 312, 313, 333
earnings, 56, 316, 323
Tax-free
cost-funding level, 129
death benefits, 138
earnings, 209, 278, 316
exchange, 300
see 1035

funding, 128, 264-266
level, 128-130, 131, 134, 264
point, 129
interest, 264
earnings, 65
rate of return, 54, 75, 85
return, 130
term funding, 65
trading, *see* Life insurance
transfer, 49
use, *see* Untaxed
Teacher's Insurance and Annuity Association (TIAA), 296
Technical and Miscellaneous Revenue Act of 1988 (TAMRA), 140-143
see Pre-TAMRA
TEFRA, 328
Term, *see* Non-guaranteed, Yearly
Term coverage, 26
Term funding, *see* Tax-free
Term insurance, 18, 19, 57, 94, 95, 119, 157, 184
see Convertible, Mortgage, Non-guaranteed, Quality, Retail, Yearly
coverage, 29
policy/policies, *see* Retail, Straight
premiums, 211
Term life insurance, 18, 25-33, 185, 210, 211
see Renewable
costs, 88
designs, 30-31
protection, 65
Term policy, 63
see Re-entry
Term premiums, 30
Termination dividend, 182
Term-insurance rider, 260
Term-plus, 31-33
Test limits, *see* Seven-pay
Third-year policy results, 266-267
TIAA, *see* Teacher's
Total
accumulated income, 18
current asset value, 191-192
death benefit, 17, 191
return, *see* Long-term
risk, 151
TRA-86, *see* Tax Reform Act of 1986
Transaction costs, 119, 138, 238
Treasury bills, *see* U.S.
Trust, *see* Irrevocable, Living

U

Uncertainty, 121-123

369

INDEX